This book is dedicated to Melanie and our sons Joe, Luke and Daniel.

You give me a reason for everything.

JOHN BISHOP

HOW DID ALL THIS HAPPEN?
MY STORY

HarperCollins*Publishers*

HarperCollins*Publishers*
77–85 Fulham Palace Road,
Hammersmith, London W6 8JB

www.harpercollins.co.uk

First published by HarperCollins*Publishers* 2013

1 3 5 7 9 10 8 6 4 2

A catalogue record of this book is
available from the British Library

HB ISBN 978-0-00-743612-5
TPB ISBN 978-0-00-743613-2
EB ISBN 978-0-00-743615-6

Printed and bound in Great Britain by
Clays Ltd, St Ives plc

MIX
Paper from
responsible sources
FSC C007454

FSC™ is a non-profit international organisation established to
promote the responsible management of the world's forests.
Products carrying the FSC label are independently certified to
assure consumers that they come from forests that are managed
to meet the social, economic and ecological needs of present
and future generations, and other controlled sources.

Find out more about HarperCollins and the environment at
www.harpercollins.co.uk/green

CONTENTS

ACKNOWLEDGEMENTS

This book is the book I never thought I would write, because I never imagined I would have lived the life that appears in these pages. I don't regard my life as anything special: like everyone else, there have been times when I have been so happy I have cried and so sad that there was nothing left to do but laugh. Yet to reach the point of putting it all on paper required the help of various people, some of whom I wish to thank here. I have to thank James Rampton who helped me sift through my thoughts to make what is on the page make sense. Everyone at HarperCollins, particularly Anna Valentine for her support from the first meeting to this eventually being printed; a support that has made all the difference. Gemma Feeney at Etch PR for getting people interested in this book. Lisa Thomas, my agent, business partner and friend who took me on when nobody else wanted me and changed my world. Everyone at LTM for their support, especially Emily Saunders, who manages to know what I should be doing when I have no idea. To the lads – you know who you are and, before you worry, this is my story, not our story, so hopefully no divorces will result from these pages. Thank you for your friendship, for the memories and mostly for the material. I have to thank my mum and dad for guiding me through childhood to becoming the person I am today, and thank Eddie, Kathy and Carol for being on that journey with me as part of the Bishop family. You were the people who made the foundations of the man I am today and I will forever be grateful for that love. My wife, Melanie, I have to thank because in so many ways she is the glue that holds these pages together and without her I am not sure there would be much of a story to tell. My three sons, Joe, Luke and Daniel, to whom I am nothing more than just a pain-in-the-arse dad but who have filled my heart in ways I probably have never been the best at showing. I have to thank my dog Bilko – he doesn't know it, but badgering me for a walk often allowed me to get my head clear when I didn't know what to write next. I finally want to thank everyone who has ever bothered to come and see me perform. Comedy changed my life, but without an audience I would just be a man talking to himself and, having done that too many times, I will always appreciate you being there, perhaps more than you will ever know.

FOREWORD

I looked around the dressing room and all I could see were legends. There were jokes and shared banter between people who had won European Cups, FA Cups, League titles, international caps: men who were known to be part of the football elite.

The home dressing room at Anfield Football Stadium is smaller and more basic than you would imagine; it could easily pass for a changing room in any sports hall across the country. Yet few dressing rooms have been the birthplace of so many hopes and dreams; few dressing rooms have felt the vibration of the home crowd roaring 'You'll Never Walk Alone' in order to inspire those within to prepare for battle; and few dressing rooms have ever held the mystique of this one, and been the place where millions of people would want to be a fly on the wall.

I was one of those millions of people, but I was not a fly on the wall. I was a member of a squad who was about to find out if he had been selected to play. Kenny Dalglish stood, about to read out the team sheet. So this was what it felt like sitting in the home dressing room at Anfield waiting to hear if you'd been selected. All of my dreams rested on the next few moments as King Kenny read out the team.

I was substitute. I had expected to be substitute. Surrounded by such legends as Alan Hansen, Gary McAllister, Jamie Redknapp, Steve McManaman, Ian Rush, Ronnie Whelan, Jan Mølby, John Aldridge, John Barnes, and Kenny Dalglish himself, I had never expected to be in the starting line-up. But at least I was putting a kit on. The magical Liverpool red. I was going to walk down the famous tunnel and touch the sacred sign that declares to all the players before they walk onto the pitch: 'This Is Anfield'. It had been placed there by the legendary manager, Bill Shankly, as a way of gaining a psychological advantage over the opposition, a way of letting them know there is no turning back.

Having first been brought to the ground by my dad as a small boy, I had always fixated that, one day, I would make that famous walk. As a child, a football stadium was a place where men shared their passions, their ambitions and their dreams with those who played for them on the pitch. You could tell that within the confines of a football ground the stoicism that reflected how most working-class men approached their lives was left at the turnstile. Football was a place where you could scream, jump for joy, sing along with strangers, slump in frustration and hold back tears of joy or pain. Anfield to me was the cathedral through which I could pass to heaven because I knew if I could be successful there, then nothing on this earth could beat it. Within a few minutes, I was going to touch that sign as home players do for good luck and warm up in front of the famous Kop. And there was a chance, a very real chance, that I was going get to play in the game itself. This would be my début at Anfield, something I had dreamed about since I was a boy.

I was 42 years of age. The match was a charity game between ex-players of Liverpool and UK celebrities versus a rest-of-the-world team that included ex-professionals and international celebrities. The game was in aid of the Marina Dalglish Appeal and the Hillsborough Family Support Group. Sitting in that dressing room, where only a few people knew who I was, I realised things had changed for me, but little did I know I was about to embark on the craziest four years of my life.

After hearing my name being read out by the legendary Kenny Dalglish, and putting my boots on in the Liverpool dressing room, I said to myself something I often say these days: 'How did all this happen?'

CHAPTER 1

HELLO WORLD

I entered the world at Mill Road Hospital in Liverpool on 30 November 1966. I was the fourth child to Ernie and Kathleen Bishop, with my siblings – in order of appearance – being Eddie, five years older than me, Kathy, four years older than me, and Carol, who was one year older than me. She had spent most of that year in hospital, having developed problems eating, which was eventually diagnosed as coeliac disease. In fact, on the night that I was born my dad had been in the hospital visiting my sister. I'm sure my dad would have been in the hospital anyway to welcome my arrival into the world, although in 1966 men did not participate in the birth, as is now the fashion.

Having attended the birth of my own three sons, I realise how ineffectual I was, despite spending months in antenatal classes being taught that whilst in the throes of labour my wife would really appreciate having me in her face telling her to breathe. I am not suggesting men should not participate in some way, and I am not belittling the wonderfully emotional experience, but, really, has any woman ever forgotten to breathe during childbirth? I can't imagine there are any maternity wards around the world where expectant fathers are being handed babies by a sad-looking nurse and finding their joy of fatherhood tarnished by the nurse saying, 'You have a beautiful new child, but I'm afraid we lost your wife. She simply forgot to breathe and because we were all busy at the other end we never noticed. If only you had been there to remind her.'

Anyway, in the 1960s men didn't have to put themselves through all that. They just waited until mother and baby were prepared and presented.

The man to whom I was presented, my father, Edward Ernest Bishop, at the time worked on the tugs in the Liverpool docks, guiding the numerous ships that arrived in one of Europe's busiest ports. Liverpool in the 1960s was said to be the place where it was all happening, but for my mum and dad the swinging sixties basically involved getting married and having kids.

My parents had grown up around the corner from each other on a council estate in Huyton and had not bothered with anyone else from the moment they became child-hood sweethearts. My mum still has a birthday card that my dad gave her for her fifteenth birthday, which I think is a beautiful thing and something I know won't happen in the future, as the practice of writing in cards is coming to an end. I can't imagine young girls of today keeping text messages or Facebook posts sent to them by their boyfriend. Having said that, for the sake of the planet, the giant padded cards with teddy bears and love hearts on the front bought by the teenage boys of my generation in an attempt to get a grope on Valentine's Day are probably best left as things of the past in order to conserve the rainforests – although the quilted fronts could always be recycled as very comfort-able beds.

My parents were married as teenagers and, shortly afterwards, started having children. That seemed to be the way with everybody when I was a child – I didn't know anybody whose parents hadn't done the same thing. I remember being at school when I was 13 years of age and my mate, Mark, telling me that his dad was having his 60th birthday party. I fell off my chair laughing at the image of his father being the age of what I considered a granddad. My dad was young enough for me to play in the same Sunday league side as him when I was 16, although I was under strict instructions to call him Ernie. Apparently shouting, 'Dad, pass!' was not considered cool in the Sunday league circles of the early eighties.

Having young parents had a massive impact on the way I saw the world, and perhaps was the driving force behind me wanting to have children myself very shortly after I got married. Or, to be fair, that may well be the result of me being a better shot than I anticipated.

When I entered the world, my dad was 24 and my mum was 23. They had four children, all born in the month of November. All my life I thought the fact that we were born in November was a coincidence; it wasn't until I was married myself and I became aware of the rhythms of marriage that I realised the month of November comes nine months after Valentine's Day. If you're married, you'll know what I mean; if you're not, you will do one day.

The first eight months of my life were spent living a few doors away from the hospital on Mill Road in a house that my dad had bought from a man in a pub for £50. You could do that sort of thing in the 1960s. The house was about a mile from the city centre and proved to be perfectly placed, as it allowed my parents the opportunity to walk to the hospital to see my sister Carol, in between looking after the rest of us.

As Carol's coeliac disease meant she couldn't digest gluten, throughout our childhood my mum was constantly baking separate things for her. This meant our house very often had that warm smell of baking – although if you have ever eaten gluten-free food you will know the smell is a lot better than the taste. Nice-smelling cardboard is still cardboard.

I don't have any memory of that first house, and it is no longer there. Someone came from the council and declared it unfit for human habitation, along with many others, as the city council progressed with the slum-clearing project which changed much of the centre of Liverpool in the 1960s. The declaration was upsetting for my dad, as he had just decorated, although I am sure the rats and lack of adequate sanitation had more to do with the council's decision than his ability to hang wallpaper.

As a result of the clearing of the slum areas, various Scouse colonies sprang up as families were moved out to places such as Skelmersdale, Kirkby, Speke and Runcorn. Getting out of Liverpool was not something my mum and dad would ever have considered; it was all they had both ever known, and Carol was still being treated in the hospital. The council offered various alternatives and, like most decisions in parenthood, my mum and dad did what they thought was best for us.

They chose to move to Winsford, out in Cheshire, the option that was the furthest from the centre of Liverpool – if not in miles, then certainly in character. Winsford had been an old market town, but now had emerging council estates that needed to be populated by people ready to work in the factories of the local, rapidly developing industrial estate.

My dad went for an interview in a cable company called ICL and received a letter saying he had a job at the weekly wage of £21.60. This was a staggering amount at the time, when he was getting £9 a week on the building sites he had moved on to after too many falls into the Mersey had convinced him that tugs were not the future. So, without further ado, we moved. When the removal van arrived, such was the exodus from Liverpool that it was already half-full with furniture from another family, the Roberts, who actually moved into the same block as us in Severn Walk on the Crook Lane estate.

When my dad received his first week's wages, he was paid £12.60.

Yes, thanks to a typing error, my mum and dad had made the decision to move all the way out to Winsford: a simple clerical mistake was responsible for where I was to spend my formative years. However, I have to say I am glad the lady who typed it (it was 1967 – men didn't type letters, as they were busy doing man-things like fixing washing machines or carrying heavy stuff) made the mistake, because I cannot think of a better place to have grown up.

If you were a child in the 1960s and somebody showed you the council estate where I lived, you could not have imagined a finer location in the world. Rows of terraced houses that were built out of white brick reflected the sun and made everything seem bright. We lived at 9, Severn Walk, which I always thought was a great address as it had two numbers in it, until I realised the road was actually named after a river. We spent the first ten years of my life at this address. Coming from a slum area within Liverpool, it was an exciting place to be, and my mum even today comments about the joy of discovering such modern things as central heating, a hatch from the kitchen into the living room and, the biggest thing of all, an inside toilet *downstairs*. Opulence beyond belief to live in a house where someone could be on the toilet upstairs and someone on the toilet downstairs, at the same time, and nobody had to put their coat on to go outside.

When I started to write this book I wanted to go back to the estate and have a look, so, six months ago, I went for a walk there. It was night-time, and I sat on the wall and remembered all the times we had had on the estate, both good and bad, and I will always be grateful for the childhood I had there.

I have to say that the town planners of our estate did a brilliant job in setting out the rows of houses in such a way that you were never more than ten steps away from grass. Every house had a back yard and a front garden, and then beyond that there would be grass. I know that 'grass' is a very incomplete description, but that is basically what it was. You either had enough grass to host a football match, an area big enough for a bonfire on Guy Fawkes or any other night you felt like building a fire, or you just had enough grass for your dog to have a dump on when you let it out.

As a child, I don't recall the concept of poop-scooping existing, and I can't imagine anything more at odds with the world that I lived in than the image of a grown adult picking up dog shit. Dog ownership involved feeding the animal and giving it somewhere to sleep. Beyond that, nobody expected anything else. Nobody took their dog for a walk – you simply opened the door and let it out. The dog would then do what-ever dogs do when left to their own devices, and it would come home when it was ready. The only dogs that had leads when I was a child worked for the police or helped blind people cross the road.

I am not suggesting that we were bad dog owners; in fact, I think the dogs were having a brilliant time, although you only have to slide into dog shit once as a child playing football before you think someone, somewhere should do something. I recall being asked to do a school project about improving the community and I suggested that dog dirt was a real problem. The teacher agreed and asked me what I would suggest to improve the matter. After some thought, I came up with the idea of the dog nappy. The teacher tried to seem impressed and not laugh, but sadly the idea never caught on – as there was no *Dragons' Den* in the seventies where my eight-year-old self could have pitched the idea, it became no more than a few pages in my school book. And, instead, picking it up using a plastic shopping bag has become the norm. However, I challenge anyone who has to pick up dog shit first thing in the morning not to think the nappy idea has some legs.

Most of what I remember of my childhood happened out-doors. All we ever did was go out and play, and mums would stand on their steps shouting for us when our tea was ready. I should explain to people not from the North, or who may be too wealthy to understand what I mean by the word 'tea', that I am referring to the evening meal, which you call dinner, which is what we call the meal in the middle of the day, which you call lunch. It is important we clear this up, as I would not want you to think I am using 'tea' in the cricket sense, and that after a few hours' play we retired for a bever-age and a slice of cake. Instead, the call for tea was an important signal to let you know the main meal of the day was ready. The shout was not something to be ignored, or your portion of scouse (stew) or corned beef hash would end up in one of the other children in the family. Or the dog.

But if you didn't hear it, someone on the estate would let you know. It is a great illustration of the sense of community we had that all communication was communal. If a mum shouted that her child's tea was ready, all the other children would pass it on until that particular offspring was located and dispatched home. It was also a great way of getting rid of someone you didn't like, but while kids can be cruel they can also be stupid. The estate wasn't that big and everyone knew all the favourite hang-out spots, so when the now-hungry child returned to the gang you had to remember to blame the prank on whichever other kid had gone home for his tea.

I learnt what the place meant to me in 2010 when I was doing my 'Sunshine' tour. I was in the dressing room of the Echo Arena in Liverpool, about to perform for the sixth night. The venue had just presented me with an award for the most tickets ever sold there for a single tour: apparently I beat *Mamma Mia!* by 15,000 tickets. I was having a coffee in the dressing room and chatting with Lisa, my agent, when Alex, my tour manager, said my brother Eddie wanted to have a chat.

When family come to shows, I always see them either before or in the interval, as often I find it easier to do that than at the end of a show. At the end of shows I prefer to be on the road quickly; there is something very exciting and rock 'n' roll about walking off the stage and straight into a waiting car. Eddie walked in with a gift-wrapped long, thin object. After kissing Lisa hello, he turned to me.

'Do you want a drink?' I asked, pointing to the fully stocked fridge that rarely opened as I only drink coffee and water before a show.

'No. I just wanted to give you this. But don't open it till I'm gone.'

'Don't be daft, you're there now. I'll just open it.'

'No, wait. You'll see. I'll see you after.'

With that he walked out, leaving Lisa and me in the room with the parcel. I didn't know what to make of it, so looked at the message on it, which read:

'We are all very proud of you, but something so you don't forget where you are from.'

I looked at it for a moment before Lisa broke into my thoughts. 'Do you want me to leave whilst you open it?'

'Don't be daft,' I replied. 'It's the wrong shape for a blow-up doll, so there can't be anything embarrassing about it.'

I tore back the paper and realised why Eddie hadn't wanted to be there when I opened it as a lump climbed into my throat.

'What is it?' asked Lisa, concerned that I was supposed to go and perform in front of 10,000 people but looked like I was about to start blubbering over the parcel contents.

'It's who I am,' I said, and showed her the street sign for Severn Walk, which Eddie had nicked from the end of the block.

When I revisited the street to get my bearings for this book, it was nice to see a block of houses built in the sixties with a brand-new street sign. The old one now hangs in my kitchen, in pride of place. You can't return to your childhood, but you don't have to leave it, either.

Football was the game of choice for all the boys on the estate. In the seventies, girls did things that involved skipping whilst singing songs, hopscotch on a course drawn in chalk on the pavement, Morris dancing with pom-poms, and being in the kitchen. I am sure my sisters Kathy and Carol did loads of other things, but if they did I never saw them. I was a boy, and boys played football and scrapped. Later, when I was given a second-hand Chopper from my uncle, Stephen, I added trying to be Evel Knievel to my list of activities. Along with the Six Million Dollar Man, Steve Austin, Evel was my first non-footballer hero – quite unusual choices, as one had bionic legs, and the other one was always trying his best to get some by crashing all the time. If you do not know either of the gentlemen to whom I just referred, then you missed out in the seventies, when a man worth $6 million was much more impressive than a person worth the same amount now, i.e. someone playing left back in League One. And, back then, the absence of YouTube meant that seeing a man crash his motorbike whilst trying jump over a queue of buses was classed as global entertainment. It basically meant that, during my childhood, I was attracted to taking risks by crashing my bike after jumping over ramps or jumping off things. Most of the time this was OK, but it did also inadvertently lead to my first discovery that I could make people laugh, more of which later.

Having an older brother who occasionally let me play football with him and his mates meant that when I played with my own age group I was a decent player, and, like any child who finds they are good at anything, I wanted to keep doing it. In terms of sport, this single-minded approach explains why I am rubbish at everything else: I didn't do anything else. There was the odd game of tennis if we could sneak onto the courts at the park without the attendant charging us, but it seemed a daft idea to play anything else when all you needed for football was a ball and some space – ideally, a space away from house windows and dog shit but, if not, you could play around that. That is one of the great things about being a boy: you can find something you enjoy like football and you don't have to stop playing it as you grow up. I played it continually for years, and I still play it occasionally now. I haven't seen either of my sisters play hopscotch since I was 10.

Football was great, but cricket was also an option. People used to spray-paint cricket stumps onto the walls of end-of-terrace houses around the estate. This meant that we always had cricket stumps, but it also meant that we always had cricket stumps that never moved. This caused untold arguments because the bowler and the fielders would often claim that the stumps had been hit, but with no physical proof of this the batter nearly always argued against the decision. This generally caused a row that resulted in a stand-off, which, more often than not, the batsman won – he was holding a cricket bat, after all. I think this is probably the reason why I don't like cricket – any game where as a child you are threatened with a lump of wood on a regular basis ends up feeling like it's not worth the hassle.

There was also the odd dalliance with boxing which was something virtually every boy I knew on the estate did from time to time; my cousin, Freddie, achieving some level of success by fighting for England. I didn't mind fighting as a boy; it was just something we did. My brother Eddie had taken it upon himself to toughen me up, a process that involved him taunting me till I got angry and flew at him, upon which he would then batter me. Older brothers never realise that they are natural heroes to their younger siblings and it was great when Eddie allowed me to hang around with him and his mates, but I would have given anything just to win one of our fights as a kid.

As a child, I would actively seek fights. If I started a new school or club, I would pinpoint the bully in the room and then challenge them to a fight. When I ran out of people in my year at school, I started looking for people a year or two above me. A challenge would be given, an arrangement made and, after school, I would be fighting someone for no reason whatsoever whilst other children stood around and chanted: 'Zigga-zagga-ooo-ooo-ooo.' While I never understood what that meant, I also never grasped the concept that by going around looking for a bully to fight I might actually have been the bully, but I did think I was doing the right thing. I was taking on the baddy and more often than not winning, where-upon I would go home and let Eddie know his attempts to toughen me up were working. Eddie, however, would usually say he wasn't interested and give me a dead leg.

As I type this as an adult, I realise this reads awfully, but that is what life was like on an estate, and none of us thought it should be different. Eddie and I were also acutely aware that my dad had a reputation for being a tough man. He had been taught as a child by his mother, whose matriarchal influence on the family was immense, that you had to stand up for yourself. My nan outlived three husbands and three of her own nine children, and her life and that of her chil-dren was one of hardship and battles. Some she won and some she didn't, but the fight was always there till the very end. She must have been in her seventies when I had to restrain her from getting involved in a fight that had broken out in the room next door to my cousin Gary's 21st birthday party in Rainhill.

As I grew up and moved in different circles, I learnt that violence very rarely resolves anything and I began to associ-ate with more and more like-minded people. The extent of this change became apparent when I received a call from my dad to say that there was a need for a 'show of strength' at my nan's house. At the time, the council had moved a young family next door and they were basically scumbags: one mum, multiple children and two dads – the kind of neighbours from hell you see on television programmes where you can't believe such low-grade people exist. There had been a row, and a threat made to my uncle, Jimmy, and my nan, so it was decided that uncles and cousins should arrive at the house to ensure it was known they would face more than just two pensioners should the arguments escalate.

It was a Sunday night and, as a young father, I had been looking forward to going to the pub with my mates. Instead, I asked them to come with me. We arrived at the house and walked in to find it full of the adult men in the family. I looked around the room at battle-ready faces of cousins and uncles, and then back at my mates – Paul, Mickey Duff and Big Derry Gav – and realised that if it kicked off I had perhaps not brought the best team. Paul was an accountant whose hair was rarely out of place; Big Derry Gav got his name from being from Derry, being big and being called Gavin, but as a trainee infant-school teacher the best he could do would be to create weapons from papier-mâchè; while Mickey Duff had perhaps the best contribution to make, if not in the physical sense – he spent most of his time hiding behind my nan – but in the sense that he was the logistics manager in a toilet-roll factory.

As it happened, the police arrived and the situation didn't escalate. After far too long, the scumbags were moved on, but I have a slight tinge of regret that the success I gained later on had not happened by then, as money and celebrity does bring you the means to resolve such matters. Or the phone numbers of those who can.

Eddie and my dad used to do circuit training in our living room, so I would join them. From the age of seven I found could do more sit-ups than anyone else in the family. This bordered on an obsession for a period, as I would forever be doing sit-ups, one night doing 200 straight, which is a bit mental for a seven-year-old child who is not in a Chinese gymnastic school. We would often then end with a boxing match. This involved my dad going onto his knees and from this position we would hit him, wearing boxing gloves, while he would just jab us away wearing the one glove that was his size. Eddie and I would then spar. One time, Eddie knocked me flat out with a right hook. I got up, dazed, but instead of stopping the session my dad just put on his glove and put Eddie on the floor. We both learnt a lesson that day: neither of us would ever be able to beat my dad.

My dad and his twin brother, Freddie, played football locally, where it was clear they had some form of a reputation. I don't think they ever sought a fight, but you can tell when people think your dad is hard; it's just the way people talk when he is around, and the sense of protection that we had as a family when we went anywhere with him. I still have that feeling now, and he is 74. My dad always told us as kids that you should never look for trouble, but never walk away, particularly if you're in the right. He also said we should never use weapons (Uncle Freddie had nearly bled to death as a youth after being stabbed in the leg), never kick someone when they are down, and, if you're not sure what is going to happen next, you're probably best hitting someone.

I think for the life we lived at that time that was sound advice, but it's not a conversation I have had to have with my sons – they have not lived the same life. To be fair, I have not lived the life that my dad lived, but he could only pass on what he had learnt. My nan had been married before to a Mr Berry and had had three sons: Charlie, Billy and Jimmy.

By the time Mr Berry died, Charlie had also died, aged nine, of diphtheria, and been buried in an unmarked pauper's grave, and my uncle, Billy, had lost a lung to TB. She then married my dad's father, Fred Bishop, and had Janet, Mary, Edna, Carol and the twins: my dad and Freddie. With eight children in post-war austerity, things were inevitably tough – in one of the few photographs my dad has of himself and Freddie as children, only one of them has shoes on. There had been only one pair of shoes to go around, so they had a fight and the winner wore them for the picture.

Although my mum lived just around the corner, growing up, she never seemed to suffer the same degree of hardship. She was one of three for a start, with older siblings (in the form of John and Josie), and fewer mouths to feed makes a difference to any family. Her mum and dad divorced and her father died the same year I was born, which is one reason why I am named after him. Her mum, my other nan, was married to Granddad Bill, a caretaker of a block of flats in Toxteth, for all the time that I knew her. As children, Eddie and I would play for hours around the flats with Stephen, my uncle, who was in fact not much older than us. Pictures of my mum in her youth reveal a slim, beautiful, dark-haired girl with plaits who grew to be a slim, beautiful woman with a beehive. My mum has always stayed in shape, and I would guess that her dress size has hardly changed in the more than fifty years that she has been married to my dad.

There are not many pictures of my parents before we started to come along, but I love the ones there are. My mum was as close to a film star in looks as could be without actually being one. There is a softness to her features that belies the toughness inside, a toughness that would often hold the family together in years to come. My dad looks strong in all the pictures, with a handsome face and tattoos on his arms and a stocky frame that suggests that he was made to carry things. My dad is of the generation of working-class men who have swallows tattooed on the backs of their hands. He has often said that he regrets getting them done as they give people an impression of him as someone who wants to look tough before they actually get to know him. The reality is, he said he got them done so that people could tell him and his identical twin Freddie apart – not the greatest of strategies, as I don't know anyone who looks at a person's hands first, but at least it beats a tattoo on the face. Personally, I would have just worn glasses or perhaps a hat. In truth, my dad has the hands of a man who suits such tattoos. He was born into a world where social mobility was limited and it was essential that you protected what you had, as there was nothing left to fall back on.

If men like my dad were to ever progress through the social order, it was to be through hard graft, and by being prepared to fight your corner in whatever form that fight took. It was the week before Christmas in 1972 when I became completely aware of what it meant to be a family and the cost of standing by your principles. I was six years old and I recall my uncle, John, my mum's brother, sitting us all down in the living room. My mum was sitting next to him, and we four children were squashed up on the couch.

'Your dad has gone to prison.'

The words hit me like a train. I didn't completely understand what they meant, but as everyone else seemed upset I knew it couldn't be a good thing. One thing I don't remember is anyone crying; it was as if it was another thing you just had to deal with. My mum sat there with the same inner strength that I always associate with her. No matter what was to follow, I knew she would make sure everything was going to be all right. She had managed to hold the family together when Carol was literally starving to death in hospital and her own father was dying of cancer. She had managed to move as a young mother away from all she had ever known for the benefit of a better life for her children. Her husband going to prison was not going to break my mum, particularly as she supported everything my dad had done.

Uncle John, his voice clear and strong, carried on: 'Some people may say bad things to you, but never forget your dad did the right thing. You need to be proud, and you boys have to stand up for your mum and sisters.' For the first time ever, I was given more responsibility than just being able to dress myself in the morning.

My dad had been sentenced to a year in prison as a result of an altercation with two men outside a chip shop. He had had a run-in with the same two men the week before, so when he'd stopped with my mum to get chips on the way home from a night out they had started another argument. When my mum had intervened, they had pushed her so hard she had bounced off the bonnet of a car onto the ground. My dad had reacted to the provocation and, as had happened the week before, both men ended up on the ground and my dad walked away.

To this day my dad is very bitter about the sentence, and even the arresting officers said the case should have been thrown out. On both occasions, my dad was not the aggressor and was defending himself, and on the second occasion was defending his wife. But for his defence he had not been advised very well, which is something that can happen when you are limited financially in the professional advice you can seek.

Months earlier, my dad and Uncle Freddie had been playing in the same football team, and my dad was sent off
by the referee for something his identical twin had done.
They appealed against the decision and the local FA had
upheld their claim that the referee had sent the wrong man
off because he could not tell who had committed the offence.

Had my dad just stood in court and simply relayed the
events as they happened, there is a very good chance he
would have walked free, or at least only been given a sus-
pended sentence. However, it was felt by many on the estates
that people who had moved to Winsford from Liverpool
would be unfairly treated by the local police and courts. As
the other two men were locals, or 'Woollybacks' as we called
them (an insult to sheep that I have never really understood),
he tried to use the same ploy in court that had worked with
the local FA. As both men had ended up pole-axed on the
ground, it would be impossible, so the plan went, for them to
know which twin had hit them. As the judge could not send
both my dad and Uncle Freddie to prison, he would have to
throw the case out, and that would be the end of that.

The defence didn't work and, as my dad was sentenced for
violence, he was sent to a closed prison. At first he went to
Walton Prison in Liverpool and then on to Preston.

He told my mum not to bring us children to visit him, but
by the time he had been transferred to Preston he was missing us too much and asked her to bring us in. I remember that day as if it was yesterday. My Uncle Freddie drove
us and we arrived early and had to sit waiting in the car,
opposite the prison. There were all four of us, Eddie, Kathy,
Carol and I, along with my mum and Freddie in the front,
yet I don't recall anyone saying anything as we just sat
and waited.

To my six-year-old self, Preston Prison looked like a castle. It was a stone building with turrets and heavy, solid, metal gates that had a hatch, through which the guards behind could check the world outside remained outside.

At the allotted time, we approached the gates along with some other families, and the hatch opened. Before long, a small door swung open, and we were allowed inside, only to be faced by another metal gate.

Standing just in front of it was a guard in a dark uniform holding a clipboard with a list of names on it, which he ticked off with the expression that you can only get from spending your working life locking up other men. My Uncle Freddie said who we had come to see, whereupon we were duly counted and moved towards the next gate. Eventually, after everyone had met with the guard's approval, the gate in front of us was unlocked and we were allowed to pass though to be faced by yet another gate.

This process of facing locked gate after locked gate was a frightening and dehumanising experience: we were being led through like cattle. We eventually walked up some metal stairs and entered the visitors' room. I just recall rows of men sitting at tables, all wearing the same grey uniform, in a room with no windows and a single clock on the wall.

When I saw my dad, I broke free of my mum's hand and ran towards him to give him the biggest hug I had ever given anyone. My dad reciprocated until a guard said we had to break the hug and I had to be placed on the opposite side of the table like everyone else. I know prison officers have a job to do, but who would deprive a six-year-old boy of a hug from the father he had not seen for months? It was not as if I was trying slip him a hacksaw between each squeeze.

'Have you been good?' he asked us all, and we each said we had.

'Good. Have you been looking after your mum?' he asked then, and for some reason it seemed like he was talking to just me.

I wasn't so sure I knew what looking after my mum entailed, but I was sure I was doing it, or at least a version of it.

'I have, Dad,' I said.

'They've all been good,' my mum informed him across the table, which seemed to satisfy him.

'Good,' he said, with a smile I had never seen before. A smile that appears when someone's face is trying to match the words that are being spoken, but not quite managing it.

I don't recall anything else that anyone said. I just remember looking around and thinking my dad didn't belong with all the other men in grey uniforms. He was my dad, and they were all just strange men wearing the same clothes as him, many sporting similar tattoos on the backs of their hands.

After what to me appeared to be too short a time, my Uncle Freddie said he would take us out so that my mum and dad could talk alone or, at least, be as alone as you can be whilst being watched by prison officers alongside thirty other families visiting at the same time. To soften the disappointment of having to leave, my dad gave us all a Texan bar each, a sweet of its era: chocolate covering something that was as close to being Plasticine as legally possible, so when you chewed it almost took every tooth out of your head with its stickiness. We didn't get many sweets at the time, so it was a real treat, even if the trade-off was that Dad was in prison. What I didn't realise at the time was that four Texan bars virtually accounted for a week's prison allowance. Not for the first or the last time, my dad was giving us children all he had.

During the year that he was away, I can only recall visiting my dad on one more occasion. It was when he was moved to the open prison at Appleton Thorn. I remember the visiting room had windows so that light flooded in, and hugs were not prevented with the same degree of enthusiasm by the prison officers. Before he had left Preston, the governor there had told my dad that he was the first prisoner he had ever transferred to an open prison: by the time you reached Preston you either went onto a maximum-security unit or stayed within the closed-prison sector till your time was served or you died.

The only reason he moved my dad was because of the support he was given by one particular prison guard, Officer Hunt, who stuck his neck out for him and pressed for my dad to be moved. It would be easy to say all prison guards of the time were bad, but clearly this wasn't the case. Despite one or two close shaves, I have not needed to visit a prison since.

I don't recall the day Dad came home. You might imagine it would be ingrained in my memory, but somehow it isn't. While he was away, I remember that things seemed harder than usual. As a family, we never actually felt poorer than our neighbours, but I was aware that some people just had more.

It was when I started junior school at Willow Wood that I was first exposed to people who had more than me – basically, people who did not live on our estate. My two friends from school were Christopher and Clive, and both were posher than I was: Clive lived in a house that had an apple tree in the garden. Despite being at least three miles from where I lived, I would happily cycle or walk there to play. By the time I was in junior school I knew the estate inside out, so leaving it to go on adventures seemed natural.

Clive was clever, and I recall his dad coming home from work once. He was wearing a suit and didn't need to get a wash before having his tea, which I thought was a really odd thing for a dad not to have to do. I liked Chris because he could draw, which I also enjoyed doing. He lived on the private estate and, to my eyes, he had the perfect life: he was the oldest, so he didn't have an older brother who always won fights; and his mum didn't seem to work, so when we played there she would sometimes make us chocolate apples, which is basically a toffee apple but with chocolate instead of toffee.

My mum was great at making cakes and I did get pocket money to spend at the mobile shop on the estate, which was a van in which a bloke sat selling all household goods from pegs to sweets, but I had never come across the concept of the chocolate apple. Chris also seemed to have more toy cars than I could imagine it was possible for one child to own. We would play with his Matchbox cars and, occasionally, I would slip one in my pocket. Once, as I did so, I saw his mum looking at me. I guiltily pulled the car out but I knew there were going to be no more chocolate apples for me. I was not invited around again.

CHAPTER 2

MY DAD AND CARS

In the 1970s, on every council estate, men were to be found under cars. It seemed to me that being an adult man meant you needed to be fixing something, and my dad was constantly fixing something for which he wasn't qualified. Because he would never give up till what he was mending actually worked, he usually managed to get things to work in such a way that nobody else on the planet was ever able to repair them again, as nobody knew what he had done. Most of the time my dad didn't know, either.

This was always best illustrated by the range of cars we had. Money was tight, but cars were a necessary luxury, so my dad bought what he could afford, then spent time underneath it trying to make it do what he needed it to.

One car that stands out for me was the Hillman Imp. The name does not inspire much confidence – any name that is one letter away from 'limp' is surely not a title to give something that is supposed to transport people around. The Hillman Imp was developed by the Rootes Group to make a small car for the mass market. The fact that most of you will have not heard of either the car or the company tells you all you need to know about its success.

The car had its engine in the back, which would be absolutely fine if you couldn't smell its workings whilst sitting there. The front bonnet was for storage. If you packed to go on holiday, this had the effect of turning any luggage you put there into a sort of early prototype airbag of clothes and knickers, should you have the misfortune to have a head-on collision. Whereas, if you were hit in the rear, a steaming engine would smack you on the back of the head, forcing you through the windscreen because, as it was still the seventies, nobody wore seat belts.

I recall a conversation with my dad about seat belts and the fact that he never wore one. His rationale was that if you ever drove into a river, the seat belt was another thing you had to deal with before climbing out the car, and that delay could be vital. He was also of the firm belief that if you rolled down a hill, there was always a chance that the belt could trap you in the car when the best thing to do would be to open the door and allow yourself to be thrown free. Needless to say, none of these theories has ever been tested and my dad now does wear a seat belt, but amongst the various jobs he has had in his life, safety officer was never one of them.

Our Hillman Imp was grey with an off-white roof – the best way to describe it is as something smaller than a single bed and less attractive than your average washing machine. And the reason that it stands out in my memory amongst all the other cars my dad had was because of one camping holiday we took in the Welsh hills when I was eight. The tent and various pieces of luggage were housed on the roof of the car as the bonnet was filled with clothes and tins of food: my mum was convinced that the camp shops would over-charge, so instead of being ripped off for tins of beans, soup and corned beef, she had stocked up and loaded the car. The fact that all this extra weight probably slowed us down to the point that we were using more petrol never entered the equation. There was no way she was going to allow anyone to rip us off.

My mum and dad sat in the front of the car, of course, while in the rear was me, 8; Carol, 9; Kathy, 12; Eddie, 13; and Lassie, 35 in dog years. Lassie was a white mongrel that I can't ever remember not having as a child. She was white all over, apart from a black patch on her eye. Every time someone new met her, they would immediately say, 'That's a nice dog – is she called Patch?' to which we would reply, 'Don't be stupid. She's called Lassie,' as if it wasn't obvious enough.

She was a brilliant dog who would dance on her hind legs for biscuits, allow you to dress her up in girls' clothes for a laugh, and was not a bad footballer. I am not joking about the latter point: Lassie could play. She wasn't one of those dogs that would see a ball and then want to bite it. No, Lassie would join in by using her nose to win the ball, and then, once directed towards the goal, would keep nosing the ball till she had dribbled past everyone and scored. Because she had more legs than anyone else on the field, she was faster than any of the other players, so she was very good at dribbling. The only problem was that she was not really much good at anything else, and if she did score she didn't have the awareness to stop, and would carry on running all over the estate, still nosing the ball, unless she became distracted by food or a cat. Also, her distribution was rubbish, so we never let her play with us too often. There is nothing worse than a greedy player, even if they are a dog.

So that was four kids and a dog on the back seat; two adults in the front; a six-berth tent along with deck chairs and a table on the roof; and in the bonnet we had clothes, sleeping bags, tins of food and the camping stove with bottled gas. All of this in a car under which my dad had spent hours making sure things like the brakes actually worked when requested to, rather than when they liked.

I cannot possibly imagine embarking on such a trip now. My kids have been brought up with rear-seat TVs and iPads: at the very least, they put in earphones, listen to music and get lost in their own world. They've never travelled for hours on holiday in an overcrowded car to one of the wettest countries in the world, where you are camping in a borrowed tent which, when you get there, takes all night to put up as there are no instructions.

We had to cram into the car, with me by the window due to my propensity to throw up every ten miles of any car journey, let alone one where engine fumes were mixing with those of dog farts. I was often given barley-sugar sweets, which were supposed to help car sickness, although how eating something that tasted of sick mixed with sugar was supposed to stop you from being sick I have never understood.

In all the excitement, we never worried about the potential dangers of being in a car that had dodgy brakes and was massively overloaded with tinned food housed under the bonnet next to gas canisters – therefore having all the potential to turn into a dirty bomb at the moment of impact. We were going on holiday and, as my mum and dad played their favourite country and western songs, we prepared to go to the only foreign country I ever visited until I reached adulthood: Wales.

The holiday was great. My memory of it was of sunshine and the beauty of Bala Lake, albeit strangely mixed with the dread of any approaching hill. Early on in the journey it became clear that, despite its name suggesting it was 'a man of the hill', the Hillman would not be able to carry us up any slope of substance, while perhaps the 'Imp' part of its name was just the start of the word 'impossible', because that was what every hill became.

Once we approached the periphery of Snowdonia National Park my dad knew that if we were to stand any chance of ever reaching our destination the weight in the car would have to be reduced. This meant that on the approach to any hill we would all climb out and, along with the dog, begin the long walk up whilst my dad slowly drove the Hillman Imp to the apex. There he would wait for us all to arrive. That said, he didn't always get there first: on more than one occasion we walked faster than he could make the car go.

There is nothing more humbling than seeing your dad at the front of a procession of cars, willing his own vehicle onwards, while you arrive at the top of the hill faster than him by walking. The frustration of those caught up in the procession was matched only by our collective desire for the Imp to make it to the top. Failure to do so would only result in the embarrassment of being forced to do a three-point turn in an over-laden car in the middle of an ascent, and start again.

When we had all reconvened at a peak, we quickly reassumed our positions in the car and would be rewarded for our efforts by a trip downhill at as much speed as the Hillman Imp could muster. It was like being in a toboggan as we weaved around the bends, until the gradient changed and we all had to get out and start walking again.

One little-known fact about my dad is that he invented the people carrier. Although his version may, by today's standards, seem rather primitive, he certainly has to be credited with the concept of taking a van and putting people in it.

After the Imp limped to an early grave, it was a red Ford Escort van that my dad brought home next. The fact that it had no seats in the back never struck us as strange; we had owned vans in the past and all we did as kids was climb in the back and sit on a few cushions.

It seems a successful way to travel until you travel with the childhood version of myself, one whose propensity for car sickness was not helped by such a mode of transport. Being in the back of a van with no windows and a vomiting child is not really the place you want to be.

I don't know if it was the car sickness or just a wave of inspiration, but my dad then decided that he did not want a Ford Escort van. He wanted a family car, and for that to happen he either had to buy a new car or change the one he had, the latter being the most sensible thing due to our lack of money.

Using an angle grinder, my dad proceeded to cut into the side panels of the van. Even in a road where people working on cars was not an unusual sight, the image of a man with an angle grinder attacking his own car so that sparks were filling the air created a fair amount of interest. After all, in a world of only three television channels something as crazy as this was bound to create a lot of interest. Oblivious, my dad just carried on. He was like Noah building his Ark: my dad had a vision, and even if the rest of the world, including my mum, thought he had lost the plot, he was still going to realise that vision.

Once the side panels came out, my dad then produced some windows that he had 'found' in a caravan. I have written 'found' in inverted commas because when I recently spoke to him about putting the glass in to replace the side panels he wanted to put me straight right away. Glass would have been dangerous (I never thought I would hear my dad say anything was dangerous when it came to cars), and what he had, in fact, put into the side panels was Perspex, which he had taken from a caravan.

'A caravan?' my mum asked. 'What caravan?'

'A caravan I found,' said my dad, and that was the end of that.

As you can imagine, your average caravan window is not made to fit exactly into the shape left behind in a Ford Escort van after the side panels have been removed. So, with the aid of welding and tape, they were customised to the space and made to fit. A seat was added in the back from another car of a similar size found in a scrap yard and, after this was bolted to the floor, my dad stepped back. The people carrier had been invented, although it was probably the most illegal vehicle I have ever ridden in.

The car must have been uninsurable and, by today's standards, it was a million miles from being roadworthy. We used to climb into it either over the seats at the front or from the rear door, which was designed for loading goods, not children. Whoever failed to get on the rear seat then had to sit in the vestibule area between the newly installed seat and the rear door. Occasionally the rear door would spring open whilst in transit, but not too often, and no kids were lost during the time that we had the car.

I loved that car, and I was sad to see it go. People would look at us whenever we were out in it and, in my mind, that just helped to enhance the magic of it. I never for one second thought the car was being looked at for any other reason than admiration. But, as Christmas approached in 1975, my dad decided it was time to sell his creation. No doubt the pressing matter of getting us kids presents played some part in that decision.

Christmas passed and my dad still had the car, which meant all his money was gone. Then he received a call from a traveller camp on the edge of Winsford.

My dad drove the car to the camp and haggled with the assembled men. It was New Year's Eve. If he could sell the car, he and my mum could have a rare night out. The deal was struck and the car was sold. After the cash was handed over, my dad asked the inevitable question, 'How do I get home from here?' The camp was a fair distance from home and none of his friends was able to pick him up. Getting a taxi to come to a traveller camp was never an easy thing to do, so he asked the man to whom he had just sold the car to give him a lift home in it.

The man shook his head. 'I'm not driving that till I've painted it, but I'll give you a lift on that.'

He pointed to a Triumph motorbike. There are few things that my dad hates more than motorbikes, but with cash in his pocket and a do to get to, he took the offer and rode home pillion, clinging tight to the driver and with a smile on his face.

The effect of that car didn't end after it was sold, because my dad used the money to take Eddie and me to the cinema for the first time ever. The film was *Jaws*, and we went because it was deemed too scary for the girls. I know, but it was 1975 and they probably had things to do in the kitchen.

I could not have been happier. I felt like we had won the pools. I was at a cinema watching the first film I had ever seen that wasn't a Western. The cinema was in Northwich, a town about eight miles away from Winsford, and the fact that it was somewhere new only added to the excitement of the evening. I loved it when it was just us 'boys' together: I saw it as an opportunity to talk to the other men of the tribe about man-stuff like football, cars, conkers – things the girls in the family just wouldn't understand. This time usually came on a Sunday afternoon, when we would sit in the living room eating our roast dinner watching the weekly Granada football highlights show called *Kick Off*, which Gerald Sinstadt commentated. It was required viewing for anyone who wanted to watch football whilst eating a Sunday roast and, as Gerald Sinstadt presented it for years, there is a whole generation of men who can't help salivating as soon as they hear his voice.

I know at times my desire to use these sacred moments for conversation did mean that I became slightly irritating to Eddie and my dad, who had the serious business of football and food to concentrate upon, so a trip out to the cinema was a male bonding experience on a totally different level. I am sure I jabbered away in the car my dad had borrowed for the evening but, once inside the cinema, popcorn in hand, I was just enchanted by the experience, and any notion of bonding over conversation disappeared within seconds.

The film was brilliant, although it did have serious implications for my swimming in the sea for the rest of my life. Like many people, I cannot now put my head under water without hearing, 'Durum, durum, durum.' However, I had been introduced to the world of cinema, a world I love to this day. One of my favourite things is going to watch films in the day. I am 46, but it still makes me feel like I am skiving school.

The best car my dad ever had was the Moscovitch. This was a Russian car that embodied the Soviet Union prior to the Wall coming down. It was red for a start, although I am sure you could get different colours. Having said that, I never saw anyone else driving one, except my dad. It was square. Very square. The kind of square you see when a child tries to draw a car, and in all honesty I wouldn't have been surprised to discover that the car was designed by a six-year-old.

In 1970s Russia, passenger comfort obviously was not a priority: if you were not in your Moscovitch, what else would you be doing? Standing in a bread line dreaming about Levi's jeans, probably. Everything about the car screamed function before purpose, the driver console being unattractive and full of things that could impale you in a collision, but I loved that car. I loved how solid it felt, which may in part be due to the tank metal it was made of. I loved that it was from the exotic Eastern Bloc that we were supposed to be scared of, but which I deduced could not be that bad if they had sold my dad a car. The car lacked mechanical sophistication to such an extent that when my dad lost the keys he began using a pair of scissors in the ignition to start the car. I actually thought my dad might be a Russian spy when he got it, and I allowed some of my mates to think the same.

But I mostly loved it because my dad did. One thing he appreciated the most was the lighter just below the dashboard, which you could press in and which would pop out when it was hot enough for my dad to light his cigarette as he drove. It was the most sophisticated thing I had ever seen. And I broke it.

Whilst sitting in the car waiting for my dad one day in Garston, Liverpool, I couldn't resist pressing the lighter in. When it popped out, I decided to test how hot it was with the tip of my tongue. Yes, I did just write that. The tip of my tongue. You do not need to be medically qualified to guess the result. I burnt my tongue and it hurt like hell. But, after the initial pain, I was still sitting in the car with nothing to do, so I kept on pushing the lighter in and out until one time when it didn't pop out again.

My dad returned to the car and immediately went to use the lighter. When it didn't move, he used his strength to pull it. The internal coil unravelled and the lighter fell apart.

'Have you been using this?' my dad asked.

I tried to explain it wasn't my fault, but due to the burnt tongue I just said, 'Ummn dun nooo.'

My dad looked at me, and I knew that he knew I had broken it. He looked me in the eye for a moment, sighed and simply said, 'I liked that lighter.'

Then we drove home. I loved that car because it always reminded me of my dad's forgiveness and that 'things' don't matter. People do. Even if those people can't talk due to their own stupidity.

CHAPTER 3

A BOY LEARNING ADULT LESSONS

It was a sunny day early in the summer of 1974 and we all went for a family day out to the swimming baths in Winsford, where the pool was outside. These days, the concept of having an outdoor swimming pool in the north of England would seem crazy, and the fact that it is no longer there perhaps proves that such a venture would be like having a ski slope in the desert (I know they do in Dubai, but they cheat). However, my childhood seems to have been full of sunny days, and we spent many an afternoon at Winsford's outdoor swimming baths.

As you entered the swimming pool, you were immediately struck by the brightness of it all. The diving board was painted red, and the bottom of the swimming pool was painted pale blue, which always gave the impression of freshness. There was a large pool housing the diving board, and it was a rite of passage one day to jump off the top. On this particular day – I would have been no more than seven – I had not reached the top, although I had gone halfway and was still edging up slowly. There was a shallow children's swimming pool at the end, beyond which was a small shop where you could buy sweets.

It was here that I saw a friend from school. He had on a scuba mask and was playing in the children's pool. We spoke for a while before I went back to the base my mum and dad had set up amongst the tables and benches, and where I knew there would be an endless supply of sand-wiches and drink. My mum has always possessed the ability to make more sandwiches than she has bread. I know that defies logic, but it's true. It's a mum thing that they can just do. I think the story of Jesus feeding the five thou-sand can probably be explained by Mary making sardine sandwiches.

I was sitting with my family when I noticed a man run and dive into the pool fully clothed. Whilst everybody else was playing, I couldn't take my eyes off the man under the water, as he seemed to be swimming furiously towards the other side.

Suddenly, he emerged from the water holding a small figure that I immediately recognised as my friend. The life-guards came running over and the pool immediately began to empty, so that I had a clear, uninterrupted view of the proceedings unfolding in front of me.

In a panic, one lifeguard tried to administer mouth-to-mouth resuscitation while simultaneously another guard tried to administer CPR. Both were working hard, but they appeared to counteract each other. It seemed like only sec-onds before the sound of a siren could be heard. An ambulance man entered the scene carrying a holdall, striding with the authority of somebody who knew what he was doing. He was tall and wearing a white unbuttoned shirt, black trousers and had black, greased-back hair.

He immediately took control of the situation, picking my friend up by his right ankle and holding him upside down with one arm. Water gushed from his open mouth. But my friend's body hung listless. Dead. The ambulance man then placed him on the ground with the least degree of ceremony conceivable and shook his head.

The body was carried away under a blanket. The lifeguards seemed just to be standing in shock, while families began to look for little children, holding them tighter as they left than they had when they arrived. I don't recall there being hysteria or panic after the event, just a sense that something terrible had happened. I saw a woman being led away in tears, and everybody seemed to move slowly and with purpose. The ambulance man had made it clear that there was little point in trying to do anything. It was over.

I understood that my friend was dead, and I knew what 'dead' meant, but I couldn't fully comprehend all that I had seen. Then I noticed that, for the first time in my life, the main pool was empty. I had never seen it empty, as we had never managed to get in before the crowds. But now the surface was as smooth as glass, and nobody appeared to want to penetrate its calm.

As the ambulance drove away with my friend's body, I felt the overwhelming urge to break the stillness of the moment. Perhaps in an attempt to recreate normality, to return the pool to a place of joy and not a place of fear and death, I ran and dived into the water. As I was in the air, I remember feeling excited at the prospect of being the only person in the whole of the swimming pool.

I broke through the surface, and my breath left me. The water was like ice; colder than it had been moments earlier, and colder than I had ever felt before.

I surfaced and scrambled up the steps before the coldness overwhelmed me, snuggling into a towel and my mother's arms. I should never have dived in; I could never have made things normal by doing so and, as the coldness entered my bones, a coldness that was not just generated by water temperature, I knew I had made a mistake. But I couldn't help myself. I had needed to stop being passive; I needed to stop being a witness. I had needed to stop standing still, even if it did result in me sitting in a towel trying to warm up from a cold that I don't think has ever really thawed.

At school the following week we had a special assembly in which the headmistress told us to pray for my friend. He was not a close friend – he was one of a bunch of mates – but I remember him being cheeky and funny. I also remember him being held up lifeless and dead. Apparently, he had decided to snorkel in the big pool against his mum's wishes and had got his leg caught in the steps underwater. People had seen him, but as he had a mask on, they had assumed he was just snorkelling. The man who had dived in had noticed the boy had not moved for some time. It was said he was already dead when he was pulled out of the pool.

My friend Clive told me his mother went to the funeral, and that our friend had been buried in a white coffin. I was seven years old, and I had seen death close up for the first time. It didn't really scare me; I knew that one day it would be coming for me. I just wanted to put it off for as long as I could. At least get to an age when I would not be buried in a child's white coffin.

Most kids play games where you count to 10 when you get shot and then you are alive again. I didn't play those games very often after that day. I knew dead meant dead, no matter how long you counted for.

I have to say that, despite gaining a sense of mortality, the experience did not stop me thinking I was indestructible. I don't know if young girls feel the same way or if it's the result of reading too many comic books where heroes have super-powers, or if it's the genetic requirement of potentially one day having to hunt or go to war that makes boys assume they will bounce rather than break. If you have ever been in a family centre where they have climbing frames and a ball pool, you will know what I mean. Little girls play and enjoy the colourful surroundings. Boys fly everywhere, and if they have not fallen off everything in the first 20 minutes they have not had a good time.

I was eight years of age and playing football on a field that we called the orchard. The sun was shining and we were getting to play out longer as spring was turning into summer, with the promise of light nights. Beside the patch of grass on which we were playing there was a fence, which I suppose would have been about eight feet high. Behind the fence there was a private garden full of trees. None of us had ever seen these trees bear fruit, but for some reason the area had become known as the orchard.

Ten minutes into the game, one of the boys kicked the ball and it flew over the fence. I volunteered to do the risky job of fetching it, thinking in my eight-year-old mind that I would be a brave hero if I got the ball back: a cross between Steve Austin and Evel Knievel.

I climbed the fence and jumped down to the other side. I ran quickly to get the ball so that I was not shot by the person who lived in the house – nobody to my knowledge was ever shot, but if you are eight years of age and on an adventure you may as well believe you might get shot for the sake of the excitement. It's either that, or the possibility of being eaten by a dragon.

I retrieved the ball and kicked it back to my friends. I then began to scale the metal wire of the fence that surrounded the orchard, until I reached the top. The fence was made of hardwire, which was spiky at the top. I don't actually remember what happened next, but I do recall the decision to jump the eight feet or so down to the ground.

Due to the fashions of the time, I was wearing flares that were so wide that the law of gravity would have allowed me to float down had I chosen to do so. However, I decided to jump, and the flares got caught on the spikes and made me fall the entire way: the first, but not the last, time I fell victim to fashion.

I woke up in hospital. I had damaged my kidneys to the extent that the doctors warned my mum and dad I may need a transplant. As it transpired, my kidneys were actually only bruised, and the doctor suggested I was lucky because, for a boy of my age, I had particularly strong stomach muscles: clearly, all of those obsessive sit-ups had not actually been wasted. I think it was perhaps the only time when something I had done alone in my bedroom had proved to be of any use whatsoever.

It was during this time, in Leighton Hospital near Crewe, that I recall for the first time being able to make people laugh. Living in Winsford and surrounded by the people who had been displaced from Liverpool meant that many on the estate sought to hold on to their Liverpool identity in the most obvious way possible: their accent. Similar to second- and third-generation Irish people in America, who become more Irish than the Irish, many on my estate became more Scouse than they would have been had they never left.

I basically grew up around people all trying to 'out-Scouse' each other, and this made my accent extremely strong.

Many people think it is strong today, but it has become much more comprehensible with age as I have learnt the importance of being able to communicate in a way that allows people to understand you – not something you immediately comprehend as a child. So, when I was eight years of age and lying in a hospital bed, I became somewhat of a source of entertainment. One particular nurse would affectionately call me 'Baby Scouse' and would keep on asking me to say things for her amusement; things that more often than not would involve the word 'chicken'. There is just something about the construction of that word which makes it sound funny when said in a Scouse accent. The nurse would even bring other nurses to my bed, so that I could say the chosen sentence of the day. It would be something like: 'Why did the chicken cross the road? How do I know? I'm not a chicken!' Two chickens in one sentence – comedy gold – and the nurses would start their shift with a giggle.

In some respects, this might sound inappropriate behaviour by nursing staff. These days there would be an enquiry, and I would seek compensation for the trauma and victimisation, as well as the anguish that has meant I can no longer eat chicken. However, I not only enjoyed the attention, I also enjoyed the sound of making other people laugh. And not only other people, but strangers, people who knew nothing about me till I said something funny. That sensation has never left me, and I feel blessed that it is now the way I make my living. The other thing that has been with me all my life is the enjoyment of entertaining nurses. However, that is not for this book. Nudge, nudge. Wink, wink. Pass the chicken!

CHAPTER 4

SCHOOL AND A FRIEND CALLED KIERAN

When I was 10 we left Winsford and moved to a brand new council estate in Runcorn. I joined Murdishaw West Primary School, along with Carol, while Eddie and Kathy went to Norton Priory Comprehensive, a 20-minute bus ride away.

Eddie at this point was very close to leaving school anyway, which suited him, as he hated it. He left as quickly as he could at the age of 15, which is quite ironic in many respects because, as I write this, having already completed an art degree in his forties, Eddie is now studying for his GCSEs in English and Maths to enable him to train to become a teacher. Prior to that, his adult life had been spent as a professional footballer playing for Chester and Tranmere, and as a welder, both careers fitting my image of him more than standing at the front of a classroom. But my own career change, too, shows that anything is possible.

Kathy, on the other hand, did well at school and left to train as a nursery nurse, knowing straight away that it was her vocation. She has now spent much of her working life looking after young children in nurseries and schools. I've visited her current school a few times to do an assembly for the children, and it is obvious why many people choose such a profession. Kids can be wonderful things – particularly when you can say goodbye to them at 3.30 p.m. Carol also went back to university and gained a degree in Community and Youth Studies, which led her to working at the young offender's institute at Appleton Thorn, the former open prison our dad had been in. She now works as my PA, which is probably more challenging at times than working with delinquents.

For me, a new school was always an opportunity to make new friends and have fun. Playing football is a great way to make new allegiances, particularly if you are quite good, and I settled into my new school very quickly. It reflected the estate that it served: it was new, fresh and seemed to suggest potential in the very fabric of its walls. The classrooms were bright, and it was the first time that a teacher had a real influence on me.

Mr Jameson was our classroom teacher. Like all junior school teachers, he was charged with teaching us everything, from spelling and painting to world geography and maths. He also ran the school football team. Primary and junior school teachers at that time were like the Google of their age; they had to have an answer for everything, and Mr Jameson managed it all with a degree of calm control.

In one game, we played a nearby school and we won the game convincingly. Mr Jameson's unruffled demeanour was notable in its contrast with the lunatic teacher from the other school, who stood on the sidelines screaming till his face went red. We almost felt bad for the lads we were playing against but, as they were from the next estate, it was our duty to hammer them.

After the game, we shook hands and did the obligatory three cheers for the opposition, which I always thought was good but belonged more in a rowing club than between teams from two council estates. I recall Mr Jameson speaking quietly afterwards to the opposing teacher, whose face quickly cooled from red to a pinkish shade of pale. None of us heard what was said, but for a day or so around the school it was rumoured that Mr Jameson had said, 'Sorry you lost, but you're a prick.'

However, what made him have an impact on me was that he recognised that not only did I like to play football and do all the other things that boys do, but I also enjoyed writing poetry and stories, and he would often allow me to continue working on a story long after the rest of the class had moved on to something else. I always valued this encouragement, and he made me feel confident, even if at times my spelling left us all confused. Every child going through the primary school system deserves someone like Mr Jameson to give them a hint that they can be something more than they can imagine.

It was good to go back to the school on the day that he retired, by then as headmaster. In the short time I was there, he made me the school football team captain, encouraged my imagination, and broke up the occasional fights I was involved in. He basically gave me confidence, and that has been an invaluable thing throughout my life (although, to be honest, I've often had much more confidence than I have had ability at times).

If there was ever a job I think I would have liked, it is that of a teacher in a junior school. I think those who work in education are some of the best of people we have. They have often chosen to take the opportunity to shape lives and influence our society rather than pursue a better-paid profession. I accept there are a fair few who fall into it because they partied through university and didn't know what else to do or couldn't get any other job. However, in my life, I know certain teachers changed the way I saw the world, and that cannot be said as readily about many people I have met as an adult.

I can still name the teachers who had a real influence on me:

1. Mr Jameson: for the reasons stated above.

2. Miss F: primary-school teacher who had a Spitfire, long blonde hair, lived in Sandbach and was, no doubt, my first crush, but as I was only six I didn't act on it.

3. Miss J: comprehensive-school teacher on whom I definitely had a crush from the age of 13. I did act on this, but not till I left sixth form, details of which will not feature on these pages, but for which I shall always be grateful.

4. Mr Hilton: comprehensive-school PE teacher who put a great deal of time and effort into the sport at our school. He made me the captain of my secondary-school football team. (We didn't have any other sports teams. There was once a lesson in rugby taken by another teacher, but a few broken collar bones and a fight later, that ended.) He also took me to all the town team games, and that eventually lead to a trial for the county under-15s team.

There were two games to be played that day, and I was put in the second group. We stood in the snow for ages till it was time to play, and then those supposedly watching didn't notice for ten minutes that one team only had nine men. I scored and had one of my best games ever. Mr Hilton assured me I was probably the best player on the pitch, and as he was not prone to empty praise I was very encouraged by his comments. Everyone knew that getting into the county team was the first real step to being scouted by a club – it was the first vital step in your dream becoming a reality.

Those in charge with selecting the team were taking a long time to do it, however. They were huddled over clip boards and team sheets, so Mr Hilton told me to take the opportunity of a lift home from my friend's dad so I could get warm. 'You did well,' he said. 'I'll call you with the good news later.'

A few hours later he phoned the house to tell me I had not got in. It was the biggest disappointment of my life, and I locked myself in the bathroom till the tears subsided. On the phone he sounded as disappointed as I was, explaining that the teachers picking the team were from a private school in Chester, and that the majority of the squad selected came from their school. It was just another example of how money can buy you opportunity.

Years later, my youngest son, Daniel, played against that same school in the final of a schools cup. The Chester school had consistently won the cup in previous years; Daniel's school had never even reached the final before. And yet they won. At the final whistle I nearly ran onto the pitch to complete the revenge by waving my victorious fist in front of the Chester school children, parents and staff. Thankfully, common sense told me that as my feelings of being wronged had occurred some thirty years earlier it was unlikely to have involved anyone on the other side of the pitch. Even so, the fact that their official school photographer was reluctant to take a team picture of our boys suggested to me that it was still an institution of tossers.

Mr Hilton had been very supportive in all my school years, using the leverage of the football team to ensure I kept up my schoolwork and didn't drift, as some of the other lads did.

In the final year the team was good enough to get into a number of the local finals, and I always felt I let Mr Hilton down when I was sent off during one final for punching the centre-half from a school in Helsby. Even to this day I don't know why I did it: perhaps it was because the lad had long hair and a beaded necklace and looked much cooler than me – he just seemed to irritate me to the point that I punched him. It wasn't even a good punch, but what hurt more is the fact that I had let Mr Hilton down. I was 16 at the time and I never managed to apologise properly. So if he reads this, I just want to say, 'Sorry, sir.'

5. Mr Logan: an English teacher who had encouraged me, along with my other English teacher Mrs Withers, through my O-levels in English Language and Literature. He talked me into returning to school when I had left, basically altering the whole course of my life – and that is no exaggeration.

6. Ms Philips: the headmistress of the comprehensive school who bent the rules to allow me to do A-levels and to comply with Mr Logan's plans for me.

There were other teachers who had more contact with me during my school life and who had more direct influence on me, but that decision, taken with no small consequence, changed the world for me. I will be eternally grateful to both Mr Logan and Ms Philips.

7. Mr Debbage: the teacher who became a friend by giving me somewhere to live when I first moved to Manchester, but who also guided me through my History O- and A-levels, giving me a love of the subject I still retain to this day. He left teaching, as many skilled people do, to move into other

areas and effectively became a professional card player. But Bridge's gain was education's loss, because he was the most brilliant of teachers, particularly at A-level standard, where he wasn't having to fight with a room full of varying degrees of interest and intellect, which is the challenge teachers – particularly those in the comprehensive system – face.

8. Miss Boardman: my class tutor through all of my senior-school years. We saw her every day, and it is impossible for someone like that not to have an influence on you. She was only a few years older than us: for many of the teachers in the school it was their first job and they were roughly 8 to 12 years older than the pupils. That is a lot when you're 11, but it's not so much when you're 16. She died too early. I managed to go to her funeral, which was both a sad and a celebratory affair, and I was glad I went. Let's be honest, you don't go to a teacher's funeral unless they meant something to you, and she did.

I am not suggesting this is my *Goodbye, Mr Chips* moment, but I do feel teachers need to be celebrated. So thank you to all the ones who have been in my life. Thanks, too, even to the ones I didn't like or who were rubbish at their job. You taught me something: the valuable lesson that some people in authority are pricks.

My education became disrupted as I entered the final year of junior school due to an operation I had on my left leg. At the time I was playing a lot of football, and the GP suggested quite reasonably that the pain in my leg must be ligament damage. As a result, his treatment was rest and a compression bandage.

However, the pain became unbearable after a few weeks and, despite the rest, there seemed to be no improvement. As I was unable to walk, my mum had to wheel me up and down the hill to the GP practice balanced on my bike, to ask if there was any other possible explanation. On many occasions they made the mistake of saying no, until she insisted I be referred to hospital.

Eventually, the referral to the hospital was made. I remember the day the ambulance came to collect me. Just as it arrived, I was sick, either with fear or illness. I don't recall very much of what happened after that, apart from being prepared for surgery with my mum and dad standing either side of the bed, and my dad leaning in to kiss me on my forehead.

This was at a time when we were years past kissing: goodnight was a nod to my mum and a handshake to my dad – I'm glad to say that my family is so much more demonstrative now than we were then. One thing I have learnt from my travels over the years is that the British approach to displaying affection needs to improve. Now, when I see my mum and sisters and female family members or friends, we always kiss – although London-based females confuse me easily with the one or two cheek thing. Personally, after one cheek, if you are going again, you may as well throw the tongue in.

Eddie, my dad and all male family members get a handshake. Indeed, after a night in a bar with a few dozen Romanian miners (which I will come to later), I always shake hands with any male group I am in. It's good manners, it breaks down barriers, and I think it shows some class – which is something you don't always expect to learn from men who spend most of their time down a hole.

Lying on a hospital trolley about to be operated on and having both parents kiss me on the head made me start to think something was wrong. Which it was. Upon arrival at the hospital, my leg had been X-rayed and checked by the aptly named Mr Bone. Mr Bone had diagnosed a condition called osteomyelitis, a bone infection which he said was akin to having an abscess inside my left femur, the size of which, he informed my parents, was a huge cause for concern. He then advised my mum and dad that the next 24 hours would be critical.

In his words, he was operating to try to save my leg, although he told them if the operation was at all delayed and the abscess burst, then it could potentially become systemic. After that, there was a real danger I would die.

His plan was to try to drain the poison out of my leg, although he felt that the damage caused was already such that my leg would probably never grow beyond its current size – I was 11 at the time. It would then either be such a hindrance that I would want it amputated, or I could live a decent life with a built-up shoe.

Of course, I knew nothing of this when my mum and dad kissed me.

Luckily the operation was a success, but I did require a month in hospital and six months with a walking stick, followed by visits to the physiotherapy unit for a further three years, till they were satisfied that the leg was growing in tandem with the other one. I quite enjoyed having the walking stick, which I used to throw for Lassie to chase until I realised she would never bring it back. There is nothing more pathetic than chasing your own dog for your walking stick, when you need a walking stick to walk.

When I was eventually signed off by the physiotherapy department some three years after the operation, I knew how lucky I was. The final sign-off meant that they believed I was fixed for life, and in reality I was: I have never had any problems with my leg, and after the rehabilitation period I was able to do everything as if it had never happened. Yet I knew that not everyone was that fortunate.

During my time in hospital I became aware of a boy in the same ward as me. He had visitors, but he never really noticed them as he lay looking at the ceiling. Sometimes his mum would just sit on a chair next to his bed and cry; other times, she would come with a priest who would administer Holy Communion, but all the time he just lay looking up, communicating using weak flicks of his eyelids.

His name was Kieran, and when I was able get out of my bed I started going over to him with my cartoons. My leg at this point was attached to a drip, which was pumping antibiotic fluid directly into the bone, with another bag to collect the putrid, black-red infection as it drained. I was not able to move all over the ward, but I could make it to the other side of the room to his bed – it only took me around 15 minutes. When the nurses saw that I was visiting Kieran, thankfully they moved his bed next to mine.

Kieran and I became good friends, mainly because we were the only ones in there for more than a few days and because we were very close in age. I would read comics with him or just talk, or show him things. Gradually his winks were accompanied by grunts, and it was clear he was on his way back from the damage that had been caused when he had been knocked over by a van whilst out playing.

When I left hospital I was genuinely sad to be saying goodbye to Kieran. We kept in touch and, during my frequent visits to the hospital, I called in to see him on the ward and later at his house, when he had been deemed well enough to be transferred home, near Warrington. When my hospital visits ended and I had no reason to visit Warrington, our communication reduced to the odd letter or card, and a very occasional phone call, although his speech still had some way to go to be fully comprehensible and his handwriting looked like it had been a struggle to complete the words.

Then, one morning, when I was getting ready to go to school, my dad opened a letter over breakfast. I recognised the handwriting as belonging to Kieran's mum. I could see from his expression that my dad had a message to pass on. He handed me the letter. Kieran had died. Despite his improvement he hadn't been strong enough to ward off normal infections and had lost his fight for life.

Kieran had died as a consequence of an accident that could have been avoided. As always with these happenings that can ruin lives, there would have been many nights spent by all involved wishing that those split-second decisions that had put Kieran in front of that van had been different. Like my school friend in the swimming pool.

I was 17 and, once again, I was reminded that nothing in life is guaranteed.

CHAPTER 5

TEENAGE KICKS

I have teenage boys now. I look at their life and not only do I not understand them because they are teenagers and their job is to be incomprehensible to their parents, but also because their life is nothing like the life I had at their age. When I was a teenager, we did not have any form of communication apart from talking either face-to-face, being on the house phone or writing. Admittedly, the letter-writing side was in reality limited to notes around the classroom, usually involving a very poor caricature of the teacher with enormous genitals. Which now seems rather odd. Why would it be funny to suggest the man in front of you had a huge cock? But, for some reason in a world before YouTube, it was the funniest thing we could think of.

Valentine's Day cards were the only other time I recall writing to communicate. They were things to be prized, and size certainly mattered. During my teenage years I would give my girlfriend a Valentine's card that was the size of a Wendy house, or padded so it was like a duvet in a box, although admittedly a duvet with a doe-eyed teddy bear on it. I wouldn't for a minute suggest that I was in any way more romantic than any other teenage boy, but from an early age I learnt that you have to invest if you want something, and an impressive card, in my mind, stood you in good stead for a fondle.

I sometimes miss the simplicity of teenage relationships, though – the ability to end it by telling your mate to tell her mate that she was 'chucked' just seems so much more honest in its own cowardly way than the text/Facebook route chosen by teenagers today. I also miss the progressive nature of the physical relationship. The gradual stages of fumbling and endless snogging to suddenly being allowed entry into unchartered waters so that you take another tiny step towards manhood – all of that held an excitement that is hard to replicate at any other stage of your life. A mate of mine said to me that reducing his golf handicap was giving him the same buzz that he received from achieving the gradual progression through the bases when he was a teenage boy. There is nothing that can define you more as a middle-aged man than having a friend who is as excited by lowering his golf handicap as he once was by learning how to undo a bra. Age is a cruel thing.

Today, the first indication that your teenage child is having a relationship is the increasing size of their mobile phone bill. The notion that teenage romance led to hours on the phone was somewhat alien in my youth: talking on the house phone at all was a rare event. The phone was for emergencies. Besides, the phone lived on a table positioned in the hallway under the stairs – the most public place in the house. Nowadays, people are suggesting that parents need to monitor their children's activities on social networking sites to find out to whom they are talking. That wasn't required in the eighties – if your mum wanted to know what you were up to, she just sat on the stairs.

Today, every individual in my house has their own mobile phone, and we have various telephone extensions around the house – to the extent that it is impossible not to be available for immediate communication. This has created a difficult situation for this generation of teenagers, as they have never known anything but instant communication. If the internet goes down in my house, it's the end of the world, and the children immediately get in touch with social services to report neglect.

But the flip side to this is that if they leave the house and I want to know where they are going and what they are doing, I just ring them. (If you are a parent, you know that I'm lucky if they bother to answer the phone or tell me the truth, but allow me my fantasy.) Telecommunication has lost all its magic for them, which is sad in some ways. They will never know the excitement of a phone call after nine at night: anyone ringing our house that late was only doing it to say someone was dead, and it was always great family fun to guess who before the phone was picked up.

Often the quickest way to converse with teenagers today is via text, even if they are in the same room. I once had a text row with my son when we were sitting on the same couch! I lost, as every adult that tries to communicate with the 'youth of today' inevitably will do when the process of communication involves only using your thumbs. Watching my kids texting looks a blur to me: it's like their two thumbs are having a race. Their head is bowed, and the concentra-tion on the face and the general stillness could easily be interpreted as meditation, were it not for the frenetic thumb action. Having a text row with them is pointless because before you can finish your text to them they have replied, told you how wrong you are, how great everyone else's parents are and how you are ruining their life.

This evolution of communication is the biggest difference between my kids and my own development as a teenager. For me, football provided a way to enter the adult world. During my teenage years my dad ran Sunday league teams. We would travel together as a squad, play the game, go to the pub afterwards and be home for the Sunday roast my mum had prepared. During those years I learnt how to be amongst men. I also learnt that if you make a commitment, you stick to it. So even on wet Sunday mornings, when your bed was calling you, you got up and went to play on whatever pitch you were sent to that week.

Trying to recall my teenage years, I can remember football constantly being there. The academy system that most clubs run these days did not exist then, so it was possible to believe you might become a professional footballer even if you hadn't been scouted by the time you were 20. There were always examples of top-flight footballers who, a few years earlier, had been playing Sunday league football. The consequence was that amateur football was very vibrant: people still had dreams, and those dreams had a chance of being realised. It wasn't difficult to get kids together either, because everyone wanted to play. In a world without computer games or, for that matter, home computers, and where children's TV was only on for a few hours after school, if you didn't go out and do something your options were very limited.

Having run kids' teams myself in recent years, I don't recall levels of parental involvement or interference being as high back then, either. I don't recollect my dad having to drop us off and pick us up in the same way my wife and I have spent the last few years doing – to the point that if there is one luxury I have allowed myself, it is to set up a taxi account. My secret ambition is to one day own a car and sell it years later, without it ever having been used to ferry them anywhere. When my oldest son recently passed his driving test, my wife and I sat back and planned what we would do with all the spare time we would now gain from not driving him around. She is considering a second degree and I am planning to learn Chinese.

The truth was that we expected less then. Youth teams barely had full kits, let alone matching hoodies and personalised bags. The parents who did come generally did so to support the lads; there was no need for rope around the pitch to prevent irate parents coming onto the field to either support or bollock their little Johnny. The level of organisation in youth football now is impressive. Team coaches have to pass an approved FA coaching course, people involved are CRB checked, and my son's under-15 team has to line up to have their photo ID-checked by the opposition manager before every game.

I think some of this can be overkill, like being CRB-checked to take your own son and his friends to a game, even though they all stayed at your house the night before. (This was actually suggested to me a few years ago – you can imagine my response.) It's great to be organised, but you don't want to take the simple pleasure out of the game. Although I do think the ID cards are a good idea, as it prevents teams playing 'ringers': I recall playing a game against one team when I was 15, which we lost. At the end of the game their bearded centre-half drove himself and his watching wife and kids home.

As a teenager the team I played for was Halton Sports. It was run by my dad's friend, Joe Langton, whose son, Peter, also played. Joe was a barrel-chested man with a bald head, the crown of which was framed by short, blond hair. He always sported a neat moustache. A strong man whose day job was laying flag stones, Joe was almost square in shape. The joke amongst the lads was that he had once been six-foot-seven and a house had fallen on him to make him the square five-foot-six he actually was. Joe took it so seriously that he would often turn up in a three-piece suit, ready for an interview with *Match of the Day* should they turn up.

The team was good. The better players from our school team played, boys like Mark Donovan, Sean Johnson and Curtis Warren – not the infamous Liverpool gangster, but a fast, ginger-haired lad who scored a lot of goals. We were joined by good lads from the schools' representative team, like John Hickey and Peter Golburn. I only list the names because none of us became professional footballers – which was an obvious ambition for us all – and every single one of those listed would have been good enough.

I would possibly suggest that playing in Joe's team was the highest sporting success most of us enjoyed, as we spent one season completely unbeaten and won most things in the years that we played. My dad kept all the newspaper clippings of my resulting football career, and I always look at the coverage of that period with affection.

•   •   •

Apart from playing football, there was not a lot to do on the estate. When I was a bit older I volunteered at a cancer hospice, but in my early teens I never went to a youth club or anything of that nature, and generally just hung around on my bike doing all the things teenage boys do. I never really got into too much trouble. Scrapping had been replaced by an interest in girls, and the knowledge that as you all grew bigger it hurt more when you got hit. I never did the drinking-cider-on-a-wall-and-smoking thing that many started to do in their mid-teens because I had promised my dad I would never smoke, a promise he made all four of us make to him from a very early age, and which none of us has broken – apart from allowing myself the odd cigar. (That habit began one night in a posh hotel in Valletta, Malta. I found myself alone with an 80-year-old barman called Sonny, drinking a glass of whisky and listening to Frank Sinatra. Having a cigar seemed the most appropriate thing in the world.)

When I was 13 and feeling the need to be more independent and spread my wings outside the estate, football things were replaced by a bicycle. It was a silver 'racer', which basically meant it weighed a ton but had curved handlebars. Due to a cock-up by the catalogue company, I didn't actually get the bike till Easter, so on Christmas Day my present was a box containing Cluedo. A great game, but not a great way to get around the estate. I hope I hid my disappointment well enough on the day when asking through gritted teeth – when my mates were all out on their new bikes – 'Was it Professor Green with the lead piping?'

With the ability to stagger repayments, the catalogue was the avenue through which many people on the estate purchased things that were out of their reach financially. Every time a White Arrow van arrived on the estate, you knew someone was getting something from the catalogue. The bike was my final present as a child. Every year previously for

Christmas I received something football-related. After the bike, all my Christmas presents were things to make me look good or allow me to go out; in other words, money or clothes. Unless it was a book voucher, which no kid wants as a Christmas present – you may as well give them an abacus and say, 'Go and try to be a bit cleverer next year.'

The progression of a boy's life can be mapped out by the Christmas presents he receives: a kit; a ball; one year I got a Subbuteo set with two teams, England and Uruguay. Nobody knew where Uruguay was, but they played in a blue kit and all the players were painted brown, so when I played Subbuteo, it was always England v the Black Everton.

As I got older, other things became more important to me, such as trying to be fashionable. I particularly remember receiving my first Fred Perry T-shirt, a yellow one with brown trim, which I don't think I took off until it was physically too small to get on and had begun to look like a bra. But the only way of providing you with something that allowed you to make up your own mind was with money. Cash became king in my teenage years when it came to presents. I could buy records, although I never went too crazy on this: I rationalised that there is always new music, so why spend your money on something you like now when something better may be out next week? These are the decisions you had to make when it came to records, as they were things of permanence, not like a download. Even if you weren't playing it, you had to put it somewhere, and I couldn't always be bothered with that level of responsibility. Besides, being the youngest allowed me to listen to the music the others brought into the house, on either vinyl or cassette. I realise for readers of a certain age these things may as well be tablets of stone, and for others they provided hours of musical joy, but to me they were just more things I had to put away.

By the time I was 15 I had discovered girls. I knew they had existed before, obviously – I lived with two of them. But I mean I became more interested in them than I was in my mates. However, it should be made clear that I wasn't exactly a lothario when it came to girls, and I had all the awkwardness that comes with being a teenage boy. These ranged from thinking that the best way of attracting the attention of a girl you fancied was by throwing something at her head (Paula); to being so unworldly wise that the first time a girl French-kissed me I pulled away, spat on the floor and shouted, 'What did you stick your tongue down my mouth for? You dirty cow!' (Jane).

This growing interest coincided with a failed car-stealing incident. It was not an unusual pastime for teenage boys on the estate to steal motor scooters from gardens. They were easy to jump-start, and you could have a few hours of fun before the petrol ran out, someone crashed or you just left it somewhere – usually always stupidly close to home, to save the walk.

Somehow, we had never been caught doing this. So, emboldened, we decided one afternoon when at my friend Mark's house that he should steal his dad's car. This was a big, golden-brown British Leyland Princess which Mark had been shown how to drive by his dad, although admittedly only for 50 yards. His mum and dad were away for the weekend, and Mark was being checked on by his older sister, but was basically left to his own devices. After some thought, we all decided it would be great to drive around the estate in the car.

Mark was a bit less enthusiastic, I recall, but, being egged on by the four of us, he capitulated. He took the keys, and off we set. He reversed safely enough and, despite it being the middle of a Saturday afternoon, none of the neighbours seemed concerned when five 14-year-old boys started driving down the street.

Mark managed to get over two relatively busy junctions and had avoided knocking over any number of kids playing in the street before the car suddenly stopped. He tried to change gear but nothing happened.

We were all sitting in a stolen car in the middle of the estate when a man in a van stopped and asked what was wrong. Not, 'What are you lot doing in the car?' but, 'What's wrong?'

With his help, it was decided the clutch had gone and that the only way back to the house was to push it. A journey of 10 minutes' driving is a lot longer when four teenage boys are pushing a car steered by their friend, and it may have been during it that the penny dropped in my head: 'My mates are idiots. I should be trying to get girls' bras off instead.'

I really was no big hit with the girls. I was never actually shy, just unsure. I understood boys. You knew what made each other laugh (farts), and you knew that if someone was annoying, then eventually someone else would punch them. It was never the same with girls. They could say something to me, and I would just be stumped. I would just think, 'Laughing must be wrong as nobody has farted, and punching them is out of the question.'

I eventually got over my awkwardness and was able to have a few dalliances, before going steady with a girl called Denise. She had hair that was a mixture of red and auburn, a great athletic figure from playing school hockey and netball, and a wicked sense of humour. And I am grateful that during my later teenage years, when I could have been doing other things, she allowed me the opportunity to fumble my way to manhood with her.

We went out with each other in that typically teenage on-off fashion for years; people assumed that we would one day get married. That is what you did on the estate: if you found someone who was good enough, it seemed to make sense to get married. I remember my dad even asking me once if I thought I would marry her. I was 17. As the father of 17-year-old boys of the modern era, I am not sure I could even ask them to commit to taking the dog for a walk without expecting a phone call telling me the dog had ran off and it was my fault because I asked them to do it in the first place.

The reality was that I wanted something more than the estate had to offer; I just wasn't sure what it was. But I was about to find out.

CHAPTER 6

ALL I LEARNT IN SCHOOL

I left school for the first time when I was 16. I had gained six O-levels and four CSEs. At that time, the education system was split between those who teachers thought were academically capable enough to achieve an O-level, and those they considered 'less able', who sat CSEs. I fell into the bracket of pupils who were regarded as a little bit of both. In Physics and Maths everyone sat the same examination, and you were either awarded an O-level or a CSE. This worked out well for me, as I achieved an O-level in both. I doubt that was what my teachers expected of me, particularly as the only thing I can remember about physics was setting my hair on fire trying to see if the central hole in the Bunsen burner continued up through the flame. If you're interested, it doesn't. And I think it is fair to say that if you are stupid enough to set yourself on fire, you are lucky to get any qualification, let alone a coveted O-level.

At my school, this batch of O-levels was a fairly impressive figure. Within my household, school was something that we all went to but never really expected much from. My mum attended all the parents' evenings, but the only time I recall my dad showing more than a passing interest was the summer I left.

'You mum tells me you've done some O-levels.'

'Yer.'

'Good, hope you get them.'

That was that, and I guess that was all that needed to be said.

With what appeared to be a healthy clutch of qualifications, I was encouraged by the school to return to the sixth form. It had only just been set up, as whilst the total student population was pushing towards 2,000, they weren't particularly successful in recruiting candidates for sixth form: there was just 11 people in it. But, after due consideration, I went for it.

This decision was based on the belief that if I were to gain A-levels I could do a degree, and if I did a degree, I could do a job where I would not need to get a wash when I came home from work, like Clive's dad. In my mind, I could end up doing something interesting, taxing, and where you wore a suit: perhaps be a solicitor. No ordinary, boring solicitor, but more of a Petrocelli-type, caravan-dwelling advocate, the sort of lawyer who stood up for the innocent poor who couldn't pay for justice. If you never saw the brilliant series starring Barry Newman, it is a great indication of how times have changed. Who would trust a lawyer now who lived in a caravan?

To be a lawyer was an impressive aspiration within my family, so I perpetuated the idea that I wanted to train to be a solicitor for many years. In fact, I'm sure there are still some family members who think it would have been better to have a lawyer in the family than a comedian.

However, my attendance at sixth form lasted all of one day. At that time, anybody staying on at school sixth form only received family allowance. This was the princely sum of £6.50 per week, as opposed to the £24 per week afforded by the government to all those on a Youth Opportunity Scheme. It was 1982, the recession was beginning to bite, and there were very few jobs around. But the government policy guaranteed all 16 to 18 year olds a place on one of these schemes.

Along with this, when I arrived at the sixth form wearing brand-new jeans, I was promptly informed that jeans were not acceptable so I would have to get some trousers.

At the time, Eddie had left home to take up residence in a flat in Southgate, an estate built to look like washing machines and with about as much practical application as a washing machine when it came to somewhere to live; Kathy was training to be a nursery nurse; and Carol was on a Youth Opportunity Scheme. My dad was trying to make a living making and selling wrought-iron furniture, such as telephone tables, which were such a staple of every home at the time. The idea was that when you used the phone you sat sort of side-saddle at the table. No wonder people of a certain age seem to droop as they get older – for a large part of their life they are having conversations on the phone at a ridiculous angle. My mum had a part-time job washing dishes in the kitchen of a factory canteen on the industrial estate. In essence, I didn't feel I could return home and say to my mum I required new trousers. Instead, I felt I should be bringing money into the household and paying my way.

I had already applied for a job at the main factory in Runcorn: ICI. Along with my mate, Vic, I received a letter saying I had the got the job, to start in the second week of September. ICI was a huge chemical plant and the job in question was as a mail lad. That was the actual job description; it was a job for a 'lad' – girlies need not apply. And to my knowledge, none of them did. Most followed other paths, like my then girlfriend Denise, who trained to be a hairdresser. At least the old system made things very simple, as I'm sure if the 'mail lad' job were to exist at all in the world of emails it would be called something like 'communications distribution individual'.

So I left school and went to work delivering mail at ICI. This involved getting a bus at 6.30 a.m. to arrive at work for 7. We would then collect the bicycles that were left at the security gate each evening and ride down the hill to the mail office. Getting up early was worth that ride downhill. Everyone should start the day going downhill on a bicycle. It was great fun – apart from the rain and snow and cold. OK, so it was great about eleven days of the year, but they were still great days.

We'd finish by 3 o'clock and, two nights a week, I would then go to night school in Widnes to study A-levels in English and Law. I may not have been in the sixth form, but I didn't want my education to stop.

One day, on the way home from ICI, and while still wearing my steel-cap ICI safety boots, my ICI safety jacket and my ICI safety trousers, I called in to the school sixth form. It was there that I bumped into Mr Logan. Mr Logan had been my English teacher during my O-level period and would have been my A-level teacher had I stayed in the sixth form. He asked me how I was getting on, and I explained that I was working and doing A-levels at night school. He asked if I'd consider returning to the sixth form in January, but as I was then earning £42 a week, to leave that to return to a family allowance of just £6.50 a week didn't seem viable.

In reality, I was beginning to have doubts about ICI and the future. I remember one day I fell into conversation at the plant with one of the men who always seemed to be walking around wearing boiler suits and hard hats, but never actually doing much. He was a friendly man in his late fifties with a warm face and a frame that suggested he enjoyed a roast dinner, and a disposition that suggested he had never seen how that roast dinner was made. He had worked at ICI all of his life.

'You've got a job for life here, son,' he informed me proudly, as he lit a cigarette, completely ignoring the No Smoking signs and the miles of pipework around his head carrying flammable chemicals. 'Yes, son, no reason you won't be taking your pension here.'

I remember looking around at the myriad pipes transporting chemicals all over the plant, and thinking, 'Is this the view I have to spend the rest of my working life looking at?'

I think one of those great things about advice is that it is often given to make one point but ends up making entirely the opposite one. I could think of nothing worse than giving my life away so cheaply. Some people are lucky enough to find contentment in such security, but for me it felt as if someone was pouring water over my bonfire so the flames would not get too high. To stay in the same place of work all my life, get married, live in the same area, go to the same pubs, see the same faces until one by one we popped our clogs was like being handed a life of limitation that I just couldn't accept. It's a life that suits many people down to the ground, and in many ways I have always been envious of them. I never thought I was better than anyone else; I just knew I wanted something different. The problem was, I wasn't sure what that was.

In the discussion with Mr Logan I had told him that the only option for me to return to full-time education of any nature was to take a part-time course at the local further-education college. If you were able to study part-time there, then you were able to claim unemployment benefits, which would mean £18 a week rather than £6.50. Still a long way behind the £42 a week I was currently earning, but at least a step to bridge the gap. The difficulty was that you were not allowed to study in school sixth forms part-time, only in FE colleges. If you were studying in a school, then you had to be classed as a full-time student for the school to receive the payment from the local education authority to cover your attendance. Mr Logan had said he would talk to the headmistress, Ms Philips, and see if there was any way around this.

I came into school a few days later to have a conversation with them both. The reality was stark and clear: I could not continue to do night-school A-levels one night a week over one year and realistically expect to pass. But, on the other hand, I couldn't afford to leave my job. After some deliberation, it was agreed that the school would give me a letter that I could take to the unemployment exchange to say that I was studying part-time. Once they accepted this and guaranteed I would receive my dole, then I would leave my job.

The school was basically gambling that the unemployment office would not get in touch with the education services who, had they found out I was only studying part-time, would not have given the school the full remittance for my place, while Ms Philips would have faced serious questions about why she had told lies.

Everything was agreed and the letter was accepted. I was to return to school to do English and History A-levels, whilst I was to continue at night school once a week to study Law.

It was a decision that would change everything I would do from then on, and it opened the door to a new world of potential opportunity.

What I had not envisaged was how this plan would sound to anybody else when I tried to explain it. The night that everything was agreed with the teachers, I went home to tell my mum and dad. I knew that they had been proud that I had been taken on at ICI as it offered one of the few permanent jobs for anyone my age in the area, but I assumed they would be pleased with my decision to leave, particularly once I had explained the financial side of things.

However, my announcement was met with blank stares. The kind of stares I would have expected if I had said I was going to join the Foreign Legion. Clearly what had left my mouth was the least expected thing in the world, and we sat talking until nearly midnight over endless cups of tea.

Although my mum was more supportive, my dad was clear and honest in his view. He did his best to convince me that having a job with prospects was so much better than taking a chance on doing A-levels and only possibly going to university. At this point, only my cousin Karen had gone to university, and it was generally accepted as something not for the likes of us.

Also, Karen was clever and known to be so. I was a boy and so intellect was balanced by my ability to carry things, and within our family history we were more greatly predisposed to the latter as a way to make a living. I knew I was going against the grain, but I also knew I had to tell them that this was what I wanted to do.

As I write these words now, it almost feels like I am talking about 'coming out' to my family that I read books. It wasn't so dramatic; it was more that I was gambling on something better and needed them to see it too, although at the time A-levels appeared as useful as magic beans. There were no jobs, so why give up a perfectly good one in the hope of another one in the future?

I set my argument out as best as I could: I wanted something more than it appeared I could achieve if I did not change direction.

After hours of talking, my dad summarised it all in just one sentence: 'I think it could be a mistake, but you have got to try. If you don't try, you will always wonder what might have happened.'

And that was that. From that moment, I had their full support and they never questioned my decision. It was a great relief that they supported me: once my mum and dad get behind you, they are there for the long haul, and you can't ask more of anyone.

So for the first time, but not the last, I left a well-paid job to try to achieve something against the advice of many, but with the support of those who mattered.

Eighteen months later, I was sitting in the passenger seat of a second-hand BT van next to my mum, as my dad was driving us north to what was then Newcastle Polytechnic. My mum could have said goodbye at home and let me travel up with my dad, or they could have put me on a train. Instead, they wanted to make the eight-hour round trip in a car none of us was sure could make it in order to say goodbye properly, because that's what loving parents do. The van had been acquired a few weeks before, and it was another in the long list of unique vehicles my dad has owned. With a top speed of 50 mph, the journey took a very long time.

In actuality, it had taken 18 years. I was leaving home and saying goodbye to start the next stage of my life.

CHAPTER 7

NEWCASTLE

Newcastle didn't exactly work out for me as I had planned. I enjoyed my first term there, and I liked the people that I met. However, I had gone to study an English and History degree having achieved a 'B' in my History and an 'Ungraded' in my English A-levels.

The English grade had shocked the school to the extent that they had paid to have the paper remarked. They had predicted at least a 'B' grade, but when the paper was returned it was clear why the ungraded mark had been given. Somewhere in the exam my brain had turned to mush, and my mild dyslexia had gone berserk: I had written some words backwards, some upside down, whilst others were just illegible. Although I certainly am not the greatest speller in the world, and had been tested for dyslexia on a number of occasions, I had never before displayed such a meltdown.

I have always put my inability to spell down to the fact that in junior school we were taught to spell phonetically, which means speaking the word slowly as you spell it. The problem with such a process is that if you speak with an accent as thick as mine, and live in an environment where you are not surrounded by the written word to counterbalance

your exposure to these sounds, then it is easy to make mistakes. I was 10 before I realised the word 'there' did not have
a 'd' in it.

What happened that day has never happened since, and it
is still inexplicable to me. But, using the grades I achieved in
General Studies and the Law exam I did at night school as a
trade-off, the school had somehow convinced Newcastle Poly
they should allow me to do a degree in a subject that I failed
at A-level. Which you have to say is no mean feat.

I began the course in Newcastle full of enthusiasm. It was
my first time living away from home and I immediately fell
in love with the city and its people. To this day, it is one of
the first places I look for when I have a tour booked. I was
living in the student hall of residence and threw myself into
the social life that this presented. I gained a casual girlfriend
called Anne and managed to get myself into the first XI football team, which provided a great social network. It also
provided fantastic trips away, as Newcastle Poly sports
teams were generally regarded as quite strong.

On one particular trip, we were to play against Edge Hill
University, a teacher training college near Ormskirk. I can't
remember the score, but I know we won, and what I can
remember is that after the game we went to the student
union for a drink – only to find out the ratio of girls to men
at Edge Hill was roughly 4 to 1. We had a whip-round to convince the bus driver to allow us to stay a few hours longer,
and at the end of the evening we returned to the team bus
triumphant. Every single player (apart from Lawrence, who
played in goal and whose cousin attended that college and to
whom he'd had to talk all night) had got at least a snog. It
was a fantastic feeling to be amongst a body of men who
had arrived in new lands and challenged the local men to do

battle on the football pitch, emerging victorious and then finding pleasure among the local women. It was probably the closest I will ever come to being a Viking.

Despite the fun I was having in Newcastle, I was quickly becoming disillusioned with the course. In truth, my experience in literature has been limited to books that I was forced to read for school rather than books I wanted to read; it was only during my A-level course that I had begun to read books for pleasure. Prior to that, if it was not a comic book or a *Roy of the Rovers* annual, I never read anything.

I regret those wasted years, and I am pleased that my three sons are avid readers. I still don't read as much as I would like, but I attempt to have at least one book always on the go. This does also lead to the accumulation of a mass of books that I have started on a train journey somewhere and never finished. I used to feel guilty about not finishing books but, as I've become older, I have come to the conclusion that this is not my fault – if the book was any good, I would have finished it.

This could be a very pragmatic way to explain my laziness, or it could simply be true. Books are the only thing that you embark upon feeling responsible for your own enjoyment of it; even if the first 50 pages are rubbish, there is a sense of defeat if you don't finish it. That doesn't happen in any other art form; it certainly doesn't happen in comedy. You can't be rubbish for 20 minutes to the extent that the audience get up and leave without seeing the conclusion of your act, and feel totally reassured that on their way home they will think it's their fault.

No, as a comedian it's your job to hold the audience's attention. This is a responsibility I take on in my job, which I have now assumed for other aspects in my life: films, plays,

TV programmes and books. Although, as a comedian, if you are losing the audience, you will soon find out because someone will tell you. That is the valid role of the heckler, to make you aware of any failings you had not realised yourself. But you can respond to a heckle, and at times it allows a comedy gig to step up a pace. You often find the act becomes sharper and quicker once the comedian has dealt with the heckle. It's not the same for an author. I have often shouted at a book, 'This is shit . . . is that all you've got?' and I have never noticed it change the book at all.

So when I embarked upon a degree in English, it is probably fair to say my literary experience was more limited than most of the people in the room. The history elements of the course I really enjoyed, but the English element I found unbelievably frustrating.

During the first term, we concentrated exclusively up on the mammoth poem, 'The Rime of the Ancient Mariner' by Samuel Taylor Coleridge. For those unfamiliar with the work, all I can say from memory is that it is a story about a sailor who leads a ship to safety with the aid of an albatross. There is a wedding involved, and somewhere the sailor goes a bit mental and shoots the bird with a crossbow, hanging it around his neck, and gets lost again. I am sure there is much more to it than that, but even now I am not prepared to find out what because my relationship with the poem was tainted by the experience of sitting in a seminar room whilst a tutor asked us first-year students to explain the interaction between the sailor and the bird:

'Why does Coleridge feel the albatross can communicate with the mariner in a way other people can't? What is the connection that binds them, man and beast, together? Why should the bird return when the gift of flight means he could leave any time? He is the master of his own destiny, but binds himself to the ship – why would he do that? What is Coleridge trying to tell us about ourselves and about him through the actions of the albatross?'

These and many more questions were put to us over a period of weeks. Although in their own right they would potentially be worth a discussion, everything is tarnished when you know Coleridge was an opium addict. When I suggested that being a smack-head and writing about ships meant that Coleridge was basically doing the eighteenth-century equivalent of shouting at buses whilst sitting on a park bench drinking Special Brew, it was clear that my days with the literary intelligentsia of Newcastle Polytechnic would soon be over.

Having made the decision to leave the course, I then faced the dilemma of what to do. I really wanted to enrol on the sports science course where I had a number of friends. The sports science faculty offered me a place, but suggested that as I had done a term already I would have to switch the following year.

So, after three months in Newcastle, I returned home with a place on the sports science degree to start in September.

Little did I know when I left Newcastle that day, I would never return to the poly.

CHAPTER 8

I DON'T EAT MEAT, OR FIGHT PARATROOPERS

The nine months that followed my departure saw me learn many valuable life lessons, including: 1) what to do with a dead man's glass eye; 2) when a wage is not enough of a reason to be killed; and 3) why I love America.

Upon returning home, I faced the financial necessity of paying my own way, but I did not know what to do to fill in the next nine months before my planned return to Newcastle. For my first job, I started working on a building site for an extension to the cancer hospice where I had worked as a volunteer since the age of 16.

This was Halton Haven, which was run on a voluntary basis and led by a very dynamic man called Dom Valdez. I cannot recall what motivated me as a 16-year-old boy to go into the Portakabin that operated as a day centre to offer my time and my skills, which were basically limited to making tea and talking to old people. I volunteered throughout my A-levels and, as residential beds were added to the facility,

I extended my support from making cups of tea to sharing the night shift looking after the residential patients. I was usually on with a retired ward sister called Grace, who had a Scottish accent so sharp you could slice bread with it.

Once midnight arrived, we would take turns to sleep for a few hours; apart from the odd patient dying, the nights were generally quiet. It would seem crazy in today's world of health and safety to leave somebody with absolutely no experience in charge of terminally ill cancer patients; however, the centre had expanded thanks to the goodwill of the local community, and in order to offer residential care at no cost, volunteers were essential, even if, like me, they didn't really know what they were doing.

My time at Halton Haven provided me with many life-affirming experiences. You learn the value of family and friends when you see people coming to the end of their life and nobody visits them. There was one particular resident called Stan who was a small, neat man with the demeanour of an accountant: organised, controlling and not particularly friendly. Stan always had a 'spittoon' with him into which he would cough up phlegm from the recesses of his damaged bronchial system. The spittoon was basically a Tupperware beaker with a lid which, over a period of 24 hours, he would fill to the top with the congealed contents of his cancerous lungs.

The job I hated most in the building, beyond the bed-pans or taking people to the toilet, or even once shaving a man and changing his shirt moments after he had died to make him presentable to his family who were just arriving, was having to empty Stan's spittoon.

This was always the first thing to do in the morning prior to helping Stan get ready for breakfast, and often prior to eating my own breakfast. The process was simple. You carried the beaker to the toilet, took a deep breath, poured the contents away whilst trying not to retch, as the previous 24 hours of coagulated mucus would by this point have often merged into one semi-solid mass, wash out the beaker and pull the flush, trying desperately to avoid any of the contents being splashed onto your hands or your clothing. Stan coughed more in the night, and most mornings the contents were virtually a single piece of green-yellow ectoplasm with speckles of red. I could not think of a more undesirable job in the world, and Stan never seemed to acknowledge it was anything more than washing out a cup, barely saying thank you most of the time.

Although he could be grumpy, I quite liked Stan. As he very rarely had visitors, I would pop my head around the door and say hello every time I visited the unit. One morning, I popped my head around his door and he was sitting sideways on his bed, his head bowed over his beaker releasing more of the sputum that gelled his lungs together. The beaker was nearly full to the brim so, when the coughing finished, I said I would empty it. As he sat back on his bed and I picked up the warm container, he put his hand on my forearm. As Stan's cancer was in his lungs, it would often take him some time to build up enough lung capacity to speak, so there was an awkward moment which seemed to last a lifetime, during which I became increasingly uncomfortable standing and holding a warm plastic container of sputum as Stan rested his hand on my arm and readied himself to speak.

After what seemed an age, he said, 'You know what I will be sorry about the most?'

Feeling slightly nauseous, and anxious to relieve my hand of the contents of the beaker which, in my mind, were not far away from dribbling through to my fingers thanks to osmosis, I just said, 'No, Stan.'

'It's that I won't be around to empty your beaker.'

Stan gently lifted his arm and smiled at me. It was a smile of acceptance and of gratitude. For the few weeks more that he was with us, emptying the beaker never seemed so much of a chore. Don't get me wrong, it still made me want to gag and throw up – no smile, however gentle, was going to make it palatable – but at least I knew it was just part of the circle of life. It was my turn now to be the beaker emptier. In years to come I would be the beaker filler. I will just have to hope someone will be there to help.

· · ·

When I returned from Newcastle, the building work to extend the hospice was well under way, and it was primarily being completed by people who were connected with the centre through friends or relatives. Clearly you cannot build something just with volunteers, and Dom was canny enough to know that, as many tradesmen were out of work, the best thing would be to get them to work for cash at a very low rate, allowing everyone the time off they needed to sign on and tell the dole office that they were working as volunteers.

I began working as a labourer by day and helping at the hospice by night. My main job was as a plasterer's mate. This meant mixing the plaster in a large tin bath with a shovel using plaster mix, sand and water. I would then shovel it onto a hod and carry it to the table where I would place it for the two plasterers I was working for.

One thing about plasterers is that they are very particular about their plaster. That day we had a new plasterer working

with us: he was in his forties, had an eighties perm, a constant cigarette in his mouth and a scowl on his face.

'This is shit,' he said of the first mix I did for him.

'This is even more shit,' he said of the second one I did for
him. Even the other lads said he was being a bit harsh on
me, but he didn't care.

'He has got to learn. If he does a shit mix, we get a shit
wall, and the building ends up a shit job just because he was
shit at his job.'

He was basically a bully and kept on at me all day, telling
me how every mix I gave him was shit, until I couldn't take
any more. So I decided to give him what he wanted and took a
dump in the mix and presented it to him. I had concealed it in
the middle of the plaster so effectively that my deed was not
revealed until he plastered the wall – whereupon he tried to
kill me with a lump hammer, whilst everyone else fell on the
floor laughing. But, apart from that, I really enjoyed working
on the site, and every time I drive past the hospice now I tell
my kids there is a part of me in the building. I just have never
explained which part.

I also enjoyed the few nights a week I did within the
hospice, which often provided moments of black humour
when you would least expect it. On one occasion, a man died
at four in the morning. It was always the case that people
seemed to die in the early hours of the morning; I remember
one nurse telling me her theory that people who died in the
night were the laziest, because they chose death instead of
getting up in the morning. I have no idea if there has been
a clinical study to look into this, but I do like the theory.
I enjoy the idea of being warm and snug and in the middle
of a dream – in my case possibly involving Girls Aloud – and
having enough conscious control of my own mortality to

decide not to open my eyes and just slip into the next life with my dream being my last registered brain activity. That would be dying with a smile on my face.

The man who had died on this occasion was called George, and he had passed on whilst not wearing his glass eye. That night the only people on duty were me and Sister Grace. She decided that we should try to return George's eye to him in order to make him look as respectable as possible. This meant me trying to replace the glass eye from whence it came.

I don't know if many of you reading this have ever tried to return a glass eye to a person who has recently died, but it's not as easy as it might sound. When a person dies, the facial muscles completely relax and, as a result, when you place the eye under the eyelids, they don't close. This means you end up with somebody dead in the bed looking at you. Not only can this be rather disconcerting, it is not the way you would like the family to see the body. I cannot imagine anything worse than being led into the room of your dead relative to find them sitting up in bed, winking at you.

We decided, after some deliberation, to place the eye in an envelope and give it to the undertaker. He arrived whilst we were waiting for the doctor to sign the death certificate and we handed him the envelope, on which was the name 'George Andrews'.

'Is that George from the church, the organist?' asked the undertaker.

'I think so,' replied Sister Grace.

'What a lovely man. Really friendly when we did funerals there. I didn't know he was ill. What a shame. Lovely fella, always said he would keep an eye out for me.'

As I write that it sounds like a pub gag, but at four in the morning in a hospice in Runcorn in 1985 it was without doubt the funniest thing I had ever heard.

•   •   •

When spring arrived, I wanted to try other things before returning to full-time education. There was a short stint as a vacuum cleaner salesman, which really didn't go too well as I only sold one, and that was sent back in the first week.

I then decided to join my sisters Kathy and Carol on Jersey in the Channel Islands. At the time, the Channel Islands were full of people from Liverpool and the surrounding areas who had come over for work. I have often said in my stand-up that Scousers were the first Polish people because we would go anywhere for a job, and would work longer and harder than the locals, often for less money. For a teenager, though, the money was decent, the jobs were normally good fun, and the social side could be excellent.

The year before I had gone to spend the summer in Guernsey, the smaller island, whilst Carol was working there, and had progressed from washing dishes in a hotel to running a chain of fast-food outlets called Chicken George and the Ribshack, all within five weeks. I had picked up the job in the hamburger shop by convincing the owner that at the hotel where I was washing dishes I was actually the breakfast chef. After five minutes in the kitchen it became clear that I had no idea what I was doing. But as the clientele were primarily drunks on the way home from the pub, the main requirement of the job was not the quality of the food, but the ability to get money out of people and to then get them out of the shop before someone wanted a fight. It became apparent that I was good at that side of the job and within weeks I was climbing my way up the Chicken George empire to become the manager of both shops.

It was whilst running the hamburger shops that I became vegetarian. In Guernsey there was no industrial abattoir as such; instead, if you wanted meat, you called the farmer on Monday and collected it on Wednesday. I did this, but made the dreadful mistake of going to collect the meat and then walking into the wrong room at the wrong time on the wrong day.

A cow was hanging there, a huge gaping cavity where its stomach once was and its eyes wide open, looking at me as if to say, 'You did this!' From that moment on, I never ate red meat. I spent a few years eating fish and chicken, which actually makes no sense for anyone who thinks that eating meat is cruel, unless of course you hate chickens and fish and don't care if they get killed. I have now been a vegetarian for over 25 years, and I have to say that I have not really ever missed eating meat. Having stopped because of the shock of the slaughter, now I see no point in killing something just for the sake of your palate. Really, is anything so tasty that you would kill it to taste it again?

I am not evangelical about this, and if society collapsed and amongst the anarchy I found myself unable to buy food in the shops, I would kill our dog and eat it. (So far that has not happened – but our dog Bilko needs to be on his toes!) I wear leather shoes, I don't mind people choosing to eat meat, including my own kids; but I do feel that if people were brought closer to the process of production, fewer would eat it. I also have to say that nearly every food scandal in recent years has involved meat. Until we find that the potatoes we are eating are actually carrots made to look like potatoes to enhance profits for the organised crime gangs that import the potatoes from Eastern Europe, I will always feel I made the right choice.

So it was 1985 and I went to Jersey and worked days with my sister Kathy in a café (insert your own joke here) in a beautiful harbour, and nights as a bouncer in the nightclub of the hotel where Carol worked. Though saying I worked as a bouncer makes it sound a lot more exciting than it was. There was only one fight of note, and that was amongst a fancy dress party. I had the dubious honour of explaining to the police that I had thrown Andy Pandy out because he had started on Snoopy.

The worst night to work was always Sunday. On Sunday nights in Jersey in the 1980s, you could open the nightclub and you could play music, but nobody was allowed to dance. I have not made this up, as crazy as it sounds. Yes, during the 1980s, in a place that is part of the British Isles, you were banned from dancing on a Sunday. This was due to ancient laws, which have since been repealed. (I just spent 30 minutes on Google trying to find why the law existed at all and when it ended. I couldn't find any information, which I think indicates that Jersey is so embarrassed by the whole thing they would like to just forget it.)

There is nothing harder than being a bouncer telling people to get off the dance floor because on Sunday, despite the disco lights and the nightclub setting, the dance floor is just a 'floor'. People were even forbidden to tap their feet too hard just in case that raised the spirits of the witches, or whatever other black magic we were saving the world from.

It was a Sunday night when I decided to leave the job. The 'DJ' of the club – I use that label on purpose because he could not have been more of a stereotypical DJ if he tried: open shirt, talking over songs, sunglasses in the dark, giant knob

My dad looking cool, although too many falls into the Mersey convinced him to change jobs.

My dad and some colleagues n the tugs, pulling a very ig Dick.

Iy mum and dad circa 1959: handsome couple in the lock, West Derby, Liverpool.

My mum looking beautiful aged 16.

Kathy, Carol and me in the back yard at 9 Severn Walk. I am the one not wearing a dress.

In the front garden with Eddie and his mates. I am sat at the end wearing knitte lederhosen, for some reason, and trying to copy what the big boys are doing.

Southport superb.

Southport 2 .... Liverpool Reserves 1

Southport: Moore; S. Baines, Bimson, Mooney, Smith, Bishop (Mitchell, 49), McDonald, Wellings, Holden, Livens, Gamble. Second sub. O'Brien.
Liverpool Reserves: Hooper, Jones, Harkness, Tanner, Lampkin, Hutchinson, Payne, Redknapp, Marsh, Cousins (Howard, 7), McManaman. Second sub. Carroll.
Referee: Mr N.J.Ellis (Maghull).

Great result ruined by the fact it was me rather than Redknapp who went off injured.

(*Below*) Halton Sports Under-15s, the bes team I ever played for – although I hadn' yet learnt how to shake hands properly.

(*Above*) In Crewe Park, aged 4, practising my right-foot power-drivers. I love the knitted jumper too, which my mum would have made.

was 3 when me, Eddie, Kathy and Carol had this 'posh' picture taken in our house. It was on the wall for the following 40-odd years and I love it.

A school picture aged 7, when my teeth had already decided to take over my head!

Dancing with my mum on New Year's Eve, wearing the coolest T-shirt I have ever owned.

The Bishops: Mum, me, Kathy, Eddie, Carol and Dad. I am very proud to be part of this family – they laid the foundation for everything.

Coaching 'soccer' in America,
although I cannot remember
why I am wearing a nappy.

(*Top right*) Playing for Southport,
and concentrating on the game
enough to smile for the camera.

(*Right*) Scoring for Southport.
It did go in, as you can see from
the excitement of the crowd.

The shoe at the Grand Canyon: not a great
conversationalist, but not bad company
when travelling across the US.

Our Cinderella moment:
returning the shoe to
Ged in front of another
legendary landmark, the
Runcorn Bridge.

On the night of my 21st with Sergei and Harvey. A sensible party: Harvey hadn't even opened his can!

(*Top right*) The obligatory cap-and-gown picture. When I realised you just rent them for the shot I asked myself, Why hadn't I just done that and not bothered with studying?

Sitting on the couch at my mum's house with Melanie, who was accompanied by her hair and glasses.

Lads on tour. Posing with the Manchester boys in Edinburgh, little did I know that I would perform years later just 200 yards from where this was taken.

Looking very similar to Runcorn: the Sydney Harbour Bridge the day before I set off on the ride of a lifetime.

In Poland it was clear there were Liverpool fans everywhere. (And no, I didn't write it!)

Riding with my shirt off was okay after a few months, but on the second day I learned it wasn't such a great idea ...

With Joe somewhere in Eastern Europe – an inspirational man in every sense. Except fashion sense.

A stop in India would quickly attract a crowd, who came to look at the weirdo in the vest.

When I eventually reached the top of the Daman Pass there was a thriving outdoor laundry in business.

Returning to Liverpool to be greeted by a bloke with bagpipes. Arthur, who is clapping with his hands in the air, probably had no idea what was going on either.

With Melanie in Singapore in 1992, after she had made me get a haircut as well as some respectable clothes.

Our wedding day in May 1993: she looked beautiful; I looked like I had cut my own hair.

The picture used on invitations for our 20th wedding anniversary party. She still takes my breath away.

on his head (I made that bit up) – could not have played more inappropriate records for a Sunday night. Instead of putting on what would now be referred to as more 'chillout' music, the DJ used Sunday to play his real party pleasers. Everything was bouncy. One Sunday, we were spending all our time asking people to leave the 'dance' floor, when DJ Knob-head suddenly said, 'This is a real special one I'm going play for the squadron of paratroopers over here on manoeuvres!'

With that, he put on 'Baggy Trousers' by Madness. The dance floor became filled with skin-headed men jumping up and down in the kind of frenzy all men of a certain age reserve for Madness songs. The manager came running over and informed me and my fellow bouncer, a thin lad from Glasgow called Dave, that we were to clear the dance floor.

Now, both Dave and I knew that we had been given our jobs in part because fights were so rare anyone could do it, and partly because we both had accents that allowed people to think we might be hard. A hard accent may be enough when faced with a farmer dressed as a cartoon character, but I had little faith that it would be enough to quell the throbbing mass of testosterone jumping up and down on the dance floor. So I handed the manager my dickie bow, told him to do it himself and walked out of the building. I had somewhere much better to be.

CHAPTER 9

MOVING ON

For the rest of the summer of 1985, I went to America for the first time.

One of the things that I had done whilst in Newcastle was to complete a course to become an FA-qualified football coach. Completing the course and gaining my preliminary coaching qualification allowed me to apply for a job to coach 'soccer' in the United States for the summer. I applied to a company for whom many of the Newcastle lads had worked: North American Soccer Camps. What was great about this company was that it was not a traditional residential summer camp, but was instead a dedicated organisation that offered coaching in three-hour blocks anywhere in various US states.

When you arrived in New York, you were given a car or a plane ticket, told about who you would be working with in the coming weeks, and then sent off to a region of that great land. It meant that you could be coaching at one soccer camp in the morning, then at another in the afternoon in the next town, and staying at a motel, or with families, in between.

I coached in America for four straight summers and, as a result, I have had the privilege of travelling all over the country. My first year was spent around the East Coast states of New Jersey and Pennsylvania, the following year expanding out towards Connecticut, Rhode Island, Massachusetts and the state of New York. In the third year, I covered everywhere from Niagara Falls to Key West, spending most of my time in Florida and South Carolina. And then in the final year I spent all summer working in California, which was just as good as it sounds.

It was in South Carolina that I realised that the UK and the US are two nations separated by a common language. After coaching one day, one of the young mums came over to me.

'Y'all should come to Howlers bar tonight. A bunch of us will be there and we'll teach you boys how to shag.'

'Really! I think you will probably find we can shag already.'

'No way! Ain't never heard of any English boys who can shag. Martha, these English boys say they can shag.'

'No way, sugar pie. I would love to see that, y'all.'

'Well, you will tonight, love!'

We arrived at the bar prepared for almost anything apart from what we saw. It was full of people line dancing. The mum that I had spoken to came running over and took my hand.

'Hi, y'all. We all soooo excited about havin' you here. This here is my husband, Frank. When I told him you boys could shag, he couldn't wait to get here to watch.'

'Sure thing. When Tammy told me, I thought I gotta see that! I ain't never seen an English man shag.'

Everyone within their group laughed and the Englishmen in question began to wonder what we had let ourselves in for. We were to learn, however, that the 'shag' they were all referring to is a dance which is best described as a complex jive and which is very popular in the Carolina states.

We were also to find that everyone was right: Englishmen cannot 'shag' as well as they think they can, and instead of finding ourselves embroiled in a mass orgy we instead found ourselves stepping on toes and bumping into strangers but having a great night. A very different night to the one anticipated, but a great one nevertheless.

What I loved about America – and still do – is that from the beaches to the desert to the bustling cities, at any moment you could feel like you had walked onto a movie set. I felt like I knew the place before I ever went there and, once there, the people made me feel like they knew me. Wherever I went, people were open and friendly. There is an accepted view that American people are rather shallow and the friendliness is fake, as opposed to the sincere unfriendliness of the British. For what it's worth, I would prefer a shallow 'Have a nice day' to a sincere 'Who you looking at?' any day.

Some struggled with my accent, and most believed I was Scottish or, occasionally, Eastern European. Rather than explain, I sometimes allowed them to believe what they liked until this backfired while in Arizona. A man in a restaurant heard me order and asked if I was Hungarian. When I said yes, because it seemed the easiest thing to do, he left and, unknown to me, drove across town to return an hour later, just as I was finishing my meal, with his 80-year-old Hungarian mother. He also brought his wife, his brother and two teenage children, who looked as bored as it is possible to look whilst still being awake.

He said he hadn't been able to resist the opportunity to allow his mother to converse in her mother tongue. They came and sat at the table with me, their mother opposite, the family members around me. I was alone, so couldn't even use the excuse of being with someone who had to leave. I just looked across at the 80-year-old grandmother, who returned my stare with her steely blue eyes.

'Hello,' I said. 'I'm John.'

'Dipstright metnntixed olovich, du bitettezxe ishtach wwwxxxyyy lolliocvihz itchvitch usstarllaha quitchevitch rrroollle,' she said, or words to that effect.

The family looked at me for my response, as if they had been hearing this jumble of words for years and wanted someone to tell them what it all meant. I felt terrible, as I clearly had no idea what she was saying and, as far as I could tell, neither did anyone else. I knew I had to say something so just tried, 'Daa' and nodded my head.

There was a moment's pause then, glancing at her sons before looking back at me, she smiled the broadest of smiles and said: 'Daa daa.'

The sons laughed, and one slapped me on the back as the wife gave the mum a gentle squeeze. The teenagers looked like they were aware something had happened, but couldn't decide if this was something they should be bored with or just hate for the sake of it, as it appeared these were the only emotions they allowed themselves.

We then sat for a further fifteen minutes with the old lady saying things to me that I didn't understand and which I was not completely convinced were words at all. All I did was respond with 'Daa', which seemed to satisfy her every time and, as a result, pleased her sons and the daughter-in-law, whilst boring her grandchildren.

When they left, there were many heartfelt hugs and handshakes from the sons and 'whatever' looks from the grandchildren, but from the lady herself there was a look in her eye when we said goodbye that made me suspect that the old lady was more relieved than I was that this had gone well.

I concluded that at some point in her courtship with the son's father she had tried to make her own life seem exotic by telling him that she was Hungarian. This tale had then perhaps passed on through the family, possibly with stories of being a spy in the war and running away to defect to the West; all tales that would sound credible living in Hicksville, Arizona where the story could never really be challenged. Now a Hungarian was in town, she had been put to the test, only to discover I was lying as well, and so as long as neither of us broke the code we could both be exotic. I may be wrong, but when she hugged goodbye and said 'Thank you' it was with the least East European accent I had ever heard.

I decided not to return to Newcastle Poly after that first summer in the US. I knew that I loved playing sport but didn't think I would want to spend three years studying it. I also wanted to live somewhere else. I had been to Newcastle and had enjoyed it, but I suspected that when I went back everyone would have moved on a year and I would always feel I was neither a genuine first year nor an established student. It seemed to me that the best option would be to apply somewhere completely new.

My only problem was that I hadn't applied to anywhere else. So, upon returning from America, I resolved to spend a day at Manchester Polytechnic to see what courses still had vacancies. I picked Manchester because it was far enough away from home for me to be independent, but not too far for me not to get there and back in a day on the train whilst I looked into what places were available.

This process basically involved me walking around each faculty in alphabetical order and trying to convince them I wanted to join them, but had not applied for the following reasons:

1. I have been to America.

2. I applied, but it must have got lost in the post.

3. I have been to Australia.

4. You must have lost the paperwork because someone phoned our house to say I had a place.

5. I had wanted to apply, but wasn't sure if I would be needed to look after my sick relative in Australia/America/ New Zealand/Runcorn.

Obviously these were very thin excuses or downright blatant lies but, as the courses were all starting the following week, I had nothing to lose. I eventually found myself in the Social Science faculty and, after a brief conversation with the head of politics, I was told he was not sure if they had a place, but he would ring me that week if they did. It was Tuesday and the course started the following Monday. But I still had a place waiting for me in Newcastle to start on the Monday.

I decided that I should ask for my place at Newcastle to be put back another year, during which time I would get a job whilst I tried to work out what I wanted to do. I made an appointment with the head of the course on the Friday, and explained to him that I had not informed him earlier that I could not start the following week because:

1. I have been to America.

2. I applied for a deferral, but it must have got lost in the post.

3. I have been to Australia.

4. You must have lost the paperwork because someone phoned our house to say I could defer my place.

5. I had wanted to apply for a deferment, but wasn't sure if

I would be needed to look after my sick relative in Australia/ America/New Zealand/Runcorn.

The head of sport science told me a place would always be there for me; all I had to do was let them know when I was ready to start.

Years later, when I was working for a drug company and drove past the newly named Northumbria University, seeing bubbly students outside whilst I was drifting into the corporate numbness of being a salesman for ever, it crossed my mind to turn up to see if he was as good as his word.

On the day I left his office, I felt like I had made a good decision, but not knowing why. I had no course, no job and no direction. It was late on Friday afternoon, and I called home to tell my mum I was thinking of staying up in Newcastle for the weekend with some mates from the year before. She then told me that someone from Manchester Polytechnic had called and to phone them back. I scratched the number into the wall of the phone box as I had no pen and not enough change to get a pen and call back.

I called the number and spoke to the social sciences lecturer I had met earlier in the week. He informed me that they had one more place on the politics course, and I could have it. I said 'yes', and my life took another turn in a completely unexpected direction.

CHAPTER 10

THE MANCHESTER YEARS

What never ceases to amaze me in life is that we can never predict how our world will look based on the small decisions we all make. Having moved to Manchester, I rented a room in the flat of my old history teacher, Dave Debbage, so I was slightly out of touch with the main body of the student population housed in the halls of residence.

However, on the first day of my course, I sat next to a girl with an easy smile. She was from Northern Ireland, and called Julie. I could have sat anywhere in the room, but we got into conversation and that led Julie to introduce me to her new friends from her halls of residence. Julie now lives back home in Northern Ireland, and I see her every time I tour in that part of the world. As for the lads she introduced me to, they were to become my brothers-in-arms throughout my three years in Manchester and some remain my best friends today.

The night I first met Sergei he was on crutches from an ankle injury. He came from Chelmsford, had mad, curly hair, and was the most Southern Counties person I had ever met. Next I met Harvey, a good-looking boy who had a neatness about him which suggested he was likely to be one of the few males in the building who knew how to use an iron. In later years he became a photographer, and was to take the picture used on my first DVD, *Elvis Has Left the Building*. Del was one of the other lads I met. Everyone who goes to college knows a Del. He was from Middlesbrough, and the jumper he wore that first night was the same jumper he wore for the next three years in Manchester. The final person I met was Matt who, as the son of a serviceman, had grown up in Germany, had long ginger hair and was into rock music. Every student house of the time had to have someone who was into rock music, it was a rule. The ginger hair, though, was optional. Along with John, a skinny, tall lad from Belfast, I was to share almost every day with these lads during the three years it took to gain my degree. We lived together throughout our time at Manchester Poly and I was lucky to have them as mates.

Although I don't think my student days differed significantly from those of many other people, I did play semi-professional football at that time, which limited the normal student excesses. I was committed to being out of the house either training or playing three times a week, including some games for the Sunday league side my dad was running. This meant that, unlike most other students, I hardly drank anything stronger than shandy, and never went out on a Friday. Not only did I love playing football, I also needed the income. The £40–£75 a week I earned made a huge difference to the life I could have, and I never in all that time had to ask my mum and dad for money. I was independent, and enjoying the many things that student life had to offer as much as I could.

We didn't live with any girls for those three years – it was just us six lads together, plus additional members depending on the size of the house, primarily Blainey, Wiggy and Big Dick – the first two being nicknames derived from their surnames, whereas Big Dick was a lad who was six foot seven tall and his Christian name was Richard, hence a funny nickname that was also factually correct. The largest population we had in one house was ten. In that house, I was the only one who didn't smoke. Sitting in a living room watching the TV whilst nine people smoked was not only a significant health risk, it was also pointless because you couldn't see across the room to see the telly. So I had to guess what was going on based on the sound. We should have saved ourselves some money and just put a radio in the room.

I don't know if you have ever walked into a house where ten male students of varying levels of immaturity and hygiene live; it is hardly surprising that not many girls wanted to come back. We were used to landlords keeping their deposits when our tenancy was over, but that was irrelevant in one particular case when we were forced to move out because the building couldn't take it any more and had decided to fall down around us.

I grew to really like the Didsbury area of Manchester, and I look back on those years very fondly. From Manchester Poly I gained a degree (a 2:1, as it happens, in case you're interested), fantastic memories, life-long friends who are the closest people in the world to me still and, something I wasn't expecting, a person who would change the whole course of the rest of my life.

It was the end of second year and I was in the library one day doing some of the studying I should have done earlier in the term. It was May and the end-of-year exams were looming, so the library was much busier than usual. It is often said that the only way to get students to use a library is to put a bar and a DJ inside, and to an extent my student experience mirrored that view. As far as I was concerned, the library was like the clap clinic: you went when you really had to, and not before.

I had ridden my pushbike from the communal house in Didsbury I was sharing with the 'famous five' and a bloke none of us knew who already lived there and was obsessed with milk theft. The landlord, Smedley, was a builder. He would call around covered in plaster dust on a Friday and, standing at the bottom of the stairs, would shout 'Duke of Kent, lads.' Student chequebooks would then be produced and payments made. That, of course, was at the start of the year. By the end, money would be running low, so a few of the lads would play hide and seek. But as Smedley was a builder, he would turn up with some mates off the site. Though they may have just been calling in for a cup of tea (bring your own milk), it ensured that cheques were waiting next time. I liked Smedley, particularly when he told our paranoid fellow resident that the best way to keep milk safe was to get a cow, lock it in his room and just get the milk when he needed it.

Within the library there were private study zones, which were basically desks surrounded by small, two-foot barriers, so once your head was down you couldn't see anyone else and they could not see you. I preferred these as places to study because I have always loved the opportunity to people watch. ('People watching' is a much more appealing phrase than 'looking at people', which sounds sinister and wrong, but is basically the same thing.)

On this particular day I raised my head for a stretch and locked eyes with a girl sitting a few desks away in front. She then stood up whilst messing with some books and looked at me again. She had a mass of dark brown hair that had the kind of curls you only saw in the 1980s – no era in history has ever combined hair volume, curls and length as that decade did. What made this girl even more attractive was the fact that she had almost tamed the hairy mass with the aid of a scarf wrapped around the crown of her head. In effect, it was like trying to control the sea with a handkerchief – there was just too much of it.

She was wearing a loose, white shirt; faded stone-washed jeans; and ankle-length white Reebok trainers. From what I could see of her face, she had olive skin and was beautiful. I say 'from what I could see', because most of her face was hidden behind a huge pair of glasses, similar to the type that Christopher Biggins wore, but without the brightly coloured frames that he preferred. Instead, hers were a light tan colour which, from a distance, made it difficult to know where her glasses ended and she began. She could not have looked more eighties without being a member of Bucks Fizz.

For my part, I was wearing my usual attire of narrow tracksuit bottoms and a pastel-coloured, blue Adidas sweat shirt. I thought I looked cool but on reflection I looked like a children's TV presenter who had just nipped out for a jog.

What struck me was that she held my stare. Normally you catch a girl's eye and, after a fleeting fraction of a second, she looks away or calls the police. Not this girl – she just looked back at me. Had she been a bloke, I might have seen this as a classic 'Who are you looking at?' moment. But, instead, she went beyond just looking into my eyes to lowering the glasses down the bridge of her nose and peering at me for a few seconds before, with a dismissive chuckle, walking away to return some books to the shelves.

I sat there dumbfounded. Not only was I impressed that she was able to slide those huge glasses down her nose without allowing the momentum of doing so to tip her over; I was blown away because I had only seen the 'peering seductively over the glasses' move in films that involved a boss and his secretary.

It was the single most sexy thing I had ever seen in my life.

For an hour I did nothing. Part of this was being cool, the kind of cool you are when you're 21 and you think things like this will always happen (if a woman was to pull the 'peering seductively over the glasses' move on any man over 40 he would be over in a shot if, of course, he hadn't suffered a heart attack from the excitement of it all). So I played it cool, in part because I thought that was what you were expected to do when a girl gave you that look, and also because I didn't want to embarrass myself.

I had seen the sexiest thing ever, and I was wearing tight tracksuit bottoms. Even with the confidence of youth, I didn't think it would be appropriate to make the first approach with my intentions too apparent.

After an hour or so, and with a few furtive glances away from the books – which reassured me that there was still some interest – I approached the study area where she was sitting. She raised her head from her notes and looked at me once again by peering over her glasses. Luckily, the study booth walls and mass of books in front of her hid my initial reaction to the look, and I made a mental note that tracksuit bottoms should never be worn when trying to chat a girl up.

Me:

'I'll be back in a minute and we can go for a coffee.'

Her:

'What makes you think I want to go for a coffee with you?'

Me:

'Because you do.'

Her:

'Do I?'

Me:

'Yep.'

I walked away and didn't return for nearly 45 minutes. Then I took her for coffee.

BOOM! If anyone is reading this in disbelief, I can assure you that this moment only happened once in my life. This was my *Top Gun* moment but, believe me, there have been many other times when I have crashed and burnt.

When you see someone who is so far out of your league, why not try something straight out of the how-to-be-cool guide book? Confidence with the opposite sex is often tainted by fear of rejection, but if you expect rejection there is not too much to lose. That is my theory as to why so many beautiful women end up with ugly men: they were the only ones who took the chance. The rest of us stand there ogling but never acting, whereas Mr Ugly thinks, 'I may as well get told to take a hike by a good-looking woman than by an ugly one.' So as they are the only ones providing these beauties with options, they win. Love is like the lottery: you've got to be in it to win it, even if you are ugly.

So I took the girl to the canteen. I bought two coffees, and we began to talk. Quickly the bravado of our body language relaxed and the conversation flowed, and then she laughed. It has often been said that if you can make a girl laugh, you can win her over. What is not often said is that when you hear a girl laugh for the first time it can become a sound that you find yourself chasing for ever.

At one point during the coffee she took her glasses off and

I finally saw her whole face for the first time. I had seen her chin, her mouth, and most of her nose and her hair, but the rest of her face had been hidden under those glasses the size of bin lids. But now I saw her smile properly for the first time. I heard her laugh properly for the first time. I heard her speak properly for the first time. All those things I grew to know like second nature in years to come first happened across that table.

In every relationship, there is always the first time you see something.

This is how I look when I laugh.

This is how I look when I smile.

This is how I look when I kiss you.

This is how I look when we make love.

This is how I look when my heart is ready to burst with love.

This is how I look when I say 'I do.'

This is how I look when I give birth.

This is how I look as an exhausted mother of three.

This is how I look when I am sitting alone because you are away.

This is how I look when I know you failed me.

This is how I look when you know I failed you.

This is how I look when I hate you.

This is how I look when I am lost.

This is how I look as I leave you.

This is how I look when I know I have broken your heart.

This is how I look when you don't know me.

This is how I look when I wipe away your tears.

This is how I look when you are the loneliest man in the world.

This is how I look when you can dream no more.

This is how I look when we both say sorry.

Across the table, I knew nothing of the faces to come. I just knew I liked the one in front of me. Her name was Melanie, and we arranged to meet later that evening at the cinema known locally as the fleapit to watch *The Last Emperor*.

It was now getting late because of the time I had wasted in trying to be cool and waiting to regain my composure in the tracksuit region, so I had to get pedalling home to change. There was no way I was going to risk tracksuit attire for a first date. I already knew that would be a disaster.

I rode the 40 minutes or so home and, after leaving my bike in the hall, bounded up the stairs in the way you do when you're 21 and are about to meet a girl you fancy. At that moment one of my house mates, Harvey, came out of his room.

'What's your rush?'

'I'm going to the pictures with the girl I'm going to marry.'

BOOM! That is what I said. I know that, reading this, many women will think, 'Oh, isn't that beautiful,' and many men will think, 'What a cock.' The truth is, that is what I said.

Harvey duly responded with the supportive comment of 'Bollocks,' and I could hardly blame him. I was not in the habit of making such grand statements. In fact, I was very much enjoying my student life and was at the top of the chart we kept in our communal kitchen indicating success with the opposite sex, as measured by a complicated algorithm calculating everything from love bites to home runs. As the kitchen was the room where we also brought our girlfriends, we had disguised it as a job application chart with each conquest appearing to be another job application. Any girl coming to our house would have thought us the most enthusiastic job seekers in the world.

Truth is, I meant it. Something about Melanie hit me that day and has never left me. With all of my failings and indiscretions along the pathway of our relationship, she has always had one thing over me that nobody else has ever managed: she has always felt out of my league.

I rushed to change and, no doubt, put on some Amaris to enhance my appeal before quickly jumping on the bus to the end of Burton Road and the cinema. Unfortunately for me, the cinema was around the corner from a pub. I got off the bus to see two further house mates, John and Sergei, emerging from said establishment. John and Sergei remain two of my closest friends but, at that moment, I would rather have bumped into any two people on the planet than those two clowns.

John is six foot three inches tall (three and a half inches taller than me, as he has continued to tell me for 28 years) and, being from Belfast, spent a large part of his student days believing most situations were resolvable by a drink or a fight. Basically, if he wasn't drinking with you, he was arguing with you as to why he wasn't drinking with you. Sergei, on the other hand, has the aura of sophistication granted to him by his Russian descent and the poshest accent I had ever heard, which contrasted with the blond, tight curly hair that made him look like a fat Art Garfunkel.

Within the community of our house they were inseparable, because one of them was always ready to accompany the other to the pub. So it was that at seven o'clock on a mid-week night they stumbled out of the pub to greet me as I stepped off the bus in my cleanest clothes and smelling of Amaris – the aroma of desperate men the world over. Very anxious not to be late, I tried as hard as I could to get past them without being noticed, with no success.

John:

'Where are you going?'

Me:

'Nowhere.'

John:

'Sergei, where are we going?'

Sergei:

'Nowhere.'

John:

'Good. Let's all go nowhere together.'

Me:

'No, I want to go somewhere.'

Sergei:

'Good. I'd rather go somewhere than nowhere. Wouldn't you, John?'

John:

'Yes, I would, Sergei.'

Sergei:

'Good. Let's all go somewhere because nowhere is shit.'

They fell about laughing, and I knew I had no choice but to confess all to get rid of them.

Me:

'I'm meeting my sister at the flea pit.'

John:

'Sergei, he's meeting his sister at the cinema.'

Sergei:

'That's what he said.'

John:

'Have you met his sister?'

Sergei:

'I don't know. Bish, have I met your sister?'

Me:

'No.'

Sergei:

'No, I haven't met his sister.'

John:

'Well, I think we should meet your sister.'

Me:

'It's not my sister, it's a girl.'

Sergei:

'Is your sister not a girl?'

At this point they nearly collapsed laughing, and I had to join in. I agreed they could meet Melanie and say hello, but on strict instructions that they kept their manners and left after two minutes.

As first meetings go, it was, I suppose, an honest representation of what she was letting herself in for: Sergei nearly climbed into Melanie's bra with his eyes, and John thought it was sensible to mention that rattling noises woke him at night. I have been apologising to Melanie for my choice of friends ever since.

The first date was as all first dates should be. The film was long, so there was plenty of time to do the obligatory arm-over-the-shoulder thing. This was also aided by the fact that the flea pit had 'love seats'. These brilliant things were double seats at the back so that courting couples could cuddle without the discomfort of a middle armrest. The cinema is now a supermarket, and I always regret not buying one of those chairs for memory's sake.

The relationship I had with Melanie was very much as it is with everyone around that age and that stage in their life. She was due to graduate that summer; I had another year left. She had a boyfriend she was breaking up with in stages, and I had my mates I wanted to spend time with. So, it was a stop-start thing, until I graduated the following summer and was given the offer of a lifetime – which I had to refuse.

CHAPTER 11

THE GREAT U S OF A

When I graduated in 1989, I had the usual picture taken with the rented cap and gown, which my mum and dad still have on their wall, and I felt some sense of achievement. However, I knew that the biggest change in me had come from mixing with people from different backgrounds more than from the lectures. Perhaps that is the most important aspect of a degree course: to learn who you are.

I knew I would have to find work but I had one more trip to America planned and I couldn't wait for another summer in the US. I flew to America in June 1989 to once again join the North American Soccer Camps. This time I was going to work exclusively in California, and I immediately fell in love with the place. I spent the summer working with Ged McCann, a teacher from Liverpool who, like a Scouse Cinderella, managed to leave one of his shoes behind when he left. I said I would post it to him although I kept forgetting, so the shoe joined me as a sort of mascot when I decided to stay in Los Angeles after the summer soccer camps had ended.

I began working on building sites, living in a shared house in Redondo Beach, just outside LA. My ability to work on a building site had not improved since the dump-in-the-mix incident, and I was once again chased off the site by an irate co-worker when I nearly blinded him with a nail gun by mistake.

After a few weeks scrambling around for jobs, I decided that with no work, and rent to pay, I should return home to England before my plane ticket went beyond its six months' validity period. The small problem was that the plane ticket was from New York to London, and New York was 3,000 miles away.

The only way to get across the country economically was either to hitch, which basically meant standing on the side of the road and hoping a psycho was not about; get a bus, which took for ever and was again limited in its appeal as the psycho you had avoided by hitchhiking could easily be seated next to you; or take a drive-away.

A drive-away was a scheme where people who were moving from coast to coast would have their car driven across for them, rather than face the exorbitant cost of shipping it, or the effort of having to drive it themselves. All you had to do to qualify as a driver was to have a valid driving licence, pay a $100 deposit and give them your passport details. The only problem was that, I was told, you had to register at a drive-away office and inform them which direction you wanted to go and sit waiting till a car became available. Sometimes that wait could take weeks, but I didn't have weeks; November was approaching and I had rent due too, so I visited the office in downtown LA every day and sat waiting.

One day I arrived and there were four English lads in the line in front of me. We got talking and I found that they were friends from Cambridge University who had also just graduated and spent the summer travelling around America. They still had a few months left before they each had to return home for their new positions and internships awaiting them in January. They had no agenda and were just waiting for whatever car came in that was going a long way. It was all just a bit of a wheeze to them, and if they didn't get a car it didn't matter, as they would get to where they were going anyway. I told them that I had been coming in every day looking for a car to New York as I had to catch a flight home by November.

We were the only five English people in the building and, as we sat and waited, I began to realise I had nothing in common with them. They were rude to the staff in a very subtle way, the way that makes you know that they think they are better than you, but not to the extent that you can justify punching them in the face. They were full of in-jokes, which is what happens when you are friends, but it seemed more than that: it seemed like they were all part of the same club before they had even met.

They carried the sense of assurance that comes with entitlement. Some people are told early in life that the world is for them, while the rest of us spend forever trying to find our place in it. To them, I was as foreign as the Puerto Rican man, Pedro, who I had got to know as he had been there, like me, on a daily basis hoping for a ride to Alaska. I never imagined Alaska having a large Puerto Rican community, and I never found out if he got a ride because my car came first, although not until the Cambridge boys had provided me with more reasons to dislike them.

A car became available for New York. Those boys, who had arrived in the office a fraction before me that morning, jumped.

The Cambridge Boys:

'We'll take it.'

The Man from the Office:

'But this guy has been waiting for days for a New York car.'

One Cambridge Boy (with a shit American accent):

'But your sign says, "Cars will not be reserved and they are allocated on a first come, first served basis."'

The Man from the Office:

'I guess so.' (To me.) 'Sorry, buddy.'

The Cambridge Boys to Me:

'Yer, sorry, mate. No hard feelings and all that.'

Me to the Cambridge Boys:

'Fuck off, you twats.'

The last line is a lie. I am not sure I said 'fuck off', but I did make it clear they could have chosen any car, and after a week of waiting they had now taken what might be my last chance to make my plane home.

They conferred and decided to take the car anyway, so I called them twats again and we went our separate ways.

Within minutes, the man from the office returned. 'Man, am I glad they've gone. This is your car. You have to collect it at this address and deliver it in New York in eight days. I think you'll be pleased.'

I didn't understand his wink as he handed me the address. I thanked the guy, wished Pedro luck and walked out into the LA sunshine. There, I saw a small brown car that looked like it could not get around the block, or even splutter out of the parking lot.

The Cambridge boys were crammed inside looking uncomfortable and unhappy. I held up the sheet of paper, smiled and waved. They didn't wave back, but I didn't need them to. I didn't need anything from them and gladly knew I never would.

I had instructions about what bus to take across town to the address in Lynwood, and boarded the first bus that was heading in the right direction. The driver was a huge black woman who looked like she would not be out of place singing in a smoky blues bar somewhere else in the world, rather than driving a bus in central Los Angeles.

'One to Central and Florence, please,' I said.

'Whaaat you say, boy?'

'Erm . . . one to Central and Florence, please,' I repeated.

I thought I must have pronounced it wrongly, as she just shook her head, making an 'Urrgh, urrgh' sound. Then she looked down the aisle of the bus and shouted: 'There's a white boy here wanting to go to Central and Florence.'

I followed her eye line to see that, although the bus was almost full, I was the only white person on it, with the passengers coming from every other possible ethnic group. It was as if they were being driven to a Benetton advert shoot. The whole bus started laughing, along with the jovial driver who resolved the situation by informing me: 'Ain't no way I am dropping a white boy at Central and Florence. No way, sugar. Your ticket's $2.'

As I paid the $2, she started to move the bus, but kept on talking. 'I'll drop you somewhere better. Where do you need to go?'

'Lynwood.'

'Whaat?' she exclaimed, again turning to everyone down the bus. Whilst still driving. 'This boy . . . where you from boy, Germany?'

'No, England.'

'Same thing.' (To the rest of the bus.) 'This German boy is going to Lynwood!'

Again an eruption of laughter, and I suddenly felt I was in the oddest sitcom ever. What I didn't know was that I was going to an area in East LA known as Compton. That area is now synonymous with the LA riots; gang violence due to the turf wars that have been well documented in news stories; and movies and gangster rap music that really put Compton on the map for the rest of the world. My kids know Compton is not a place for a white German boy to hang around because they have an impression of the place from the songs they have heard. In the mid-eighties my only reference point was a bus driver who looked like she should have been singing 'Sweet Home Alabama'.

When I got off the bus – under instructions from the driver to change onto another bus – I had to wait for around 15 minutes. I would say it may have been the longest 15 minutes of my life as I suddenly found myself in an area where nobody wanted to look me in the eye. I stood at the bus stop and a car drove past, then suddenly did a U-turn and drove past me again, very slowly. I looked inside at the passengers, all Hispanic men ranging from 16 to about 25. They were each wearing bandannas of the same colour, either on their heads, around their neck or tied around their wrist.

Within minutes, the same thing happened again but with a different car. I don't care who you are – you only need two different cars to drive past you, windows down, all occupants looking at you without the glimpse of a smile, to begin to think that if this was better than Central and Florence I should have hitchhiked to New York and taken my chances with the psycho!

To try to look nonchalant, I called my mate, Jimmy, in England. One thing that amazed me about America was that you could call England from a pay phone. I am not sure if you could do the same at that time in England – I had never tried, as I would never have enough coins and in England the 'magic number' I had would not have worked.

The magic number allowed me to make free calls and had been given to me by Ged, he of the lost shoe fame. He had memorised the number the previous year while working for North American Soccer Camps: it was an account number that all phone calls related to the soccer camps could be charged to. He had been told by one of the other coaches that the account was closed, but if the phone company had not deactivated it there was a chance you could make calls for free. This advice was to get me into serious trouble, but at that moment in time it allowed me to make a call to a friend just when I needed to do it most.

I had known Jimmy for a few years as we played football together, and he remains one of my best friends to this day. I was in LA, he was in England, so God knows what time of night it was, but he answered.

'Hello.'

'Jimmy, if you hear a shooting noise, it means I have been shot.'

'What?'

'I think I am in a bad area and some cars are driving past, and I saw a story on the news about drive-by shootings, and I think they may shoot me because I am German and don't belong on their turf.'

'What?'

'Jimmy, I am just saying if you hear a bang, then it means I have been shot.'

'Not necessarily – what if they shoot and miss?'

That was typical of Jimmy, missing the central point that I feared for my life to argue that not all bangs necessarily meant that I had been shot. Fortunately, my bus came before either of us could test the theory.

When I arrived at the address, the door was opened by a

middle-aged man, behind whom stood a very attractive Hispanic girl in her early twenties. It was her car I was to take to New York. She had come to the West Coast to live with her boyfriend, but things had not worked out, so she had decided to go back home and was staying at her uncle's house until the car was collected.

They took me to the garage and showed me the car. A brand-new black Ford Probe. A sports car. My mind immediately went back to the wink from the man in the office and the jalopy the Cambridge wankers were driving, and an even bigger smile crossed my face.

I handed over the $100 – to be returned when I delivered the car – and set off to empty my room and head east on a road trip that I could never have dreamt of.

·   ·   ·

In the eight days it took me to cross America, I went to as many sights as I could whilst covering the near 3,000 miles. I planned to sleep in the car to keep costs down, but after the first night in Las Vegas I felt this was not the best idea. The Ford Probe was a great car for driving; it had been designed to get you from A to B and to look cool whilst you did so, but it was not designed as a make-do caravan.

I stopped at the Grand Canyon, drove across the flat Arizona desert and up through Denver where, after a night's sleep, I then drove 19 hours to Chicago.

I was doing this to see a friend from college called David who was training at a Christian centre, prior to going to be a missionary in Africa. We had been on the same course at Manchester Poly and, despite our differing views of the world, we always got on and I liked his company. He would be leaving in a few days' time, so if I was to see him it had to be on that day or not at all.

I drove through the night to get to his house, but when he opened the door I walked right past him and fell asleep on the couch for 10 hours, cancelling out any progress I had made.

That evening, when we went out for dinner, I used the magic number to allow us to talk to our friends from college, Jane and Julie. One was in Newcastle and one was in Belfast. We made the call from pay phones next to each other and then, after we had each spoken to them for a considerable length of time, we held the receivers upside down so the girls could talk to each other – surely the most expensive call ever made between Belfast and Newcastle.

All the way across America, I thanked Ged for two things. One was the magic number, which allowed me to be constantly in touch with people in England for free, and the other was his lost shoe. The camera I had didn't have a self-timer on, and as I was taking the trip of a lifetime alone there was every chance that I would end up with a handful of slightly dull photos of various views. So I decided to take photographs of Ged's shoe.

At the end of my road trip I had a collection of shoe pictures, which I gave to Ged when I returned his shoe. The shoe in Vegas. The shoe at the Grand Canyon. The shoe in Denver. The shoe in Chicago. The shoe in New York. I know Cinderella got more when her shoe was returned, but I thought it was an impressive effort.

The value of the magic number became apparent again when I was in Chicago. A message had been left at my mum's house saying that I was to call the North American Soccer Camps office in Norwich, Connecticut. In today's world, where we are all connected via the internet and mobile phones, it seems crazy that if someone wanted to contact you in America they had to call your mum in England. Anyway, I made the call and was told that if I didn't want to return to England I should make a detour on my way to New York as the president of the company, Gary Russell, wanted to interview me about a full-time job.

I took the detour and the interview went well, Gary offering me the job there and then. It was paying $20,000 a year, one week's paid holiday (Americans never have enough paid holidays, which might explain why when they retire they are everywhere), and all travel expenses covered. My job was to travel through Texas and California, where I was to spend the winter months selling the camps to soccer organisations and schools before returning to the Connecticut office to co-ordinate things in the summer. The company would take care of my visa and assist with the aim of acquiring a green card.

I had left Manchester Poly barely five months before, and now I was being offered a job in America involving football. What could possibly go wrong? I immediately thought about Melanie. For some reason, American girls just never did it for me, and though we were still involved in the shadow-boxing of a noncommittal early relationship, I had spent a lot of time thinking about her, and a lot of time phoning her as I travelled across the country.

At this stage, we had been going out with each other for nearly a year and in many ways it was still very early days for me to consider her in relation to taking up such an offer, but the truth is she had a hold on me. I knew if I took the job one thing was certain: it would mean the end of any relationship with her.

I told Gary that, before I accepted, I wanted to phone home and asked if I could use his office phone. 'Don't worry,'

I said, 'I have this magic number; it won't cost you anything.' I did what I always did, dialling in the magic number,
followed by the number I was ringing. Gary watched intently
then left me alone to talk.

When he returned to the office, he looked more concerned
than I was expecting him to look if he just wanted to know
what my mum had said. He was with his right-hand man,
Paul Lawrence. Paul was from Preston and, like all the
lads who worked in the office, had progressed from being
a coach to establishing a full-time life in the States. As Gary
was American, it was clear he was bringing Paul in as a
go-between.

'Gary says you have a magic number,' Paul said. 'Where
did you get it from?'

I knew something was wrong and didn't want to drop Ged
in it, so I replied unconvincingly, 'Just one of the lads. I can't
remember, but it's OK. The phone company rents them out
and then forgets to cancel them, so nobody has to pay for it.'

Even I was beginning to suspect this logic was a bit
flawed. They asked me to write the number down, which I
did. They were out of the room for less than five minutes
before Paul came back in and dropped the bombshell.

'This is Gary's personal credit card number. A few years
ago, when the company was started, he allowed people to
use it to call the office, but for no other reason. How many
calls have you made?'

'Only a couple.'

I returned to England before the full picture came out.

To his eternal credit, Gary still maintained his offer of the
job, suggesting I could work off the debt somehow, although
this was before the size of the debt became apparent.
However, I knew the trust would be gone, and besides, once I

returned to England, I realised there were places and, more importantly, people I would miss if I left.

A few weeks later, an itemised bill arrived, from which it was possible to plot my journey across America. It revealed I owed a staggering $6,400, which at the time was roughly £4,000. This is a lot of money today, but in 1989 you could almost buy a decent left-back for the price. I had no income and barely £100 to my name. However, I vowed to pay every penny back, and I did.

Even though I never worked for NASC again, the organisation had given me such a brilliant experience that I did not want my name to be besmirched even further by not accepting my responsibility. It took time, but I am glad I never ran away from the debt as I could have done. For what they had given me, they deserved at least that.

The truth was, although I made multiple calls, one person probably accounted for half of the total, and maintaining my relationship with Melanie, no matter how long distance, had seemed something worth paying for.

CHAPTER 12

FOOTBALL

When I returned from America, in November 1989, I was in debt for the first time in my life, and had no immediate source of income apart from football.

I was a good footballer at a lower level, but once I moved up to non-league it was apparent that there were many more skilful players than me around. I decided to make up for my lack of skill by being a good worker, and by that I mean running and tackling.

At that time, it was expected that within every non-league team there would be one or two players whose job it was to stop the better footballers in the opposing team from playing. This was often achieved by the type of tackling that would result in you receiving an ASBO in today's game.

That was my job and one I did reasonably well. My semi-professional football career included a number of clubs. The general pattern was that I would sign for a team and after two seasons move on, either because I had fallen out with the manager and wasn't getting picked, or I had a better offer.

Whilst playing for Southport in 1991 we played against Liverpool in the Liverpool Senior Cup. This was a tournament that involved the local non-league sides and Liverpool and

Everton, who would play their reserves. That night I marked a young lad who Liverpool had just signed from Bournemouth called Jamie Redknapp, and though we both have different memories of who was the better player on the night, neither of us could have imagined we would become good friends some 20 years later. For anyone interested, I was the better player ... it's my book so that's what is going in!

I devoted a lot of my life to football and, in many ways, I regret this because I never did any other sports or engaged in activities such as going on weekends away. I needed the income from the semi-pro football on a Saturday, and I also got great pleasure from playing in the Sunday league sides my dad ran. I'm now starting to take up other sports, although it's quite apparent that I am pretty rubbish at them all.

I also played for money, which changes the whole *raison d'être*. You turn up three times a week because you are paid to be there, not because you choose to be there. When I stopped playing non-league football for good after around 14 years, I never missed it. I missed the dressing-room banter and the lads that I played with, but I never missed the travel and the commitment. You only have to draw 0–0 away at Bishop Auckland on a cold, wet and windy Tuesday night in front of 50 people and a dog a few times before you start thinking there must be better things to do with your time.

I had two epiphanies during my non-league career. The first was at the end of the biggest game I played. I was playing for Hyde United, and we were in the semi-final of the FA Trophy against Telford who played in the Vauxhall Conference, the league above us. This is basically the FA Cup for non-league sides, and the final is played at Wembley. The semi-final is a two-leg affair, and we went into the game a goal down from the home leg, but still feeling we had a chance. We scored early and for a period it felt like we might make it, but eventually Telford went through as well-deserved winners.

I hadn't played particularly well and was substituted with 15 minutes to go. At the end of the game I was completely deflated. That morning I had been 90 minutes away from Wembley. By the time the final whistle blew, that dream was over and I felt I would never get there. I had been given a chance and had blown it.

It was 15 April 1989. In the dressing room, amidst the disappointment, news started to come through that something had happened during Liverpool's FA Cup semi-final at Hillsborough. In the time it took to shower and change, it became apparent that a disaster was unfolding, and people began talking about fatalities. I have always been a Liverpool fan and almost certainly would have been there had I not been playing. Within minutes of my biggest disappointment, football didn't seem to matter at all. Writing these words, it still seems incredible what unfolded afterwards and that families are still fighting for justice. If ever a day changed my view of the importance of football, it was then.

The second was to come years later. I was married with a new baby, had a full-time job and was playing for Caernarfon in the Welsh League. Caernarfon was a two-and-a-half-hour drive from my house. My son, Joe, was a few months old and I was still training twice a week. On a Saturday, I would set off around 10.30 a.m. and return when he was in bed around 8.30 p.m., and that was for home games. In the Welsh League, you could be in mid-Wales or even down south, which was an even bigger commitment.

I can't recall who we were playing against, but it was spring and, as the sun lowered itself in the sky and began to signal its departure by unfurling a beautiful red aura across the sky just behind the corner flag, I found myself standing in the middle of the pitch, with the game going on around me, as I looked at this brilliant splash of colour on the horizon. I stopped running and just watched the day end.

I looked around the small ground at the 70 or 80 spectators, and it hit me. I was in my thirties, I was never going to get any better – if anything, I was getting worse. I was just making up the numbers in the team, and if I wasn't playing, someone else would have my shirt on. I offered nothing unique and gained nothing except some extra money, which is what I had used to justify not being at home. But yet another day was over and my son had not seen me. He had grown another day older and I had missed it.

For the rest of the week I would be away again, working. I was giving up the opportunity to be a better father in pursuit of extra cash, cash he didn't even know existed. It wasn't the cash from playing football that made him laugh, it was me pulling faces. It was me who bathed him, who changed his nappy, who read him stories, who tickled him and who rocked him to sleep. It was me who did all of those things, but it was also me who had chosen to give that time up so I could chase a ball. I realised the only place I was unique was at home being a father, being a husband. Only one person on the planet could do that job, while there was a queue of people who could stand in mid-field and tackle.

'Bish, what the fuck are you doing?'

The game was still on, and whilst everyone else was defending an attack I was down the other end of the pitch gazing at the sky.

The manager's voice broke my trance. I ran back to defend, but finished my non-league playing days shortly after. I had more important things to do, which didn't involving kicking someone – well, not often.

I still played football locally for a year or two and now I play every week with my mates on the five-a-side pitch I have had put in my garden. I even had a dug-out installed, which Melanie says only proves I am still a little boy wanting to be a professional footballer! I also still have season tickets at Anfield and go regularly with my dad, my brother and the two sons who like football. We had a season of a family table in the corporate part of the ground where you can get a four-course meal before the game before we all agreed it wasn't for us, and went back to our normal seats. I love going to the game, and it's also one of the places where I seem to be left alone. People know I am just going with my family, and it's really nice that this is respected. I never mind giving people photographs or autographs – it's a privilege that they ask. But it is nice sometimes to be left to do something normal. As my brother says, 'Who's going to be arsed with you when the match is on?'

•   •   •

One thing that has been great about living the dream I never expected – that of being a comedian – is that I have also been granted the opportunity to live the dream I wanted by playing in celebrity charity football matches. I took part in the Hillsborough memorial game for the Marina Dalglish charity at Anfield, and also played at Old Trafford with Soccer Aid, as well as taking a penalty at Wembley on *A League of Their Own*.

Of course, you are only there because you are good at something else, so it's not like being a real professional footballer. But as a friend of mine said, 'If you get a beautiful woman because you're rich not because you're good looking, you still have a beautiful woman. Even if everyone looking at you thinks you're a perv.' If you play football at the best grounds in the world because you're a comedian, not because you're a good footballer, you are still playing at the best grounds in the world, even if everyone looking at you thinks you're shit. There is logic in that somewhere.

CHAPTER 13

TIME TO GROW UP

In debt, and with a girlfriend in Manchester while I was living at home in Runcorn, it quickly became apparent that I needed to get a job with some form of transport.

I had a friend who was selling an ice-cream round. This entailed buying the van and the right to drive around the estate selling ice cream after rousing everyone from their houses with some chiming music – a bit like the Child Catcher in *Chitty Chitty Bang Bang*. Although I was tempted, I decided that in the fledging stages of my relationship with Melanie, turning up in a Mr Whippy van would not convince her that she was on to a winner.

I was in the position that many people find themselves in upon leaving university; you have been independent for three years and then you move back home to your old bedroom at your parents' house. Even if you enjoy a great relationship with your parents, as I did then and still do now, the reality is that once you leave you need to stay gone. There is nothing like going back to your teenage bed to sleep under your teenage posters to make you want to get a job and move on with your life. Also, parents get out of the rhythm of having children to look after; even if you are a man with more body hair than either of you would like to admit, bumping into your mum on the landing after a rushed shower still makes you feel like a naughty boy who shouldn't be getting the carpet wet.

As the youngest, I was the last to leave home, and despite all children thinking that their parents have nothing better to do than to take care of them forever, as the last one leaves, I am sure they have a 'Oh, will you just sod off and get on with your life?' sort of feeling. I know this, as my lads are coming closer to moving on – or at least reaching the age where I will be saying, 'Isn't it time you moved on?'

After a few weeks it seemed right that I should again leave and 'have my own space'. I moved into a house with my brother Eddie on a neighbouring estate and started looking for work.

The old adage that it is not what you know, it's who you know proved true as I moved on to the next phase of my life. My friend Mark had a sister who worked for a pharmaceutical company, and she in turn knew someone who had a vacancy for a sales rep calling on GPs in the Liverpool area.

It seemed to tick all the boxes. There was a car; pharmaceutical sales had a reputation for being one of the better-paid sales jobs you could get, so I could earn enough to clear my debt; and it was close to where I lived so I could carry on playing football and seeing Melanie. All I had to do was convince the company I was the man for the job and add a few more science O-levels to my CV. In fact, I realised it was surprisingly easy to gain an O-level in biology and chemistry once you'd left school: you just added them to your CV and hoped nobody checked. As I had nothing to lose, I put them down and went to have an interview with the area manager of Syntex Pharmaceuticals, Mark Scrutton, in the Adelphi Hotel in Liverpool.

I borrowed a suit from my friend Jimmy, which was slightly too small, but which managed to look OK as long I didn't stand up: once on my feet, everyone could see the trousers were too short and were only held shut with the aid of a belt, because doing up the button made the waist too tight. Coupled with this, the jacket shoulders began before my collar bone ended, so the sleeves barely reached my wrist; and if I moved my arm forward, the jacket sleeve shot up to my elbow, so that I looked like I belonged in a Wham! video.

The suit looked smart on Jimmy, which was why I had borrowed it; on me, it looked like I had fallen into a washing machine on a hot wash. I should have tried it on prior to the morning of the interview but, as I stood in front of the bathroom mirror, I knew I had no choice but to wear it. Unless I went dressed as I had been for the previous three years, as a student or in a tracksuit, I had no other option.

I arrived at the Adelphi Hotel before Mark and took a seat in the impressive lounge area. The Adelphi was for many years the premier hotel in Liverpool, and though it was past its best in the 1980s my mum and dad were still impressed by the fact that I was meeting someone there to discuss a job.

'If he wants to meet in the Aldephi, it must be a good job,' my mum said.

'It's just a first interview, it may not go any further.'

'Well, even if you don't get the job, you're still going places by going to the Adelphi.'

I did think of saying to my dad that everywhere was in fact a place, but I didn't think trying to be clever when I was

jobless was such a good idea. They were just being more optimistic than I was.

One tradition that the hotel had continued into the 1980s
was the serving of tea in the lounge by waiters in tuxedos
with starched white aprons. It was a touch of Edwardian
grandeur that had persisted, in marked contrast to the
recession-blighted city in which the hotel stood.

I took a seat in the lounge and, within a few minutes, one
of the waiters approached me. I was a jobless, 22-year-old
man in debt, sitting in a borrowed suit that didn't fit, so I
half-expected him to tell me that I didn't belong in such a
place and that I should just leave.

Instead he asked, 'Can I get you anything, sir?'

I automatically looked over my shoulder as I assumed he
was talking to someone else. When it became apparent that
I was the 'sir' to whom he was talking, I asked for some tea
and sat swimming in the reality that I was growing up.
Whatever was to happen with the interview, someone had
called me 'sir'. Even today, I am not keen on being called 'Mr
Bishop' – if people know my name, I would rather they call
me 'John'. But the first time someone calls you 'sir' sends a
message that at least on some level you have acquired a
status of respectability.

Shortly afterwards, the waiter returned with a tray containing a china cup and saucer, a matching jug of milk and a
traditional stainless-steel teapot which looked very impressive to a person who had only seen such things on *Upstairs,
Downstairs*. He placed the tray and the bill on the table.
I took the only £5 I had in the world out of my pocket and
gave it to him for the £1.50 requested on the bill. He left to
get change, and I tried to pretend that I had not nearly
fainted at the idea of paying so much for a cup of tea.

I then tried to pour myself a drink, at which point I discovered the design fault inherent in making a teapot completely out of a material that conducts heat: the handle was as hot as the rest of the pot, so that I nearly dropped it as it burnt my hand, while my resulting loud, 'Fuck's sake!' punctured the hum of low, polite chatter in the lounge.

Before I could consider a way of pouring a cup of tea without suffering third-degree burns, the man I was waiting for arrived. Mark had said he would be identifiable as he would be wearing a red tie and a grey suit and, sure enough, he walked in looking every inch you'd expect a Liverpool-based businessman to look: he had dark, neat hair, a moustache, his suit fitted much better than mine did, and he was carrying a Filofax.

For those people reading this who are not aware of what a Filofax is, imagine putting everything you hold dear – your Facebook contacts, your work diary, your innermost thoughts and your receipts – into a leather-bound folder: that's what a Filofax is. In the mid-eighties it was used as the barometer of success and importance. If you had a big one, you were top of the tree, or at least wanted the world to think you were. Mark's was nearly the size of the table. He sat down just as the waiter returned my £3.50 change. I thought it would be rude to pocket it straight away as Mark and I were exchanging introductions and I was trying to shake his hand without ripping my suit.

I had experienced one formal interview in America for the coaching job; this was my first interview for a 'proper' job with someone I had never met before. Though I was slightly nervous, within a few minutes I relaxed, as Mark seemed such an easy person to talk to. I perhaps relaxed too much as, after we had been talking for around 40 minutes, the waiter returned to collect the remains of the now cold pot of tea and, spying the £3.50 that had been left where he had placed it, took it upon himself to assume it was a tip.

The final money I had to my name jangled as it fell into the waiter's pocket, making a noise as if to remind me of what I had lost.

'Thank you, sir,' he said, as he turned to walk away.

I suddenly realised that being called 'sir' wasn't always a good thing. It had disarmed me, but I was in the middle of a job interview and I didn't feel able to turn around and say, 'Hey, you robbing bastard, give me my £3.50 back!' Nobody who had just been called 'sir' could say that. So I just watched my money walk away, and vowed to myself that if I didn't get the job I would come back and kill the waiter.

Fortunately, I was successful and entered the pharmaceutical industry, a place where I would stay until I left to become a full-time comedian at the age of 40.

•   •   •

The only break I took from work during that time came in 1992. I had been in the job for nearly three years at that point and was enjoying it. I was out of debt; I was enjoying my football; I had some money in my pocket and I had a 'proper' girlfriend. By 'proper', I mean I was at the stage where we were invited to things as a couple, relatives knew Melanie's name and everyone was waiting for something to happen.

By 'something' I mean a commitment of some sort. Clearly I had a different view of what 'commitment' was, as I thought I had shown an enormous amount of it by spending every Saturday night with her after playing football. This didn't involve clubbing or all the things we should have perhaps been doing, but involved going to the pictures or Pizza Hut, then back to the house she shared with her friend, Jane, where I would stay before getting up in the morning to play Sunday league football.

Little did I know such an arrangement was not being enjoyed as much by Melanie as it was by me. Women, I often find, have a relationship sat-nav in their brain that lets them know where they should be, at what stage, with a voice telling them what to do if the relationship is going the wrong way. Men tend to approach relationships in the way we approach directions: we carry on convinced we are right and refusing to ask anyone the way until we are completely lost.

This is what happened with us. I had a decent job, a nice company car, a gorgeous girlfriend and, with my football, had all I felt I needed. I never considered what Melanie wanted because I never had to.

Then it happened. Jane got engaged. Suddenly, all the conversations I had been trying to avoid – the 'Where are we going?' conversations – were back on the agenda. Melanie was ready for a commitment, and I wasn't. Something had to give.

I still had a feeling that there was more I wanted to do before settling down into the pre-ordained route of marriage, kids, mortgage, two holidays a year, job, pension, death. I had travelled all over America and kept coming back to the idea of travelling to or from Australia over land. I saw myself riding a motorbike with a flowing beard and a sleeping bag on the pillion, sleeping under the stars, as I let the road decide where I spent the night.

I suggested to Melanie that this might be something we could do together, as a life-affirming adventure, with her riding pillion to my dreams. I am not sure if she said 'Fuck

off' straight away or took a breath first, but basically it was
a non-starter.

Melanie then applied to work as an air hostess for Emirates,
an airline that had recently started and was based in Dubai.
I thought she was trying to call my bluff, but when she got
the job and decided she was going, it was me who began to
think we should have at least got engaged. I now risked
losing her for ever and all because I couldn't commit.

I also knew that if I was to get married I would want children; I always knew I wanted children, so I suppose I feared
that any commitment would be life-long as kids would come
shortly after and then any bohemian ideas I had whilst driving round in my Marks and Spencer suit in my company car
with my salesman's bag would be well and truly squashed.
Like a lot of men, I didn't want to commit in case there was a
better life around the corner. I just didn't have the bottle to
go round the corner and look.

It was a horrible day when I took her to the airport. We
were both in tears as we said goodbye. Neither of us knew
what was to become of our relationship, but we both knew
that we loved each other. Due to my wanderlust, I just
couldn't make the commitment that Melanie was after, and
she couldn't wait any longer. We resolved to try to keep a
long-distance relationship going and see how it would work
out. Melanie had a two-year contract, and I had that time to
get whatever was holding me back out of my system or let
the relationship die.

I left Melanie as she walked through the departures terminal at Manchester airport and set off to drive to the Syntex
office in Maidenhead.

Timing in life is everything. Those small decisions that at
the time seem fairly innocuous can change the whole course

of your life. On the way, I stopped for a cup of tea at Solihull, where Jimmy was living with his new wife, Diane. Jimmy was a friend I often went to for help or advice, although often that advice made little sense. (Jimmy was the person who told me that being shot at by a gang in LA did not automatically mean I would be killed, and he was also the person who lent me the ill-fitting suit for my first interview knowing full well it wouldn't fit, but explained later he thought it would make me look more desperate for the job.) Basically he was the person who always gave me a different perspective, whether I wanted it or not.

'Well, you've dropped a bollock there, son. She was the best girlfriend I've ever seen you with,' were the words he consoled me with as he poured me a cup of tea. Jimmy has always had the ability to tell me what I already knew, and once again he was right. But, on the other hand, something told me I had to follow through with my plans to travel.

After the refreshment of tea, which for anyone English immediately makes the world a better place, I started to drive back towards the M6, where I saw a hitchhiker.

Having hitched around the country myself a few times in the past, I used to have a policy of always picking hitchhikers up. I still do it, although I am now much more selective after picking someone up a few years ago who was returning home from a festival where he had clearly not used any washing facilities for days. He smelt so much, I had to kick him out at the next junction. I did try to pretend that I had changed my route, but in the end I had to say, 'Mate, you stink, and if I keep you in my car I will be sick. So get out and hope a tractor transporting sheep comes along. You'll fit right in there.'

On the day that Melanie left, I had no such problem. The hitchhiker was not only clean, he was a very nice man and we fell into easy conversation. His name was Tim Sumner and he was returning home to his mum's house in Oxford, having been to see some friends in Birmingham.

Within minutes, I was telling Tim about Melanie leaving, about the fact that I was in a good job, but felt I wanted to do more travelling before settling down, so had resolved to ride a motorbike from or to Australia, even though I had never ridden any other motorbike apart from the odd scooter we used to nick to ride around the estate.

I could have picked up any hitchhiker that day. Tim could have been picked up by the car in front of me. A million things could have happened that would have resulted in us never meeting. But meet we did, and it changed everything.

Tim had recently returned from a trip where he had ridden a bicycle the length of South America with some friends for charity. He suggested that as I had never owned a motorbike, why didn't I go on a bicycle and do it for charity, like him.

The suggestion hit me like a lightning bolt. *That* was what I would do! A bicycle seemed so much simpler to manage than a motorbike and, as I owned neither of them, it would make sense to use the easier – and cheaper – one. The charity element gave it a purpose beyond not just wanting to get married yet, and if I rode back towards England it would always feel I was coming home.

When I told Melanie and my mates, there was a general consensus that this sounded like a good idea, but as I was probably talking out of my arse nobody got overly excited. My mum and dad reacted in much the same way. It was rather as if I had told everyone that I had decided to become an astronaut. If that had been the case, my dad would never have said I could not be an astronaut, but he would have suggested I get a rocket first. In this case, he simply said, 'Get a bike and go for a ride. See if you like it and then decide.' Sound advice, but something I didn't manage to do till two weeks before I left, by which point it was a bit too late to change my mind.

The point when it became a reality and was not just me talking hot air was when I told my boss, Mark. Once I had told him I was leaving, I knew I could not change my mind. He listened, then said he would speak to his boss about my resignation. Amazingly, he gained the agreement of his boss to keep my job open for me until I planned to return, in ten months. Not only that, but Nic Holliday, the CEO, said they would contribute to my expenses and make a donation to the charity. It was far more support than I could ever have anticipated, but it also meant there was now no turning back.

Now I had to find a suitable charity. I settled on the Save the Children Fund and wrote to them asking, 'Can I raise money for you, and would your chairperson, Princess Anne, be a patron of my trip?' They wrote back saying, 'No, thanks.' Apparently, people often claimed they were doing things for charity when actually all they just wanted was a bit of a holiday. As if . . .!

I was disappointed they had said no, and it didn't help that the day the letter arrived I was to meet the Lord Mayor of Liverpool, Trevor Smith, as I had written to him to ask for his support, too.

Although I felt embarrassed about not having a charity to do the ride for, I kept the appointment and I am so glad I did, as it transformed everything. Trevor was the kind of Lord Mayor you get in cities like Liverpool, where there is a history of a strong Labour council. He was in his early fifties, had an accent thicker than mine and, despite the suit he was wearing, looked like he had driven himself to the town hall in his own van.

I explained to Trevor that I now had no charity to raise the money for, but still wanted to do the ride for the benefit of someone, ideally a children's charity.

Trevor listened whilst stroking the thick moustache on his top lip. He then picked up the phone and organised a meeting between myself and Arthur Johnson from the *Liverpool Echo*, drafted a fax to his counterpart in Sydney, and agreed to be a patron of the ride. In 10 minutes he had put plans into place and shown more enthusiasm than anyone, and I started believing again it was going to happen.

I met Arthur that same week and he introduced me to Rick Myers of the NSPCC, which became the designated charity. Arthur was a complete star. He put wheels in motion for me to meet people in Australia, including Scouse ex-pat groups and Rotary clubs along my route. He got support from companies like BT and made everything come together. He even kept the public interest up during my time away with regular pieces in the *Echo* and by organising radio calls with the Linda McDermott show on Radio Merseyside. There is no doubt that without his support I would never have got the trip off the ground.

I spent so much time organising the trip, in fact, that I neglected to deal with the essential factor, which my dad had noted: weeks before I was due to leave, I still didn't have a bicycle. This was resolved by Quinn's Bike Centre, a shop based in Liverpool and run at the time by two brothers, Mal and Mel Vasey. They gave me one of their own-branded bikes on the basis that when I brought it back they would sell it to me as a second-hand bike.

When I was to return, some ten months later, they would both look at the state of the bike after its 10,000-mile journey and say in unison, 'Keep it!'

CHAPTER 14

LEARNING TO RIDE

In January 1992 I left England to travel to Sydney, Australia and ride back home on a bicycle that I had been given just two weeks earlier.

I didn't really know what I was doing. I had no experience of riding a bike long distance, I had no fixed route planned, and I had no idea if I would actually be able to complete the ride at all. But I knew I had to do it. It felt like I had managed to climb to the top of that diving board in the swimming baths: if I didn't jump now, there was a chance I would never do it. I also knew that if I was not going to commit myself to Melanie, there had to be a very good reason: riding a bike home from Australia for charity seemed like a good one; thinking of riding a bike home from Australia but not doing it didn't seem like such a good one. I could not face the humiliation of not even trying, particularly when so many people had offered me support. As my dad had told me when I had decided to go back to sixth form, I had to at least give it a try. Sometimes in life that seems the best reason to do anything.

I left England full of anticipation. My mum and dad, Kathy, Carol and Eddie came to see me board the Cathay Pacific flight, which was the cheapest ticket I could buy. I was to fly to Hong Kong, then on to Australia, over a 30-hour period. The fact that the time zones meant I would land before I had set off caused much amusement.

'Let me know the football scores so I can get a bet on,' was one of the last things my dad said to me as I walked through to departures. Making a joke was a good way to reduce some of the emotion, as my mum began to cry before putting a golden St Christopher in my hand, which had been bought by Eddie, Kathy, Carol and Mum and Dad. Before I became too choked, I went through security and prepared to travel to the other side of the world.

I have to admit to loving long-haul flights, and this love has only been enhanced by the ability to sit in posher seats in recent years. The idea that your main purpose of being on the plane is travelling means that anything else you do in addition is a bonus. You get on the plane to go from one place to another, but if you happen to watch a movie, read a book, do some work, drink some wine, eat some food, have an afternoon nap, even do leg exercises to avoid thrombosis, it's all a bonus. The older I get, the more I relish any activity that involves me being seated, eating, drinking and watching a film, whilst still doing what is being asked of me.

Even in the economy section of the Cathay Pacific flight on 14 January 1992, I was excited at the prospect of the journey. Only to find that we were landing at Frankfurt airport two hours later. The travel agent had failed to inform me about this short stop-over, but I felt sure that German efficiency would not delay my journey too much. Little did I know at the time that it was going to delay me by four days.

As we set off from Frankfurt, I began talking to the man next to me, a mechanical engineer from Swindon called Paul. As we chatted, we became aware that the cabin crew were passing through the plane and asking people to identify their hand luggage. This obviously aroused some suspicion, which was confirmed when the pilot came on the intercom:

'Ladies and gentlemen, this is your pilot speaking. I have asked the cabin crew to check all hand luggage and request you identify your own luggage as we have been informed by the authorities in Frankfurt that they have received a phone call saying there is an alien package on the plane.'

As you can imagine, this was met with varying degrees of stunned silence and panic as people deduced that 'alien package' was code word for bomb, although not everyone worked this out straight away and seemed to roll their eyes at the inefficiency of the baggage handlers for putting luggage that was intended for a UFO onto an earth-bound plane. The worst thing was that the English announcement was after the Mandarin and German version, so Paul and I had had to watch Chinese people, then German people, hold their hands to their mouths, look around suspiciously and then rush to identify their bags without knowing what was going on.

It was appearing more and more to me that my great adventure was to end before it had begun, and that the last person I was going to talk to in my life was a bloke from Swindon called Paul.

I don't think I could have been any more disappointed with the situation. I am sure had the plane been blown out the sky I would have felt aggrieved anyway, but something told me I would have felt happier talking to a couple of supermodels going to Hong Kong for a bikini shoot.

As it happened, after an unscheduled night in Frankfurt and then another in Hong Kong, I found myself arriving in Australia four days late.

I immediately knew that I liked the country. Coming from England in the middle of winter, Australia looked like someone had just gone outside and painted everything: the grass, the flowers, the trees, the sky, the buildings – everything looked shiny and new.

I spent a week in Sydney preparing for the trip, during which time I made contact with a group called 'Scousers Down Under', whom Arthur had put me in touch with. Now I know 'Scousers Down Under' sounds like a fly-on-the-wall documentary involving lads in tracksuits having BBQs whilst their numerous kids and wives jump in and out of a swimming pool somewhere sunny until the whole thing ends with a fight and one of the women shouting, 'Leave it, Tony, he's a dickhead anyway,' but the reality was that it was a network of people from Liverpool who had moved to Australia at various times and now supported each other where they could, as well as offering support to strangers with the same accent, like me.

I left Sydney for Cairns on 26 January 1992. The date had been chosen by Ray Pont, a 'Scouse Down Under', to coincide with the ex-pat football competition held at Centennial Park. It provided a good opportunity to send a picture back to Arthur of myself surrounded by well-wishers dressed in Liverpool and Everton football kits. The picture looked good and was used in the *Echo*, but the reality was that football is, after all, an important game, and the players' interest in the lad on the bike riding home for charity lasted the duration of the automatic wind on.

I put on my brand-new white helmet, having first checked that my green rear panniers with reflector strips were secured to the rack of my bright red, spanking new bicycle. I put my hands inside my blue cycling gloves and, waving goodbye, dressed in my new cycling kit of blue and grey shoes, black shorts and the cycling shirt which managed to combine the colours yellow, blue, pink, white, red and black, I turned left out of the park.

I was beginning the greatest adventure of my life. After so much build-up, there was now no turning back, and I had to muster every ounce of self-confidence I could find, because if ever I needed faith in myself, it was at this point. Never before had I thought of my own limitations to this degree. Taking a deep breath, I glanced at my reflection as I rode past a glass-fronted building.

I looked like a half-chewed packet of liquorice allsorts.

• • •

It took 30 days to ride the 1,600 miles from Sydney to Cairns, and along the way I learnt a few invaluable lessons:

1. *Riding a bike on your own for days on end is boring.* I mean mega, super boring. Of course, the scenery was beautiful and there was something spiritual about transporting yourself through a country at a pace where you could absorb the environment around you. But this was 1992 – there were no iPods to listen to, no mobile phones to text mates during breaks, and no internet cafés to pop into when you arrived at a town to check your emails or Skype people back home. In 1992, if you were riding a bike in Australia, you were alone with your thoughts whilst sitting in the saddle for seven or eight hours a day, and it's surprising how quickly you can get bored of yourself.

2. *I quite like being bored.* I learnt, however, that I liked to be on my own and, after the first two weeks of talking to myself, I liked the silence of the road being disturbed only by the sound of my very slow peddling. Even now I am very happy with no external stimulus, and I have often driven to London and back without noticing that I have not turned the radio on.

3. *The vast majority of people in this world are warm, caring and helpful, while some people are twats.* That is an obvious statement and the words have been chosen carefully. There are some people in the world for whom there are not adequate insults, but I have always found the word 'twat' useful in these circumstances. I am not sure that I even regard such an onomatopoeic word as swearing; it is just a great way of describing a contemptible person that everyone who speaks the English language understands, and even if you don't speak it, the sound of the word lets you know something is wrong with the person you are talking about. The poetry inherent in the word allows all of us who use to it express our opinion and then move on. 'Twat' is a beautiful word.

In Australia, I was introduced to the random acts of kindness that make you feel blessed: from people offering a place to sleep and food to eat, to others giving me cash for the charity. But I also came across a few twats, only a few, but I think they deserve listing here before I balance it off with a story that epitomises the beauty of the human spirit.

TWAT NUMBER 1

The man who put the sign up near Bundaberg saying, 'Come Visit the Whitsunday Islands, only eleven hours away.' That is like arriving from France on the ferry and in Dover seeing a sign saying, 'Come and visit the Isle of Skye.' I knew Australia was big, but seeing something like that when you are travelling on a bicycle, it is impossible not to think someone, somewhere, is taking the piss.

TWAT NUMBER 2

The cartographer who drew the map I used. Australia is so devoid of people, it is very easy to find your way from Sydney to Cairns because there is basically only one road going north, so as long as you are on the Bruce Highway you will get there. The big problem is that, despite the majority of the country living along this coast, there are very few towns. As maps of Australia would be virtually bare if they just showed towns, instead they just put 'stuff' on them. When I say 'stuff', I mean everything from bridges to collections of trees.

The problem is that these places are marked with small dots on the map. In England, if a map gives something a name and a small dot, you expect to find a community, a place where there are people, shops, garages, banks, things that you may actually need when riding a bike alone. Instead, in Australia you find that the town called 'Two Mile Creek' you rode two hours to get to is, in fact, a bridge.

TWAT NUMBER 3

The person who stole all of my valuables. When I reached Cairns I had the number of two people I could call for a bed: Gus and Bill were doctors from Ireland who were working in the local medical centre for a few years as part of an exchange programme. Their number had been passed on by a friend of theirs in Townsville, Queensland. When I called, though, it was clear they had not been warned of my impending arrival. They still insisted that I take the spare room in their house, however, and that night we went out to celebrate me completing the first leg of my journey.

In true Irish fashion, the drinks flowed till the early hours. When we returned to the house, we found the patio screen door had been forced open and my bag, which contained my traveller's cheques, credit card, passport, camera and cash, was gone.

TWAT NUMBER 4

The person who investigated the robbery. A policeman arrived shortly after we reported the theft and, taking one look at the crime scene, said, 'It was an Abbo who did it.' I couldn't believe my ears, not only at the speed of the decision, but also the certainly in which it was delivered. 'How can you tell?' I asked him. This is where the tremendous Australian detective work came in. 'Well, you can see,' he said. 'It's the Abbos around here who do all the stealing, and if you look at the hole in this mesh, it's two inches away from where the lock is, and it's only a small hole. That means it's got to be a small, thin finger, but long enough to get round. So, that's a long, thin finger, and if you ever look at a black hand, they've always got long, thin fingers.' Needless to say, with crack detectives like that, I never saw my belongings again. The most heartbreaking loss was the camera, which contained pictures of the ride that I would never get back.

4. *We take communication for granted till we have none.* Travelling alone, I had nobody to talk to all day and, because of costs and logistics, it was not possible to ring home, Melanie or mates for a chat. Instead, letters became

my life-blood, and I would eagerly await collecting them from American Express offices along the way.

There is no greater joy than turning up in a strange town and then walking out of an American Express office with a handful of letters. The day after I was robbed in Cairns, I collected some mail from the Am Ex office and amongst them was a letter from my mate, John Hickey. He had been raising money in his local pub for the NSPCC, and when I opened the letter $AUS20 fell out. There was no mention of it in his letter, but I could not have been more thankful; at that moment it was all the money I had in the world, and I will forever be grateful. Coupled with the fact that Gus and Bill had not known me for 24 hours, yet offered me free food and lodgings and further cash advances when I needed to pay for things like a replacement passport, it illustrated that human kindness can offset any setback.

5. *Dead kangaroos smell.* This may seem like an obvious statement, but it is not until you are hit by the sickly-sweet aroma of a rotting carcass that is being gradually cooked under the heat of the sun that you really appreciate how powerful a smell can be. Kangaroos can be big animals: a few of them I saw were the same size as me, so if you want to know what a dead kangaroo looks like, think of a man in a kangaroo suit. I didn't *see* many dead kangaroos because they were generally in ditches beside the road having, presumably, been hit by one of the lorries that would sometimes come thundering along out of nowhere. However, if the wind was blowing in your direction it was possible to smell them for hundreds of metres before you passed them. It was the kind of smell that you feel in the back of your throat before you register in your brain that

this is a smell, rather than just a feeling of nausea. Peddling through the pong was a real reminder that that was what death smelt like, and, if a kangaroo could be put in a ditch, so could a cyclist – each time I passed one I reminded myself it could have been me instead.

6. *New South Wales is not North Wales.* Another obvious statement, but an important one that people need to be aware of, so they do not repeat the mistake I made on my second day riding through New South Wales. As a child on holiday in Wales, it was a common sight in the seventies to see children with pink or peeling skin as a result of sun exposure. Today, such an attitude may be regarded as neglect, but in those days parents were ignorant of the need to protect their children from sunburn and the attitude was very much 'Go out, get pink, it will peel and eventually it will go brown.'

So I adopted the same attitude, and decided to take my shirt off. I then rode for five hours bent over the handlebars, which only allowed my skin to stretch even further across my back.

Bearing in mind this was the skin of a man who had come from England in January, it could hardly have been whiter. I am sure that passing planes would have been able to see the reflected rays bouncing off my white back. Other road users, if they weren't already wearing sunglasses, quickly did so to avoid being blinded by the glare. Meanwhile, I was oblivious to the burning that was happening to my back because, as I rode, the wind was providing a cooling effect that masked the reality of the situation. It was not until I arrived at my destination and climbed off my bike that it happened.

By 'it', I mean the pain.

As I straightened up from my bent position, creasing my burnt skin as I did so, the pain was like being hit with a bed of nails, but more like being hit with a bed of nails that had been in a fire and had bits of glass on the end. I had to lie face-down in a hotel room for two days and have the rather attractive receptionist apply cream dispensed to me by a local doctor before I could continue. I can't tell you how hard it is to ask a stranger to apply cream to your burnt skin, and it is a testament to Aussie friendliness that she didn't bat an eyelid at the request: it was as if such things happened every day. Needless to say, I never took my shirt off again for the whole trip, which meant I was never burnt again. But it also meant I never had frequent visits from attractive female hotel staff to my room, so there is always a downside to anything positive. Afterwards, I was so careful to wear the right clothing; in fact, wearing Lycra becomes very normal after a while and you even begin wondering why nobody else does the same in their normal life, to save having excess fabric wafting everywhere.

By the time I left Australia on 6 March, nearly two months after my arrival into the country, I had fallen in love with the place and the people (the odd twat mentioned above excluded, of course). I made a promise to myself that I would go back, which to date has never happened, but I hope it will one day.

However, my sadness at leaving was quickly replaced by the sense of adventure. I was going to continue my ride through Singapore, Malaysia and Thailand, a part of the world I had never thought I would visit. I also had a date with the person who had mainly occupied my thoughts during those long hours on the bike, a date I was desperate not to miss.

CHAPTER 15

ROAD TO BANGKOK

I arrived in Singapore on 9 March, where Melanie was waiting for me at the airport. We had always planned to meet at this point in the journey. She had managed to book a week off and, using a crew concession, had travelled on a cheap flight from Dubai.

I had last seen her fleetingly in January when she was on a flight back to England, but that had been perhaps for an hour; now we were to spend a week together. We both knew it was either going to make or break us, as the difficulties inherent in a long-distance relationship had been further compounded by the fact that I had no fixed abode, so phone calls were extremely infrequent. This week would either consign our relationship to the dustbin or would inspire us to continue to try to make it work.

I knew Melanie had arrived a few hours before, so I eagerly looked out for her as I entered the arrivals lounge, scanning the airport with a mixture of anticipation and apprehension. Our relationship had always had an element of volatility, and as Melanie was now building a new life in Dubai there was every reason to suspect that any little argument could see her decide her life was elsewhere and that she wanted to end things with me. I also had to admit that, though I was prepared for this, I was a 25-year-old man who had not seen his girlfriend for months and who had spent weeks anticipating sleeping together again, so I just didn't want it all to be over before the first night. If she dumped me in the morning I knew I would be able to cope a lot better.

The moment I saw her, though, all my doubts melted. She looked wonderful. She was wearing a pair of dark trousers and a white shirt with a patterned collar, her hair was much richer-looking than I remembered, and her skin had the glowing sheen of a new tan. I walked over and held her in my arms, and the distance between us disappeared in an instant. We kissed, then she looked into my eyes:

'God, John, you look shit.'

Although I thought this was a rather negative thing to say within the first thirty seconds of our reunion, as I stood there in kung fu pumps, a washed-out green T-shirt and a pair of canvas trousers that had managed to become colourless in the same way as well-used dishcloths do, I knew she had a case.

One other aspect of spending the vast majority of your time alone is that you quickly forget how you may appear to other people. In my defence, it is also difficult to carry anything that you may regard as an extensive wardrobe on a bicycle. My hair was the worst problem. I have hair that just seems to get thick before it gets long. As a result of eight weeks' cycling, during which I had barely looked in the mirror, let alone considered visiting a barber, I now had a helmet-shaped hairstyle. I looked like a Beatle tribute act dressed for the worst festival in the world.

We stayed for a few nights in the Carlton Hotel, which further exacerbated my sensitivity over my appearance as the staff would only let me in if I was accompanied by Melanie; when I arrived at the hotel alone, they would call the room to ask her to vouch for me, no matter how often I had been in the hotel that day. Eventually, Melanie became tired of this so she took me to buy clothes and get my hair cut. I felt like I was 10 again in the week before school term started, being made respectable by my mum.

Towards the end of our week we were joined by David Swift. I played football with David's brother and, during a conversation after one game, he had mentioned that he was in a rut and would be keen to join me on the ride. It was one of those situations where a brief conversation had become a commitment, and he had actually come out to Singapore to ride the rest of the way home with me. I had told him that there were no guarantees that we would get on as we didn't really know each other and that if he managed to come he could ride with me until one or both of us decided it wasn't working.

The truth was, I was now used to being on my own and I preferred the idea of carrying on alone. However, when someone has travelled across the world to join you, it's not an easy thing to turn around and say, 'Sorry, mate. I want to do my own thing now.'

A cock-up involving the Indian High Commission losing my passport meant I said goodbye to Melanie twice: once when she was leaving after our week together, and then again when she returned a few days later for work as I was about to set off with David. The second time, we were also joined by Jimmy and Diane, as she worked for BA and he had tagged along on a flight to say hello and offer his usual misplaced advice:

'If you can get a gun in Thailand, it might be handy in case someone tries to rob you with a knife.'

'What if they have a gun?'

'Then it's a shootout!'

Saying goodbye a second time was made easier because Melanie had received her roster and was scheduled to fly into Bangkok on 28 April. This gave me a month to get there and something to look forward to, along the way.

•   •   •

Although I wasn't sure how long I would last with David, we rode out of Singapore on 25 March. As it was, we rode all the way to Bangkok together. When we split up in India, six weeks later, there was nothing to say we had fallen out, although there was not much to say we had bonded, either. This was probably in part my fault. I was so used to riding all day and not talking that I didn't speak for hours without noticing. I was also a few months further on in terms of cycling fitness. All the stages we did through Malaysia and Thailand were long distances, so David had to work hard to keep pace right from the first day, which to be fair to him he did, but it took a lot of effort.

There were two reasons for having to keep the pace up: David was only given a 14-day visa at the Thai border, which put pressure on us to make the distance to Bangkok and deal with all the other matters we had to do, prior to going on to the next stage in India.

I was going to be a father. Melanie had informed me during a call from somewhere in Malaysia that her period was late but, as an unmarried woman in Dubai at the time, was not allowed to take a pregnancy test until she returned to England, which was to happen before I saw her in Bangkok.

The news turned everything on its head for me. I was a 25-year-old man enjoying the adventure of riding a bike around the world. When my dad was 25 he already had four children, so the notion of 'getting something out his system' had never been there. For me it had been the purpose of doing the ride, and now, all of a sudden, everything had changed.

What I was afraid of – commitment – was staring me in my face. A child was a lifetime's commitment, but I was overwhelmed by excitement at the prospect. Whatever I had had to get out of my system went after that phone call. I now had another priority. There was something else more important than me, and now I just wanted to get home in one piece.

This was a feeling which was even more acute when cycling in South East Asia, where the ability to drive seems to be mainly dependent on how prepared you are to pick a direction and keep going along it, regardless of obstructions such as other cars, pedestrians, cyclists or even buildings.

This was most apparent in Thailand, where huge, colourful lorries populated the roads with designs on them that looked like they had been modelled on the carousels you find at fairgrounds. These trucks were invariably driven by men who looked 12 years old and who all wore flip-flops.

I don't want anyone to misunderstand my flip-flop comment here. Now, I like flip-flops: they can look great with shorts in the summer and stop your feet getting too hot or having small stones hurt the soles of your feet. However, I think when you are driving an over-laden, 40-ton lorry, you need to have footwear on that is unlikely to slip when you are deciding when to accelerate or brake.

Progressing through Thailand, it was not unusual to find a truck abandoned in a ditch, on its side like a wildebeest that had been injured and was now waiting for the vultures to feast on the carcass. Having experienced the driving in Thailand, I was not surprised so many of them had crashed, but what was strange was that it was always on straight roads, where you could imagine the driver would have seen any oncoming hazards. However, the straight roads were also where all the overtaking went on, which basically meant that every driver was engaged in a giant game of 'Chicken'. This worked by one truck trying to overtake another truck without really considering the oncoming traffic. Either someone would give way or they all went for it to see who died first.

With my new change in circumstances, I would regularly move into the side of the road. Once or twice, I ended up in the ditch, but figured that climbing out alive was better than staying on the road and being dead. David, on the other hand, had a very British attitude to the situation and would regularly just continue on the line we were cycling, despite the oncoming tons of metal in front of him. At one particularly hairy moment, I looked up from out of the ditch to see the oncoming truck swerve to miss him by a matter of inches, whilst its horn blared, along with every other vehicle on the road. When I asked him why he hadn't moved out of the way, he just replied, 'It's my right of way.'

There are many occasions when I think it is admirable to stand up for your rights. But, to my mind, riding on a bicycle towards a 40-ton truck driven by someone who can't even tie shoelaces is not the time to do it. I didn't want my future child to be told, 'Your dad is not here and he never managed to see you because he was squashed on a road in southern Thailand. But it was his right of way!'

Knowing that I could see my potentially pregnant girl-friend the following week meant I wanted to do all I could to move quickly, and with his visa restrictions David was happy to up the pace. About 150 kilometres south of Bangkok, however, the road forked. We could either go straight to the capital, or north to Kanchanaburi and from there get the train into Bangkok. This would allow us the opportunity to avoid riding into one of the world's most polluted cities and chok-ing to death on the way. And it would also allow me to do something I had promised Melanie's dad I would do if I could.

Kanchanaburi is a regular tourist destination because it is within easy reach of Bangkok and is home to the famous bridge over the River Kwai, which was another reason for wanting to go. Upon arriving in the town, we made our way to the Chungkai cemetery. It could only be reached by a ferry, which was a five-minute journey across the river.

I had been expecting white crosses. Instead, each soldier in the cemetery was commemorated with a small, neat, white gravestone upon which was written their rank, name, the date they died and their age. After searching for hours, I found what I was looking for.

The headstone simply read: Brigadier C V C Cornall. Died 15.9.43, aged 31.

I was standing at the headstone of Melanie's grandfather. He had gone to war when Melanie's dad was one year old and had been captured by the Japanese. He had suffered horrendous treatment in the POW camps that had built the railway but which now proved such a profitable tourist attraction. I was the first person with any connection to the family to have ever been to the grave and, as I stood there, I realised that that connection was potentially growing by the day.

When I called Melanie's dad to tell him where I was, he thanked me for making the effort (little did we know that a few years later we would go there together to stand at the grave of the father he never knew). He then said, 'I believe congratulations are in order.' Melanie came to the phone to say she was definitely pregnant and would be returning to Dubai to hand in her notice.

The anticipation that she may be pregnant had buzzed around my head since we had spoken two weeks earlier. Knowing it was a reality made that buzzing explode, and whatever doubts we had both harboured about our relationship were now replaced by the knowledge that, as parents, we would be bound to each other for life through the child we had created. All of a sudden, everything had a new meaning, our relationship had a purpose and my life had a point to it that it had lacked previously. I could not have been more in love.

That night I told David my news and we went out to celebrate in a bar in Bangkok. It was also a celebration of finishing the South East Asia leg of the journey. We were beginning to work together on the road and the long silences no longer felt uncomfortable. I was also pondering the prospect of fatherhood and all that this meant. It was one of those moments, for both of us, where you know your life is going to change and you are sharing that moment with someone who you think is the most likely person to understand. It was probably the closest we ever got on the trip, and we may have bonded more had a woman on the bar not started firing ping-pong balls at us – without using her hands. There is only so much introspection anyone can do under those circumstances.

When Melanie arrived a few days later, David had already gone to India – where we would meet later – his visa having run out. I was overwhelmed when I saw her enter the hotel reception. She looked radiant, and I spent as much time as I could in those few days together stroking her stomach, which showed no sign of pregnancy but which I knew would when I saw her next. Melanie was keen that I should complete the trip, despite our change of circumstances. We calculated that she would be seven months pregnant if I kept to my timetable and returned home in September.

During our short time together in Bangkok, I took her to her grandfather's grave. The continuity of life can never be more transparent than when a granddaughter stands at the grave of a grandfather that neither she nor her father knew, whilst the next generation grows inside her.

It was hard to say goodbye to her when she left. I knew she had been enjoying her life in Dubai and would not have returned had the pregnancy not happened. But we also understood that the indecision that had surrounded our relationship was now over. There was no more 'Will we, won't we?' because we had, and now we had to get on with it. Part of me wanted to go home straight away and prepare for fatherhood, but a greater part of me knew that this time would never come again. I would never have just me to think about. I needed to complete the journey because I had made the commitment to do so for the charity, but I had also made a commitment to myself. Now that my future looked so different from how it had when I left England, I knew I would never get this unique opportunity ever again.

CHAPTER 16

INDIAN DAYS

When I arrived at Calcutta airport on 4 May, I thought the pilot had got it wrong and had just landed in a car park somewhere. There was nothing 'airporty' about it: the steps from the plane looked like a decorator's step ladder; the terminal was better than a shed but less impressive than a disused garage. When I tried to change $20, I created 35 minutes' work for seven men, who each had to count the money and sign a piece of paper to say they had done so before the person standing next to them did exactly the same.

David met me at the airport in a taxi that was held together with string and hope. We drove through the night streets with no lights on, not because the driver hadn't turned them on but because a tangle of wires was hanging from the front of the car where the lights should have been. David and I sat in the car and prepared to die.

We spent a few days in Calcutta trying to sort out the bikes and to allow David time to get over a stomach bug. The brief pause enabled me to explore the city and to form an opinion of it that I also ended up extending to the whole country. In my view, India is like onion-flavoured ice cream: it has the potential to be something special, but no matter how good the good bits are it still leaves you with a bitter aftertaste.

People have said to me that you can love and hate India within the same minute, but I don't think it takes that long. The biggest issue I found in the country was the poverty. Even though you could see some people had money, the level of accepted poverty was incomprehensible. People would use the main street as their toilet, and I'd see children with twisted limbs that had been bent at birth by parents who had sought to give them a chance to earn some money begging on the streets.

It was the poverty that the children faced that upset me the most. How could you blame them for chasing Westerners for change to buy food? I hated the fact that you would see children no older than five living on the streets and wearing rags, with nobody to look after them, as they scrambled for whatever food they could get. But what I hated most about India was that I got used to this level of poverty; so used to it, in fact, that I found myself waving children away as they stood with their hands out. There were excuses: there were too many of them; I had often been riding for hours in oppressive heat; it is wrong to reward begging as it confirms to them that that is their lot in life. There were many excuses, but you can't help feel some small part of your soul dies when you refuse a child some pennies.

David and I split after the first day in India. His illness had taken its toll and he needed time to recover, but I needed to press on home. It was evident within the first few hours that India was going to be hard work. The drivers made the lunatics in Thailand look like grannies on a Sunday afternoon. This was proved within the first hour when we rode past a smartly dressed, middle-aged man lying in the middle of the road, with deep red, almost black blood oozing out of him, the injuries making it clear he was taking his last breaths in life. Around him people paused for a second, then carried on with their day. The driver of a truck with a smashed wing mirror stood by, smoking a cigarette. There were no sirens, no police or emergency services, just a man dying on the road. A reminder, if I needed one, that our hold on life is so fragile it can be broken at any time, and I owed it to more than myself to try to ensure the same did not happen to me.

I continued alone. Mistakes such as riding 100 kilometres the wrong way due to misreading road signs did not enhance my enjoyment of India. In each village or town I rode into, I was immediately surrounded, mainly by men who just stood and stared. There is nothing stranger than walking into a chai house or shop and turning around to find 30 or 40 men standing within five feet of you, staring intently. Being English, I assumed the locals could speak English. This proved wrong as, even if I spoke to them, they just continued to stare. Which was good practice for a future life where audiences did the same.

In a town called Bankura, I needed to find a hotel and decided the train station would be a good place to ask. The station in Bankura is like many in India, the best building in the town, a proud Victorian construction and a monument that stands as an indication that the British once ruled and that, despite the persecution and theft of the country's natural resources, we did at least give them a decent railway.

I went to the transport office and spoke to a proud, uniformed man with a neat moustache. 'Can you tell me where there is a decent hotel, please?'

He just shook his head at me, looking slightly bemused.

'Do you know where I can find a hotel, please?'

Again a blank look. So I raised my voice, repeated the question and started to engage in a game of charades where I acted out sleeping in a building with a roof called a hotel.

'A HOTEL. I need a HOTEL. With a BED to sleep. Do YOU know a HOTEL with a BED in it?'

He creased his brow again and then replied, 'Walk half a mile down this road, take the first right and the next left and you will find a reputable establishment. If you are in India, you should learn to speak English. I am sure you will find it very useful.'

CHAPTER 17

A DAY IN BUXTON CHANGED EVERYTHING

I rode across the border at the Nepalese town of Hetauda after a long day riding in the late May sunshine. The heat of the days and the dust on the roads in India had begun to take their toll, with my eyes feeling constantly sore. I was hoping Nepal would allow some respite from the assault of my senses I had experienced in India, yet my mind was pre-occupied with getting to Kathmandu to speak to Melanie again. I could only call her from a telephone shop where you booked a long-distance phone call, and these facilities only seemed to exist in larger towns.

I immediately liked Nepal, and it was to become my favourite country on the whole trip. The mountain ranges provided a beautiful and inspiring backdrop, and with the increasing altitude the air felt fresher and so cycling was not the same, grinding ordeal it had felt like in India, despite the difficultly of riding uphill for hours on end.

The level of poverty seemed similar to India, but there was a much greater sense of community there. This was illustrated one night in a village on the road to Pokhara where I had taken a room in a guest house for the night. The house utilised the fact that it was clinging to the edge of the mountain by having a squat toilet – a hole in the floor through which you could see the mountain pass below. If you didn't want to go before you walked in, you certainly did shortly afterwards.

I bathed using a bucket of water and was about to go to sleep to recover from the long day's ride when I heard a commotion outside in the village square. I walked out to see virtually the whole village in a huddle watching something with much excitement and amusement. Not wanting to be left out, I walked over to find the source of the entertainment. It was a cockerel attempting to have sex with a duck. Now there *is* something mildly amusing about the thought of a cockerel attempting to have sex with a duck, but it is only mildly amusing at best. In a Nepalese village in 1992, it entertained the whole village and an English cyclist for at least an hour.

My first night in Nepal was spent in the Hotel Avocado, which at the time was run by a dwarf who could not see the funny side of me suggesting that the bucket of water he gave me to use for a shower might be enough for him, but I would need two. I was to discover later that the hotel had a guest book in which a number of cyclists either coming from or going to Kathmandu had written. After spending weeks battling through India alone and preoccupied with Melanie and the baby, it was nice to feel a connection to other people, even though some were clearly mad, like the Danish couple who had visited as they cycled around the world and said they had been on the road for two years. There was a photograph of them beside their entry: they were well into the sixties and were sitting on a tandem. Can anyone who is married imagine being on a tandem with your partner for more than a Sunday afternoon, let alone two years? It's hard enough being married and looking at the same face every morning over breakfast; imagine looking at the same arse all day long! And, if you're at the front, how can you know if the person at the back is peddling as hard as you? What a great way to get your own back: just lean back, read a book and let the other one do the work. I'm sorry, it's a great idea, but to make it work you both have to be slightly mental. Or Scandinavian.

The reason the hotel was popular was because it was at the bottom of the old road to Kathmandu. The new road took most of the traffic, so this one was quiet when it came to cars. It took you over the Daman Pass, famous for being one of the highest passes you can cross on a bicycle at 2,488 metres, from which there is an observation point where you can see Mount Everest.

I rode the 150 kilometres up to Kathmandu in 14 hours and arrived exhausted but happy. The height of the pass sounds impressive, but another reason the old road is attractive to cyclists is that the gradient of the climb is reduced by the road being cut into the side of the mountain at a shallow angle, so that you zigzag up, increasing your altitude steadily. This made it longer and slower than a more direct route, but also scenic and enchanting. It is the route that has been used for centuries, and when Kathmandu was closed to the world the Nepalese used it to reach the capital to bring their goods and animals to trade. I had experienced something unique: a bike ride you would never repeat in one of the most interesting places in the world.

I had said that I would phone Melanie when I reached Kathmandu, but as I didn't know when that would be, I had not been able to arrange an exact day, and so I was not unduly concerned when there was no answer when I called the following day. I took the opportunity to see the city and catch up on some rest.

One of the first things I wanted to do was to go and visit the American Express office to see if anybody had used their mailing service to send me any letters. When I got there, however, the man behind the counter told me that he had sent all the letters to Delhi as apparently I had written to him to ask him to do so. The fact that I wasn't in Delhi obviously confirmed that I hadn't actually written to him, but he was able to show me a fax that had come from the American Express office in Delhi requesting that the letters for David Swift (which would have been written to David Swift care of John Bishop) be sent to Delhi. Deciding that if David Swift wanted his letters there, then perhaps John Bishop would do too, he had sent the lot.

My disappointment was immense. I knew Melanie had written during the days we had not been able to speak on the phone and I was desperate to read those thoughts. I had also not picked up any mail from anyone else for over a month, so to know that I would never read what was in them was a crushing blow. There is no greater loneliness than the feeling of never knowing what has been said.

In desperation to have some contact with home, I booked another call at the phone shop and tried to get Melanie.

When she answered the phone, I knew. As she broke down, she told me she had lost the baby. I was standing in one of five phone booths in a shop in Kathmandu whilst people either side of me held conversations in various languages, and my world collapsed. I couldn't speak. The thing that had been a surprise had become all I had thought about for weeks. Surprise had turned into excitement. Excitement had turned into hope. And now it was gone. I was on the other side of the world trying to speak through a piece of plastic to heal a broken heart in England, and as my five minutes of call-time passed by in a flash, the line went dead.

I was unable to book another call due to a long queue, so I walked into the streets of Kathmandu in a daze. I was lost, confused and lonelier than I ever imagined possible. I could only imagine what Melanie was going through. Our future had been changed by the pregnancy and now it had been stolen from us.

I decided that I had to see her. I was ahead of the schedule I'd imposed on myself, but now all my motivation was gone. I just needed to put my arms around her. I found out that there was one flight a week to England, and that was not due again for six days. So, the following morning, I went to the airport and with the aid of a $20 bribe managed to get a seat on the only plane travelling to Delhi that day.

In Delhi, I bought a ticket to London via Frankfurt from a man in a shop in the city centre who sold household goods such as brushes and dustpans, and airline tickets. I was not convinced till we were in the air that he had even sold me an actual ticket, although my promise to come back and murder him if he was ripping me off may have convinced him it was worth making sure my ticket was valid.

Melanie had no idea I was coming but, just over 24 hours after leaving Nepal, I walked into the back garden of her father's house where she was sitting in the sunshine. She saw me and, after a second's hesitation, she ran into my arms. We said nothing, but just held each other for an age. We both had our own personal pain and disappointment to deal with, but in that hug we allowed ourselves to share our loss together for the first time.

I could have turned around and gone straight back because, in that moment, all my questions were answered; whatever happened, I wanted to be connected to Melanie for the rest of my life. I stayed for a week in England without letting anyone except my family know. During the time home, I went with Melanie to a guest house in Buxton. I had already asked her father's approval and so, after emerging from the shower one evening, I went down on one knee and asked her to marry me.

I must say that when I asked her father for his daughter's hand in marriage, I never mentioned I would pop the question with all I had to offer on show. Had I told him, I am not sure he would have granted his approval, but I think it was the best way to do it, nothing hidden. I had no doubt that I loved Melanie, and I wanted us both to have something to replace what we had lost, something for us both to look forward to, something to move our relationship on to another level. I guess I wanted the commitment I had run away from months before.

She said 'yes', and I returned to continue my journey through Nepal and India a man engaged to be married the following May.

Had Melanie not become pregnant, she would not have lost the baby when she did and I would not have proposed when I did. I was beginning to learn that, in life, circumstances often shape you and not the other way round. Had none of those things happened, I think it's unlikely this book would ever have been written. I am writing this book because

I am a comedian. I am a comedian because I married Melanie. I married Melanie because I learnt I loved her. I learnt I loved her because we lost something special.

Naked on one knee in a guest house in Buxton, I planted the seed that led to you reading this book, when I was actually supposed to be on the other side of the world riding a bike.

CHAPTER 18

A YANK CALLED JOE

After returning to Kathmandu, I rode on to Delhi with renewed vigour. Like the pregnancy before it, the marriage gave me a sense of purpose. I wouldn't be riding a bicycle for months on end again because I was getting married less than a year after I returned to England, so I knew I had best enjoy it.

The final leg of my trip began in Istanbul. In 1992, it was virtually impossible to get from India to Europe on a bicycle, unless you were mental and wanted to risk death or imprisonment in one of the various countries that bordered India. Melanie, for her part, wanted us to move on to the next stage of our lives and though she was very keen I should complete the ride, she didn't want me to take unnecessary risks, which was why I had decided to fly from Delhi to Istanbul to continue the next leg of the journey; a leg which was to take me through more countries than any other and which was to be influenced by one person more than any other.

I knew of Joe's existence before I met him, because when I first checked into the youth hostel in Istanbul I saw his unique bicycle chained against the railings behind the reception desk. It was unique to me because it had a mountain bike frame and wheels with multiple panniers, an extra-thick seat and the drop handlebars of a racing bike combined with the newer aero bars of time trialists, rather than the straight bars of a normal mountain bike.

I also heard Joe before I spoke to him. I was returning to the hostel on the second day after purchasing a long-sleeved shirt to combat the refreshing coolness of the European night (it was so refreshing, it was almost giving me pneumonia). Behind me, I heard the loud American accent of someone speaking about his cycling trip so far. So, I eavesdropped as he told the assembled group at his table that he had set off from Germany in the winter, had moved down through Italy before spending some time in Greece, and was now taking a bit of time to rest in Istanbul having spent three months cycling in eastern Turkey.

I casually looked in the direction of the American accent. The speaker was on the edge of his seat, oozing enthusiasm about riding in eastern Turkey where they all wore Reebok trainers and nobody spoke English, even those who had MTV. His dark, shoulder-length brown hair was unkempt and parted in the middle, so that it looked like a set of curtains that framed a round face upon which sat a goatee beard. The face was tanned from sun as well as with an obvious genetic connection to some European country, and I would have guessed, as much from his American accent as anything else, that he was of Italian stock.

He also seemed to have a thick frame, which made me believe that he spent more time talking than cycling. He wore the clothes of a latter-day hippy: tie-dye baggy Turkish pants and an open-necked, collarless sweatshirt under which lay a leather string, holding a stone around his neck.

His overall appearance gave me the impression that he was, in fact, a wanker.

I resolved to avoid the loud Yank and make my own plans to leave as soon as the bank's computer released my funds, which had been held up since I arrived. Yet, as before, fate intervened to my great benefit.

On the third day in Istanbul, I woke in my bunk to be greeted with rain, so I decided to spend the day phoning the bank, checking my bike and planning a route. It was while sitting at a table, drinking coffee and looking at a borrowed map, that somebody joined me at my table and said, in a strong American accent, 'Hi, I'm Joe. Are you the other cyclist?'

I looked up to see the wanker. 'Yeah, how did you know?' I replied.

'The lady at the desk told me,' he said. 'Where are you going to?'

'West, back to England,' I replied.

'Really? Me, too. I'm sort of heading that way, although I really fancy going to Eastern Europe. Man, that's got to be a place of interest.'

Two hours later we were still talking, and the wanker was now becoming a friend. I felt guilty about my prejudices as I rapidly became a disciple of his new-age cycling church.

When it came time to leave Istanbul, it seemed natural that we should ride together. Joe had impressed me with his knowledge of cycling and his openness of character, but we had no illusions about how long we would stay together. After all, we both had different agendas.

I was riding back to England and had 12 weeks to reach Liverpool on the date I had set when I had originally left in January, six months earlier. Joe had spent the last seven years on and off his bicycle and was in no rush to go anywhere. The only date he had to keep was to meet some of his family on holiday in Switzerland in July.

We camped in his blue igloo tent on the first night, after riding 130 kilometres along the scenic coast road. The next morning, we returned to the main road, only to see a sign saying it was 40 kilometres to Istanbul. The first day had been nice, but not worth a 90-kilometre ride in a circle.

Joe was a very strong cyclist so, in spite of the detour on the first day, we made steady progress towards the Bulgarian border, even though the head wind seemed to be permanently in our faces. At one point, I was beginning to suspect that in order to keep the Turks out of Bulgaria, the Communist regime had built a giant wind machine to blow everyone back.

After a final night in Turkey, we approached the border, not knowing what to expect. We were both children of the Cold War and had been educated that those countries that lay behind the Iron Curtain were police states in which Westerners were at best treated with suspicion, or at worst simply disappeared. The demise of the Soviet Union had happened barely 12 months previously, and it was not an unlikely suggestion that we would be amongst the first Westerners to cross from Turkey to Bulgaria: certainly the first on bicycles.

After having our passports stamped out of Turkey, we cycled the 500 metres or so to the building that represented the Bulgarian border. The gun turrets were unmanned, but the armed guards who greeted us acted as though they would happily return to pointing their weapons across the border.

Our passports were handed to a woman at the reception desk who had a face that looked like it had been trained to never smile . . . ever. Without saying anything, she disappeared into an office. A few minutes later, a large man followed her out. He had a thick moustache, stubble and an eye that suggested he had just left a bar-room brawl to deal with us.

'Who is the American?' he asked.

Before Joe could say anything, I answered: 'He is.' If one of us was going to be thrown into jail for being a citizen of a Western imperialistic capitalist nation, then it was not going to be me.

'Welcome, my friend. I have personally stamped your passport,' he said, flinging his arms out to Joe and slapping him on the back in a kind of border-side-male-bonding session. Without bothering to turn to me, he said, 'British citizens have to pay for a visa. It is thirty-three US dollars.'

I couldn't believe that Americans, who had spent the Cold War pointing nuclear missiles in the general direction of Bulgaria, were able to enter for free, whilst the British people who had spent the Cold War making James Bond movies had to pay to get in.

We had crossed the border and had started the descent into the first border town of Bulgaria when Joe signalled for us to stop. Out of his pannier he pulled out two bottles of Turkish beer, the last things we bought at the border to use up the remainder of our Turkish currency.

Joe proposed a toast: 'Look at us, man, drinking Turkish beer in Bulgaria. Our only problem is finding a place to sleep. Haven't we got life by the balls?'

I could hardly argue with that.

CHAPTER 19

A TOWN THAT DIDN'T EXIST

I was to learn that being American first and from New York second made Joe a celebrity everywhere we went in Eastern Europe. People would continually ask us questions about life in the West, but it was always Joe they wanted answers from and it was always Joe who they thought would be best placed to help them get in contact with their uncle, cousin, brother or school friend who had managed to escape to the West and from whom all contact had stopped. I, on the other hand, was just a source of minor interest, somebody who was travelling with 'The American'. That was, until we reached a town that did not exist.

It was the fourth day on the road in Bulgaria and the grey skies had soaked us in rain when we pulled into what we thought was a café but – as we were now becoming accustomed to – was actually a café without food. There seemed to be food shortages everywhere we went, so we asked the lady who was trying to run a café without food the best place for us to go. She indicated a position on the map, which had no town marked. We both thought she was possibly a bit mad due to the lack of food but, rather than spend the rest of the day in the company of a hungry, mad woman, we rode in the direction she suggested.

From the main road, we found a smaller road, again unmarked on the map, but which seemed to be in the direction of the phantom town. We rode slowly down the empty road till we arrived at an unmanned checkpoint. Lifting the barrier, we rode into the town of grey, square, pre-fabricated buildings that we were to learn later was called Belene.

The town felt like it had been plonked there no longer than 10 years previously and, looking at the buildings, it seemed unlikely that it would be there in 10 years' time. As a place, it provided an ugly contrast to the old country villages that we had been progressing through.

Amongst the characterless buildings, we found a small, empty café and quickly ordered hot chocolate and toasted cheese sandwiches before we lost the energy to talk. When the food and drink came, the relief was immediate and we ordered a repeat.

Whilst we sat there drying off and wondering if one of the square boxes was a hotel, four middle-aged men entered the café. Before Joe or I had time to think what their intentions might be, all of them sat at our table.

'Hello. My name is André. Where are you from?'

The speaker had a warm face that held the friendliness of a child in a school playground meeting new friends, although his greying hair was testament to the fact that it had been some time since André was in a school playground.

Before I could speak, Joe had once again become the Ambassador of the West and told the four-man greeting party that he was from New York. As expected, this was received with approval, and one of the men leant forward to slap Joe

on his back as if to congratulate him on the fact that he was
born in one of the most famous places in the world and was
now in one that didn't even feature on the map.

André then turned to me and asked, 'Are you also American?'

For a moment, I almost lied so that I could be greeted as
somebody whose place of birth was a personal achievement
rather than my mum's decision. However, a thread of patri-
otism found its way through beyond my desire to be a hero
in Belene, so I confessed to being from England.

There was audible disappointment, so I decided to be as
specific as Joe and mention the city of my birth in an
attempt to gain some kudos from being best friends with
the Beatles.

The reaction was immediate. As soon as the word 'Liverpool'
left my mouth, all four men in unison said, 'Kenny Dalglish!'

Joe sat bemused whilst I was slapped on the back and
given the wide smiles of approval that had so far been
reserved for members of the Stars and Stripes brigade.

'Who the fuck is Kenny Dalglish?' he asked me, as other
people in the café came over to shake my hand.

'He is a footballer who used to play for Liverpool and then
became the coach,' I informed him, before elaborating, 'He
was a great player and is a really nice guy, as well.'

'A nice guy,' André interrupted. 'So you know him?'

'Yes, I know him quite well,' I lied. 'We are not best friends,
you understand, but I do see him occasionally.' I flashed Joe
a 'stick your Robert De Niro up your arse' look and enjoyed,
for the first time, being the main man of our double act.

André told us of his passion for football and that Liverpool
was his favourite team. Before reporting restrictions were
lifted in 1989, André and his friends would risk severe pun-
ishment to tune in to foreign radio stations and listen to

games on the radio. Occasionally, the state television would show a match, but things were much easier now for distant supporters because, as André announced with pride, English football was so popular, Bulgarian newspapers were printing the results.

It had grown steadily dark outside and Joe and I needed to make some arrangements for the night. I asked André if the town had a hotel. Like everything else we had said to André apart from the words 'Kenny Dalglish' or 'Liverpool', this had to be, in turn, translated to the men.

A short discussion began amongst them that involved a lot of pointing, shrugging of shoulders and nodding of heads. André eventually turned to us and said, 'I have a place for you to stay.'

We followed him out into the cold, wet night and the three other men said their goodbyes with vigorous handshakes and mentions of Kenny Dalglish in the middle of sentences in Bulgarian. I assumed this was them telling me to say hello to my mate Kenny next time I saw him. Alternatively, it could have been them shaking my hand and saying, 'We know you're a lying bastard and that you don't know Kenny Dalglish. But, luckily for you, it is not the old days when we would have shot you.'

We followed André through the dark streets to another ugly building, where a man stepped out of the shadows and approached us. He was six feet tall with dark hair and a clean-shaven, pale complexion, and was wearing a pair of grey canvas trousers with a crease so sharp it would have cut paper. Either he had learnt to iron his clothes with the precision of an army recruit, or he had an obsessive wife with a new steam iron.

'Hello, I am Jordan Jordan. You will be staying with me.'

We spent two days in Jordan Jordan's apartment. In the past, he had been a senior party member but now, like everybody else in the town, he was adjusting to a new life. He was clearly still held in high esteem around the town and, in his small apartment, he had begun using his party contacts to sell 'things'. We were to learn that these 'things' ranged from potatoes to parts for Russian tanks.

Jordan Jordan also informed us that the town was not on the map because it was built to house a nuclear reactor. As it was close to the Danube and the Hungarian border, the authorities had not wanted its real purpose to be known. Then the Soviet Bloc had collapsed, the nuclear reactor was never finished and a town populated with nuclear physicists and party workers no longer had a meaning. It was perhaps the strangest town I have ever been to, and this was made even more apparent on the last day when André revealed himself to be a nuclear physicist who had moved into potato growing, as there was no work in his chosen profession. He then tried his best to get us to carry off 10 tons of overproduction on our two bicycles as a parting gift.

We attempted to get directly from Bulgaria into Romania, but were prevented from doing so as the border crossing was purely for nationals of those two countries. This meant we had to enter Yugoslavia, a country at the time in the depths of a savage civil war.

We were only there for 24 hours, during which time we could easily have failed to notice anything amiss. In fact, the chaos of war would have completely passed us by had I not attempted to change 20 US dollars at the bank so that we could buy some food. Outside the bank, there was a small crowd, containing mainly men. In our naïvety, we thought that this was because it was the centre of town and people were using it as a meeting point. It was not until I entered the mayhem inside that I saw there was something different going on.

The small bank was crowded with people carrying boxes, cases and buckets of money fighting to get to the counter. The counters didn't have the protective barrier glass common in banks nowadays, and people were desperately thrusting themselves over to the other side in attempts to force their packages of money onto the staff and avoid the crush behind them. One man seemed to have been refused service, so he withdrew a shotgun from a bag that also overflowed with notes. This wasn't greeted with the screaming response you might have imagined, but with a simple nod from the bank teller the man was served and everyone continued as before.

I decided that changing $20 was not going to be a high priority, so I forced my way back through the crowd outside to Joe. We were to later discover that the reason for the panic was that as the civil war had expanded, people had withdrawn all of their money in case the banks collapsed. The government had then reprinted all the national currency removing a '0', meaning all previous notes would become worthless. They had given people three days to change the money or lose everything. This was the third day.

But for that incident, I would have been impervious to what was happening elsewhere: that night, we camped in a sunflower field and, whilst we warmed ourselves by a fire under the starlit night, people were engaged in ethnic cleansing barely a car journey away.

Camping was something that Joe had convinced me to do. It allowed total freedom and a great sense of adventure and I enjoyed it – until one night in Romania, whilst in the foothills of the Transylvanian mountains.

We had set up camp beside a forest after a long day's ride. As the shadows crept out of the forest and engulfed us, we had cleared away the pot from the fire and were preparing for sleep when we heard it.

A sound raced out of the trees. It resembled the howl of a dog, yet it was almost human. It seemed to come from nowhere, enter my ears, run around my head, jump out and slap me in the face before being replaced with dark silence.

I realised that Joe had experienced the same sensation. Neither of us spoke for a moment. We just stood there looking in the direction of the noise for some indication of its source.

'What was that?' I asked, partly to draw on the knowledge of my well-travelled companion, but mainly because the silence was becoming as scary as the noise.

'Don't know . . . probably a wild boar or something,' Joe said, trying to sound unconcerned but not managing it.

For my part, the idea that it was a wild boar didn't help. I would not suggest I have expert knowledge about the animal, but anything with 'wild' as part of its name doesn't sound too friendly.

I opened my mouth to talk to Joe, but before I could speak a shrill sound cut through the air again, firing at us from the trees like an arrow. We both stood saying nothing, until this time Joe broke the silence and attempted to make light of the situation. 'You don't think this has anything to do with being close to Transylvania, do you?'

We both laughed weakly and attempted to reassure one another by saying things like, 'I'm OK, if you're OK,' and 'I don't mind staying if you don't.' Yet within seconds of a third bark/scream we had packed up the tent and were on our bicycles without saying a word to each other.

I was preparing to start riding into the darkness when Joe stopped me. 'Hold on, man, what are we doing?'

'Running away,' I answered.

'Yeah, but look, it's too dark to see anything. We don't have any lights, we don't know where we are, we can't see where we're going and that was an ideal campsite.'

Joe was right. It was ludicrous that two grown men with pretensions of being able to look after themselves were running away from a noise in the trees. We agreed to go back and, laughing at ourselves, began turning towards the forest. Only to see a group of bats fly over our heads.

We jumped on our bicycles and rode like hell.

We decided to make for Turkiju, which appeared to be about 20 kilometres away and was the only town within reach.

It wasn't a good ride. We had been attacked five times by packs of dogs and were still at least 10 kilometres from Turkiju when salvation came in the form of what we would later discover was a miners' tavern.

The only things that suggested we were in a drinking tavern were some crates of beer and the presence of four round tables and assorted chairs and benches. We were the only people in the building, which at 9 p.m. on a Friday didn't suggest this was the most swinging bar in town. But, within five minutes, it was as if a coach party had arrived, and the tavern echoed to the noise of a dozen men talking and opening bottles. We were greeted with a brief cheer and each man shook our hands. Their wide smiles across their leathery faces revealed the loneliest teeth in the world.

As the smiles relaxed, I could see the cracks in their faces were impregnated with black dirt, like grout separating tiles in a bathroom. All the men had faces full of character, which is a diplomatic way of saying that they looked knackered. They were world-worn and looked prepared to fix a child's toy or have a fight within the same minute. We learnt they had all just finished a 12-hour shift down the local coal mine.

As the evening progressed with the opening of more bottles, the fact that we did not speak the same language mattered less and less. Every time someone left they shook hands with everyone in the room, and every time someone arrived they did the same. It was a simple touch of friend-liness that I found heart-warming. Then one of the miners remembered that it was 3 July, so it was decided that we would celebrate Joe being American as more bottles were clinked and cheers shouted.

I then told them about the noise in the woods and the fear it was a vampire, so I proposed a toast to Count Dracula. Joe joined in the toast, but we suddenly realised we were the only people in the room clinking our bottles: the miners just stared blankly back at us.

Attempts to translate through mime failed dismally, and the point where I pretended to bite Joe's neck was greeted with chair-shuffling and coughing, their expressions now turning to ones of concern. After all, these men had emerged from 12 hours underground to go to their local tavern to drink beer, talk about manly things and wash away the coal dust. Instead, they were greeted by the sight of two stran-gers dressed in Lycra shorts, one with his hair in a ponytail, the other pretending to give him a love bite. They had every right to be concerned.

As I stood there watching lasting friendships dissolve in misunderstanding, Joe had the sense to realise that the story of Dracula meant nothing to these men, since Bram Stoker had written for an English audience. In later life I was to learn how to turn an audience but, at this moment, with Romanian miners looking blankly back at me, I was struck dumb. It was Joe who brilliantly explained the whole thing away by saying, 'Hollywood,' while using the gesture that indicates a film in a game of charades.

'Ah, Hollywood.' All the bottles in the room rose to a clink, and the drinking resumed.

It was past 2 a.m. when we were eventually led away by the barman to stay at his house. Despite the time, his wife got out of bed to greet us, and we were given a bowl of water each to wash with, and a bed to share. In the morning, there was a feast prepared for us whilst the family – the barman, his wife and their parents – sat and watched us eat. We assumed they had eaten prior to us, but with hindsight I realised that there was every chance their sense of hospitality was to give us everything and see what we left for them which, after a drunken night when our bodies were craving sustenance, was not a lot.

After breakfast, we thanked them all for their wonderful hospitality and started to walk along the rutted dirt road to pick up our bikes. Our intention had been to head towards Turkiju and then advance throughout the day but, as we reached the tavern, the barman insisted we have a farewell drink.

After a peppermint liqueur, bottles of beer were opened. In an attempt to avoid having to drink the beer, I feigned a hangover from the night before. It was a terrible mistake as it meant I had to drink the most disgusting cocktail in existence: cold espresso coffee mixed with coke. Within minutes I was drinking a bottle of beer.

The bar now had a new set of miners in attendance and, despite it being only 11 a.m., beer was flowing freely. The barman explained to us that all the miners worked 12-hour shifts and their first port of call on their way home was the bar: regardless of the time of day, after 12 hours of breathing in the choking soot of the coal face, each man deserved the right to wash their throats clean with a beer. The fact that the miners would need to have eaten the coal supply of a power station to justify the amount they drank was lost in the handshaking and toasting in which I found us engaging once more.

The day wore on. Then, in the middle of a toast to Elvis Presley, I had a sudden vision of the future. In 10 years, Joe and I would still be here, coming to this very bar after 12 hours pulling coal out of the ground. Like our friends, we would have complexions that a boot maker would dream of, and before each visit the tooth fairy would have had to have made a withdrawal from the World Bank, as 75 per cent of our teeth would be missing. We would drink a crate of beer before going home to our obedient wives, our noisy pigs, our tasty poultry, our back garden allotments and our 14 children.

The truth hit me between my unfocused eyes: escape now or stay for ever. The decision was made. I drank the remains of my fourth bottle of beer, thanked the barman for his hospitality, shook hands with everyone in the room and prepared my bicycle for departure. Joe, however, hesitated for a moment: it was clear that he was closer to the pick and shovel than I was.

I could have left him, but then I would have had to return like Robert De Niro did for Christopher Walken in *The Deer Hunter* (but instead of bursting in on a game of Russian roulette, I would be trying to persuade a zombified old friend not to listen to the crowd and to put that last bottle of beer down). I could see it all ending in tragedy with Joe looking into my eyes for a second, a slight flicker of recognition upon his face when I said the words 'mountain bike', before ignoring my pleas and downing the bottle in one before going back to the mine . . .

It seemed easier to try to persuade him to leave now, so I told him the truth: 'Joe, if we stay here for another hour we are going to die here.'

Slightly dramatic, but effective. Waving to our friends at the bar, we wobbled over the small river bridge next to the tavern and escaped, barely one bottle away from the point of no return. And we paid a price for our excess – it took us two hours to ride seven miles to Turkiju.

•   •   •

I split up with Joe in Prague. We had spent just over a month together and had become firm friends, and there was no doubt that we would keep in touch, despite living different lives: I was to return to England to put my bicycle away, get married and rejoin the company I had worked for; Joe was just going to keep riding and see where the road took him.

But, thankfully, neither of us was going to be a miner.

We were not to know that, decades later, he would be in France living a sustainable lifestyle with his wife and two kids, and I would be in England with my wife and three kids, and the easiest way to communicate would be via the internet. Of course we weren't to know: the internet had not been invented.

In many respects our lives have been polar opposites, and yet I think it is fair to say that I could have easily lived Joe's life and he could have lived mine. In fact, after watching the

Sport Relief challenge I did in 2012, Joe went to Sierra Leone to work for three months on a bicycle project out there. It seems our lives will always cross paths.

I pushed on alone, riding long days, fixated with hitting my return date in September. Back in the UK, Arthur informed me that the fundraising was going well and that there would be a small reception when I returned to Liverpool. For my part, I just wanted it over. I really enjoyed the ride through Europe, but I was desperate to get home. I had spent nearly nine months riding a bike. Every day I was uncertain of where I was going to end up, and now I just wanted to stop still. So much had happened during that time, and I now felt I had a degree of certainty that I had lacked in the past. It wasn't as if I had had an epiphany and was now ready to get married and settle down; it was just that I realised who was important and I wanted to be with them. I wanted to be the person I ran away from being nine months earlier.

After splitting from Joe, I made my way home by crossing the border into Germany, then riding through the Austrian Alps into Switzerland. From there I moved through France, only pausing to spend a few days at Melanie's mum's house in the Dordogne where she lived at the time. Within days I knew I would be in Liverpool and it would all be over. I knew I was ready for the end; I was ready to stop moving and to start setting down some roots.

I rode into the Albert Dock in Liverpool on 12 September 1992 after spending my final night on the road at my nan's house. I was greeted by a crowd of around 50 people made up of work colleagues, friends, family, Melanie and a man playing the bagpipes (for a reason even Arthur has never been able to explain). It was emotional seeing everyone after so long and, after spending large portions of the previous nine months alone, it was slightly overwhelming to receive handshakes and hugs from so many people in one go.

There were numerous comments about how much weight I had lost and how much bigger my legs had become; there was even a suggestion that as I was now fitter than I had ever been, I should help our Eddie's Sunday league team out with a particularly tough game the following week. (I played and looked like a true athlete with my tanned face and legs against the all-white strip. The only problem was cycling does not help you run, so I could hardly move. We got beaten 9–0.)

There was a reception in a bar at the Albert Dock where I was told the trip had raised £30,000 for the NSPCC. In today's money, that would hardly cover a Premier League footballer's hairdresser's bill, but in 1992 it was a significant sum.

At a family gathering that evening, I allowed myself a moment to let it all sink in. I had to admit to a level of mild satisfaction: I had learnt some valuable life lessons and, at the same time, raised some money for a brilliant charity. I had also done something many people thought I was mad to attempt.

It was not the last time I would have that feeling.

CHAPTER 20

MARRIAGE, FATHERHOOD AND IDIOT FRIENDS

After returning home, my future was set out in front of me. I was 25, going back to work at Syntex, I was getting married to Melanie and I was to slip into the old life I had before. It felt like the world was telling me that it was time to grow up: I'd enjoyed my adventure and now it was time to settle down, get married and have kids. Which I duly did.

The first house we bought was two doors away from where I had lived with my mates as students in Manchester. We bought it for a knock-down price from Melanie's dad, and that gave us the funds to convert it from the bedsits it had been into a nice Victorian semi, although this involved ripping everything out. I remember taking Melanie to assess the job in progress; as we stood in the cellar looking up, we were able to spy daylight from the absent roof four floors above us.

I felt we were making great progress, and I enjoyed talking to the builders about manly things that I could pretend I knew about, like ackros, scaffolding and roofing. Melanie was watching a building being ripped apart and left nearly every visit in tears because we looked ever further away from the point of moving in.

Everyone who has ever refurbished a house will know that builders can sway from being your best friend to being your worst enemy within the time it takes to plaster a wall, and a very small wall at that. As a form of protection, I used some friends I had known from my school days, but it also illustrated how much Melanie and I didn't really know each other at that point. When I took her to the house one day, I was downstairs shouting up to my mates on the roof, John Hickey and Paul Christie, both lads who, like me, had spent their teenage years in Runcorn surrounded by people who spoke with the same accent. I had played football with John as a teenager and he was the one who had sent me the $AUS20 when I was in robbed in Cairns. He had always been more sensible, even as a teenager, although things didn't always work out the best for him. When we had all learnt to drive, John took us to the Cherry Tree, the local nightclub, and sensibly decided to leave his car there overnight rather than drive home after a few drinks. When he stepped off the bus the following morning to walk across the road and collect his car, he was knocked over and broke his leg. 'Don't Drive But Be Careful Crossing Roads' is not a government campaign that ever really caught on, but perhaps it needs looking into because we all joked he would have been safer just driving home pissed.

When I had finished shouting up to John and Paul on the roof, Melanie looked worried.

'What's wrong?' she asked.

'Nothing,' I said. 'Why?'

'If nothing is wrong, what were you arguing about?'

'We weren't. That's how we speak.'

The John that Melanie knew was the Manchester student who had friends from all over the country. Although she had obviously met my family, she had never really spent time in the world I was from because I had left it before I met her.

At the time it was a funny comment, but it also showed that perhaps we did not know each other as well as we would have hoped. The reality was that losing the baby had left a hole between us, and my asking her to marry me had been an attempt to fill that hole, when perhaps what we had needed to do was just spend time together and get to know each other properly, rather than rush into a life-long commitment.

The first holiday we ever had together, apart from the trysts of the previous year, was our honeymoon. One tip I would give to anyone in a relationship is to go on holiday before you commit. Priorities change when you go on holiday; it's surprising how not getting the right sun lounger can ruin your whole day, and from experience deciding to get drunk at lunchtime while your partner sunbathes doesn't seem to help matters either.

Our courtship had been on-off, and I guess Melanie, too, would admit there was always a sense of shadow boxing. It was a question of 'Who would concede?' or, in the vocabulary of a relationship, 'Who would compromise?' Now we were to be married, and things were no longer negotiable.

•   •   •

I had returned home in September 1992; in May 1993 we were married in St Cuthbert's Catholic Church in Manchester, and in August 1994 our first son, Joseph Michael Cornall Bishop, was born.

Joe was initially going to be called everything except Joseph. We had a list of names we had argued over:

Melanie: 'Jude.'

Me: 'Girl's name.'

Melanie: 'Gabriel.'

Me: 'Hairdresser's name.'

Melanie: 'Josh.'

Me: 'We don't have a pony.'

Melanie: 'Thomas.'

Me: 'Not naming my son after a train.'

Me: 'Zack.'

Melanie: 'With your accent? Don't be stupid!'

It is such a responsibility to give another human being something that will last for the rest of their lives, but somehow Joseph came completely out of the blue and was no doubt influenced by the fact that, the year before, I met a man named Joe who had impressed me so much.

When he was born, after a long and exhausting labour (yes, I was exhausted – it's hard work feeling useless for eight hours), I was overcome with emotion as Melanie re-gathered her composure in the manner that women instantly do after childbirth. In a way, that is Nature's defining difference between the sexes: women become mothers instantly and start dealing with the new life in their arms, while men take photographs and thank everybody within a five-mile radius. When handed the new version of themselves, if they are anything like me, they become a blubbering wreck as more emotion than any man can take flows through their body and finds its escape in tears, snot and slobber so that they look like that last person on earth who should be holding a baby.

When asked what we were going to call him, I just looked at Melanie. With tears and snot running down my face, I was in no position to speak, so out of the blue she named him Joseph Michael. As this birth process has been repeated twice since, Melanie has named each one of our three sons, always with a name that was either not in the running or was the least favourite going into the delivery room – and a good job she has done of it, too. I think Joe, Luke and Daniel suit being called Joe, Luke and Daniel, although had we gone for Zack, Jude and Gabe we may have had a boy band in the making.

The 'Cornall' in Joe's name is Melanie's surname, and all the boys have it as part of their name. Her dad, Mike, had been an only child, and Melanie was not only a single child, but also a girl. It seemed an insult to her grandfather's legacy that the Cornall name, which is unusual anyway, would be further diluted by our marriage, so Melanie kept her name when we married and, naturally, it passed on to our children.

The irony is that her dad subsequently got married to his third wife, Denise, and had two other kids, Hannah and Charlie. So the gesture was unnecessary, and we are left with the legacy of the kids having a double-barrelled name that we keep forgetting when booking plane tickets. Thus we end up in long arguments at airports as to why the names on the tickets don't match the passports. Bloody Japanese.

At least we didn't name him after where he was conceived. Parents who do that must surely plan their travel accordingly. Joe would have been called Gran Canaria – difficult to carry off in any accent.

In many ways it was appropriate that Joe was conceived in Gran Canaria, because Mel and I had flown there to see her dad Mike depart on a transatlantic voyage aboard his sailing yacht. On board was a crew comprising two of my mates, John and Paul, who had never sailed; an experienced sailor called Paul; and Jim, Melanie's stepdad. Jim was an excellent sailor and a good friend of Mike's, although we liked to joke it was an arrangement that Eileen, Melanie's mum, could have sold to a TV station: *How Two Men I Married Went Sailing Together*!

I say it was appropriate, because there would have been a time when I would have sought the adventure myself, instead of staying at home. But I was not long returned from my cycle ride and with the responsibility of a job, a mortgage and a wife I bid them farewell. Nine months later those responsibilities grew even more when Joe was born.

Having already lost a baby, Joe's arrival mattered more, if that was at all possible. When your first child is born, it changes your life. I knew there was now someone much more important than me and that everything I did from that day forward would be measured against the barometer of my being a good father or not. It changes your perspective on everything, and though your friends send cards and come to the christening they don't really know what is going on in your world unless it has happened to them, too.

I was 26 and married with a son. My dad was 24 when he had his fourth child, and many of his friends were in the same position; it seems to have been the norm for that generation. Some of Melanie's friends had by this point started a family, but most of my mates had not even reached the stage of co-habitation with a girl, unless she happened to be in the same shared house.

It was even more apparent that my mates and I were at different junctions in our lives when Sergei came to stay. Joe was less than six months old, and teething. Every parent knows that a teething baby is like having a pneumatic drill in the next-door room, and the only way you can stop the shrill ringing in your head of a baby in pain is to spend nights walking around the room rocking said baby and hoping the dummy eases the agony. The reality is that as a couple you try to share the load, which means one of you stays in bed and attempts to sleep whilst the other deals with the baby. The result is neither of you sleeps.

At the time, we had a very protective German shepherd called Sheba who felt it was her duty to be in the room with Joe, just in case some sheep needed herding or an intruder needed biting. Although her intentions were admirable, a German shepherd is a big dog. In fact, with all the baby paraphernalia taking up so much space, adding a German shepherd was like adding a man in a dog suit, but a man who couldn't hold anything and who thought lying on top of the changing mat was helpful.

It was into this environment that my erstwhile student friend Sergei came to stay the night. He was back in Manchester from London to attend a job interview. We had a spare room, and as it presented a potentially tempting opportunity to go to the pub with an old mate, I readily agreed to him staying. Actually, I will rephrase that to reflect the reality of the situation of a freshly married man with a baby. I had a discussion with/asked permission from Melanie who, to be fair, thought it would do me good to get out too, as long as Sergei knew not to wake the baby when we came home.

Kissing my family and stroking the dog, I left the house with Sergei for the same pub we had attended every Sunday as students. It felt like getting a surprise day off school, and I admit to being rather giddy with the simple excitement of it.

The night was good fun, and I enjoyed catching up. But, by 10.30 p.m., I had developed the 'new dads' face, the face that says to the rest of the world you have not had a full night's sleep for months and if you carry on being out of your bed you will burst into tears, fall asleep in the lap of the nearest person or will remain in a semi-catatonic state till less troubled friends escort you out of the building. It's the face that says, 'I used to belong here but now there are records in the charts I have never heard of, my clothes feel like they belong to my dad and I want to tell every single person in the room to leave the pub and get to any hedonistic gathering before it's too late.' It's basically the face that says, 'Look at me! Do you want to be me? Run! It's too late for me – save yourself!'

I said to Sergei it was time to go home because I knew that if we went now I could do the last feed and give Melanie a break.

He looked at me as if I had gone mad. With eyes that sparkled with frequent sleep and lacked any hint of fatigue, he surveyed all that was in front of him and declared that the night was still young and that he fancied a club.

Saying that to a man in my position was like saying to a marathon runner he had gone the wrong way and would have to do it all again. There was not a chance I was going to a club, so I gave Sergei an ultimatum: come with me and stay in the spare room, or go clubbing and do not return till the following morning.

He said it was no problem and he would see me the next day. What I should have realised is that ultimatums do not exist in the world of twenty-something single men without real responsibilities. In their world, what do they have to lose by not sticking to an ultimatum? In the world of the married man, you lose your dinner, conversation, access to the bathroom, clean clothes, sex and, in extreme cases, the television controls. Ultimatums matter to us: they are a bond, and accepted as such.

The doorbell rang at three in the morning and the dog started barking, which woke up Melanie and the baby, who had both been asleep for less than thirty minutes from the last bout of teething (please consider what it must be like to be a genetic product of me and have gums that hold teeth like mine – teething is hard for any baby, but for ones whose teeth are emerging and expecting to be in a horse's head, it must be even harder). I knew that the ultimatum had not worked.

I opened the door to find Sergei swaying on the doorstep, while eating a kebab.

'What are you doing?'

'Eating a kebab – I got you one.' He pulled something flaccid from his pocket that was wrapped in paper. 'It's vegetarian, which means it's just lettuce and shit. I didn't get Melanie one. I thought she would be asleep and all that.'

'She was! Dickhead!'

'I was right not to buy her one, then.'

There are some people with whom reason will work – a drunk friend holding two kebabs in the early hours of the morning is not one of them. Melanie was now walking zombie-like to Joe's room to deal with his crying, whilst the dog proceeded to growl at Sergei in between being fed bits of kebab. I decided the best course of action was to throw him into the spare room and for the rest of us to try and salvage whatever sleep we could.

In the morning, after barely any sleep, Melanie decided to take the still-awake-and-still-crying-with-teeth-pain Joe out in his pram – she felt it best to be out of the house and away from any kitchen knives when Sergei woke up.

After she left, I went into the spare room.

'Get up and be gone by the time I get back from walking the dog.'

'What have I done wrong?'

'We've had no sleep because of you.'

'You should have come with me. It was a great club.'

'GET OUT!'

'Is that an ultimatum?'

'YES.'

'Fair enough.'

I walked the dog and returned 45 minutes later. Melanie was still out, so I went to the spare room. The bed was unmade and there was still a half-eaten kebab on the bedside table, but at least he was gone. I softened slightly, knowing it was not Sergei's fault or that of any of my mates. Nobody knows what pressures you are under as new parents, and I knew once Melanie and I got some rest – which felt like it would not happen for a few years – we would see the funny side. At least he had done as I asked and left so we could get on with our day. I walked into the bathroom.

Sergei was sitting in the bath, which was filled to the brim with bubbles, having a cigarette and drinking a cup of tea. To some people, the word 'ultimatum' is just a good score in Scrabble.

CHAPTER 21

BABIES, A SURPRISE I DIDN'T WANT AND THE SNIP

Our second son, Luke, followed 18 months later, and his birth was just what you would wish for. Joe was staying with my parents the night Melanie's waters broke in bed, at about two in the morning. We had the bag ready, and of course I knew the route to the hospital, so I guided her downstairs and into the car and prepared myself.

For the first and only time in my life, I could drive like a madman and nobody could complain. I had seen it done so often in the movies, so I was ready for the moment the police would stop me after I had sped through a set of traffic lights. I would storm out of the car and shout, 'My wife's having a baby.' Immediately they would escort us to the hospital with lights flashing and sirens blaring.

I drove to the hospital as fast as I could and went through every red light I saw; I even slowed down at a few so they changed to red when I went through. Not one single police car. I even contemplated doing a few laps of the route till at least one police car appeared, but Melanie's insistence that this would result in the baby being born in the passenger seat (another potentially terrible name, 'Passenger-Seat') meant we went straight to the hospital and I never got to cash in that literal 'get out of jail free' card.

It was lucky we did go straight there as, within less than two hours of leaving the house, Luke made his arrival into the world as if he was on a water slide. It was a smooth, beautiful birth, which contrasted again, 20 months later, with Daniel's.

Daniel's birth was not entirely straightforward, and he arrived weighing a massive 10lb 5oz, which made me ask if he had been born with shoes on. However, it was immediately clear that something was wrong. Instead of Daniel being handed to us, he was taken away for the doctors to examine him. That first night he stayed with Melanie, but when I arrived the following morning we were told he had a hole in his heart. They said it might heal by itself, it might stay the same forever and, if so, there was no telling how it would affect him, or it could get worse, which would result in long-term health problems.

To be holding a new-born child who looked perfect in every way and be told he had a potentially life-limiting condition was crushing. The only thing worse than not achieving full potential is to have that potential removed at the beginning. I sat holding him with no vision of what the future held for him.

As it happened, Daniel's hole closed, but it felt like someone had reminded us that having children is a lottery: after reaching the magical 12-week threshold we take it for granted that they will be born healthy. When you experience that moment of doubt, it really hits you how lucky you are, and perhaps how you should not push your luck too much.

Dan was the last child we had. As a friend said to Melanie when she arrived home with our third son, 'There is something about being the mother of boys that makes you lucky.' I am not sure that Melanie would always agree, but for my part I feel blessed to have the boys we have. They are all teenagers now, which means tensions are sometimes high in the house because, as I have learnt, arguing with a teenager is like arguing with a foreign policeman: there is a lot of shouting, you don't understand each other and there is a chance someone will get shot. Yet I know that, despite everything, they will be good men. That is all you can ever ask of a son: to be a good man.

After Daniel's health scare, we decided that three was enough. People kept commenting that we must be disappointed because we'd had another boy and would surely be trying for a girl, as if having children is like collecting football cards and you have to keep going till you get the full set. For us it was never like that, and I liked the idea of having a house full of sons. That was, of course, until I had a house full of sons.

Anyone who has boys will know that the one thing you have to get used to is the noise. Boys leak noise. It just comes out of them constantly, in the form of cries, shouts and body wind. When we had three under the age of four, our home reverberated with these noises and with the sounds of toys made in a Far Eastern country where noise pollution is clearly not a consideration in the production of items of amusement.

Even if a boy attempts to be quiet by saying nothing, the effect is ruined by his constant fidgeting, which results in whatever he is sitting on making a racket. The truth is, you have no idea how noisy your boys are until you go to a house where they have girls. Walking into these homes is like walking into a yoga class: everyone seems calm, there is no shouting, no fighting, and occasionally somebody will do a handstand in front of you without putting their foot through a window or the telly.

Within six weeks of Daniel being born, I made the decisive step towards removing the chance of us ever having a daughter by getting a vasectomy. This was not a decision I took lightly. I had discussed it with Melanie, and for us as a family it seemed the most efficient way to proceed. I loved my sons and never felt that we would be missing anything by not having a daughter and, after three children in quick succession, neither of us felt the need to have any more. Anyone who has ever been through the process of a vasectomy will know that it is not something that you can enter into without thought. Indeed, you are counselled to ensure you know exactly what you are doing.

The operation was performed quickly, because when I registered at the local family-planning clinic three weeks after Daniel was born I was greeted by Pat, the mother of Melanie's best friend, Jane.

She informed me that there was a waiting list, but that she would move me up it so that I could be operated on by a surgeon who was a senior registrar, and who was leaving soon to take up a consultant's post in New Zealand. She said he was very good at his job, and she would feel happier if he did the procedure.

As it was an operation involving the most precious part of my anatomy, I was not about to quibble. I was not used to jumping queues and, had I been paranoid, I could have come to the conclusion that being moved through the system more quickly because of my wife's connections was perhaps a sign of Melanie's desire to get the job done, rather than that of the surgeon's imminent departure.

As the family-planning clinic was only 15 minutes' walk from our home, I decided to walk there on the day of the snip. I had been told it was a 10-minute operation under local anaesthetic, so I thought it would be easier than having the hassle of finding somewhere to park.

The first advice I would give anyone who is considering having the snip is, don't walk to get it done. Rather than 15 minutes, the return journey became nearly an hour and a half, during which an invisible horse kicked me in the testicles every second step.

The operation itself was perhaps the most bizarre 10 minutes of my life. After the local anaesthetic had begun to take effect, the surgeon ushered me in from the waiting room and onto the operating table. He was a dashing man in his early thirties. A neat haircut was parted to one side, but he had a five o'clock shadow which suggested he had spent a long day saving lives and being fascinating to the nurses. The fact that he had spent all day messing with men's bollocks somewhat diluted the Mills and Boon persona he exuded.

I was fully awake as he stood on one side of the bed and his colleague stood on the opposite side. The surgeon did an initial pre-operation examination, like a golfer checking the lie of the land before deciding which club to use so he doesn't end up in the rough – which, if it happens during a vasectomy, has serious implications that cannot be resolved by simply dropping another ball.

I couldn't help it. I caught myself thinking: 'I am lying here with two people I don't know looking at my manhood, which has just been injected with a local anaesthetic and cannot be looking its best, and I have never felt more self-conscious in all my life.'

'How are you feeling?' the surgeon intoned.

'I'm fine, thanks . . . How are you?'

I have no idea why I asked the man holding the scalpel that was about to cut into my scrotum how he was doing, but at the time it seemed a valid question. Had he said, 'I've a terrible hangover and I can't stop my hand shaking,' I would at least have had time to halt proceedings.

We then engaged in a conversation revolving around his impending move to New Zealand and how he and the family were looking forward to it. All the while, I could feel the odd numb tug and pull as his fingers isolated the vas deferens tube, which he then cut and clamped with titanium clips. He was thus nullifying my right testicle's ability to sire children, whilst at the same time, in my mind, turning my testicles into something special.

I now had one of the strongest metals known to man in my balls so, as I lay there, I imagined what would happen if it all went wrong and by a freak accident I acquired a super-power through the new metal in my body. I could spend the rest of my life fighting crimes and being known as Titanium Bollock Man.

'There you go. The right side is done. Now, as I am going away, my colleague, Dr Kumar, who is in training, is going to do the other side.'

I felt this was not the right time to undermine Dr Kumar's confidence by suggesting I would prefer someone who was not 'in training' – after all, I only had one set of testicles and would have preferred they were handled by someone who knew what they were doing. I once had a friend who allowed a trainee hairdresser to practise on him for free. Without going into too much detail, his hair eventually grew back and within 12 months it was almost acceptable. Although I am not medically trained, I don't suppose you could do the same to correct a mistake in the testicle region.

The conversation stopped as Dr Kumar concentrated on the job in hand, and I concentrated on not moving, as the last thing I wanted to do was to make it more difficult for him.

I had already been on the table for around seven minutes. Although I suspected that Dr Kumar would be a bit slower, I was still guessing that I would be out of there within ten minutes when Dr Kumar interrupted his pulling and tugging – which even with a local anaesthetic was much more forceful on the left testicle than it had been on the right – by exclaiming, 'Oops, I've dropped it!'

I quickly explained to Dr Kumar that despite my lack of formal training, I would have suggested it might be prudent when you have your hands inside someone's scrotum that 'Oops, I've dropped it' is perhaps not the best choice of words. He thanked me for my advice and then continued about his work, and I just lay there hoping the anaesthetic did not wear off.

•   •   •

Having 'the snip' was just part of a wider picture of me doing what I thought was right for my family. I was the father of three young children and was doing what I was expected to do: I got my head down, and I worked my socks off to provide for them. I became obsessed with trying to ensure my kids did not have a childhood defined by financial restrictions, as mine had been.

In my job as a sales rep in the pharmaceutical industry, I progressed into the specialist area of immunology and transplant therapy, and also started studying for my Masters degree in Business Administration. This meant working long hours, and this was not helped that it was a job that was hard to talk about when I arrived home.

'How was your day at work, honey?'

'Great. I went through this double-blind randomised trial in liver transplant recipients with the transplant unit in Leeds, illustrating that cold ischaemic time could have a direct impact on immune-suppression dosing, and then showed the sales team this graph.'

Lots of jobs are like that. They exist in their own world and only have relevance to people within that world. I remember that when I was promoted to the position of running sales and marketing within the UK I told Melanie we should go out to celebrate. Joe, who was around five at the time, sensed the excitement and asked what my job was.

'I take care of the sales and marketing side of things for the UK, which will mean I have to attend international strategic meetings in Europe and the US.'

After a few moments of thought, in which he digested this, he asked, 'Is that like driving a digger?'

The dad of his best friend from nursery worked on building sites and, one day, both boys had gone to visit and sat on the digger, which in Joe's world was the most exciting thing ever. I could hardly compete with that by showing them how to put a good Powerpoint presentation together.

'No, son, it's not that good.'

The job began to seem incompatible with my home life. By its very nature it did not lend itself to conversation, and the increasing travel demands meant that Melanie and I started sharing less space together. Melanie had her hands full, and we gradually began operating in the same family but in different worlds. I was the provider and did all that was deemed necessary to achieve that, while Melanie was in a constant cycle of child care: for six years there was always a child in the house in nappies. We made little time for each other and, as most of our friends were not at the same juncture in their lives, it was easy to feel isolated.

I recall that on my thirtieth birthday I was lured home from an Italian meal Melanie had arranged with the promise that as the kids were away we could have an early night of passionate sex.

I didn't need asking twice. So, with the tiramisu barely off my spoon, I hailed a taxi, already imagining the joy of making love in rare abandonment without one of us saying, 'Shhh, you're going to wake the kids.' I also reasoned that there was a good chance I would even catch the second half of *Match of the Day* as well. Who could want more?

I turned the key in our front door with great excitement, only to be greeted by the lights being turned on and all of my family and friends standing there shouting, 'SURPRISE!'

Yes, it bloody was! I reasoned that the night of passion I had envisioned was not going to happen, and that it would be regarded as rude in most social circles to turn the TV on to watch the footie in the middle of your own surprise thirtieth birthday party.

I tried to hide my disappointment from Melanie and all the smiling faces looking at me with glasses in their hands but, with three young children, the thought of football and sex had felt like a much rarer commodity than a birthday party you have once every thirty years.

I hardly saw many of the friends who were at the party

any more. Few were married and even fewer had children, so we were increasingly losing the common ground that had bound us together through the college years and beyond. I saw them with their girlfriends enjoying weekends away, nights out when they wanted and Sunday mornings in bed reading the papers, instead of changing nappies or taking turns to try and catch up on sleep. It was hard not to feel jealous.

At the party, one of my mates pulled me to one side after we had been jumping around the living room to 'A Town Called Malice'. Stepping away from his girlfriend he said, 'Look at you, mate – you have everything. A beautiful wife, a beautiful house, lovely kids, a decent job . . . What have I got? A 23-year-old in boots and a short skirt who has just told me she's never heard of The Jam.'

In that moment my resentment disappeared. He was absolutely right, of course. I had a beautiful family that I adored. Little did he know it, but he had summed up the dilemma of most men, particularly those caught within the fog of marriage: you can see what you haven't got, not what you have got.

CHAPTER 22

BAD HAIR DAY, REMOVAL VANS AND BROKEN HEARTS

Our marriage didn't end in a single dramatic moment: there was not a huge fight with one of us storming out, or the revelation of someone else; it just faded until removal vans arrived and we went our separate ways.

When a marriage ends this way, it's like a tree in autumn. There is a moment when you almost believe the leaves will not fall. Yes, they have changed colour and the tree no longer looks as healthy as it did, but it doesn't look damaged – it just looks changed, and you can believe that this is how it will continue, changed but together. Then, one day, when you're not looking, the leaves fall, and when you look at the tree again it's bare, its imperfections no longer concealed by the foliage. We were among many marriages that withered and died, a gradual, painful death that the rest of the world never really noticed.

In the vortex of a marriage breakdown, the things that you do as a matter of course – doing the weekly shop, putting the bins out, walking the dog, dealing with the kids, sitting in the same room to watch the telly – all become areas of tension, and are reminders that the person you wanted to share your life with no longer wants to be with you, and you don't want to be with them. All the natural movements of family life feel like walking with drawing pins in your shoes. You can do it, but it doesn't stop hurting.

I wanted to try to work things out; I wanted to try to fix it, because that is what I thought I should be able to do, to fix it. Work harder and fix it, isn't that what a man ought to be capable of? But you can't be married to yourself, so if the marriage is dead for one person, it is effectively dead for you both.

Melanie had grown so cold towards me, to the extent that, one night, I sat in the bath and decided to shave off all my hair to see if she would notice. I am sure some would say it was a desperate cry for help; others that I was being a bloody idiot. Looking back now, I am not sure what camp I fell into, but I would not recommend it as a way of working things out in your relationship. For a start, you look terrible. Instead of the smooth, skin-covered scalp I was expecting, I climbed out of the bath and looked in the mirror to see myself wearing what appeared to be the worst swimming cap in the world. I'd always had my hair short, which I now know never really suited me, but when it was down to the skin I looked terrible: somewhere between a right-wing thug and someone who people run marathons for.

The following day I had to fly from Manchester to the office in London. When I boarded the plane I could see people looking at me with expressions that suggested they assumed this was part of the trip of a lifetime to Disneyland whilst there was still time. When the air hostess asked if I was OK as I lifted my bag into the overhead locker, I just said, as a joke, 'Yes, thanks, every day's a bonus,' and I swear she almost burst into tears. When I realised she thought I meant it for real, I said, 'It's OK, I'm not dying. I just shaved my hair off in the bath to wind my wife up, but she never really noticed.' Which probably made me look even sadder than someone on treatment. When the same members of staff saw me on the shuttle flight back that evening, they seemed slightly less supportive.

Although I never wanted us to split up, it had reached a point of no return, so we put the house up for sale and proceeded to look for separate places to live. It was such a civilised split that we both went to look at each other's new places, and engaged in conversations about décor and kitchens for homes that we would both visit to collect our children from the person we had once loved, but would never now live with.

I was determined not to be a distant father: seeing the kids on a Sunday afternoon and sitting in McDonalds, trying to replace a stable family unit with a Happy Meal. The boys were aged one, three and five, and I couldn't imagine not seeing them every morning and every evening. The reality was, however, that I didn't see them every morning or every evening anyway, because I was busy working to make our life better; and, by doing so, I had played a part in making it worse. I had become boring, remote and preoccupied, and had failed to see the signs that leaving Melanie at home facing endless days of child-centric activities was driving her mad. I was just working hard believing that was my role. I thought if I did that, wouldn't everything else just fall into place?

Due to my work commitments, I couldn't say what days I could have the boys in the week, so I said that I would have them every weekend. That meant collecting them from school and nursery on Friday afternoon and taking them back on Monday morning.

I bought a nice, small, three-bed semi 15 minutes from Melanie's house. I was in one room, the boys' room had bunk beds and a cot, and the third room had just enough space for me to have a desk.

Whoever thought of the phrase 'box room' got it right in my new home, as the third bedroom made you feel you were inside a shoe box. I think there should be a rule that if you open the door of a room and the width of the door is longer that the rest of the room, it should not be called a 'box room' but a 'box with a door'.

When we sold our marital home, Melanie's house purchase was delayed for the first few weeks, so the boys came to live with me full time. It was only then that I realised I didn't have a clue what I was doing: I burnt nearly everything I cooked, clothes came out of the washing machine the wrong size, or pink – regardless of what colour they went in. When a child needed attention, I was on the phone to work or dealing with another child. That meant they went unattended or, more usually, just increased their volume so that they could not be ignored any more.

It wasn't that I was incapable; it was just that, within the preceding years, we had fallen into a very traditional marriage. Melanie had given up work to look after the kids, and I had become the company-car-driving bread-winner. I still retained the ability to cook vegetarian stir fry in a wok, which had been one of my staple diets as a student, but it's surprisingly unappetising for boys aged one, three and five to be faced with a plate of crisp vegetables soaked in soya sauce.

For Joe's fifth birthday, he asked me for a Manchester United kit, which was understandable. He was living in Manchester and, as a five year old, had no concept that such a decision changes the whole course of your life – particularly if your dad is a Liverpool supporter and will never speak to you again. As a compromise, I bought him an AC Milan kit which was blue with black stripes, and which allowed me time to get him to Anfield before he made a final decision.

I remember washing the kit for the first time and reading on the label that dark colours had to be washed separately, which completely threw me: if something had black stripes in it, how could you wash the stripes separately? What was worse was that I was so incapable, I had to phone my mum for advice. It is no surprise that for the first six months or so after we separated I never even went on a date. A man in his thirties working in middle management, with three kids and a failed marriage, who has to phone his mum about how to wash a football kit, is not a great catch.

Life had not turned out the way I would have liked, but I just had to get on with it.

Once we got into the weekend routines I started to enjoy my time with the boys. I began to call them my three amigos, which is why I gave the production company I set up years later the same name. For months I would work in the week and if the opportunity presented itself to stay at a hotel I would take it – anything to avoid returning home to an empty house. But on Fridays I would always make sure I was there to pick up 'the amigos' and take them home for our time together.

I got to know them and they began to know me. I am not pretending it was all easy, but we had a garden and lived close to a park, and I ensured I had no distractions from the moment I collected them to when I took them back. Girlfriends was not something I was interested in, and though after a few months I did see one or two really nice girls, nobody ever met the boys or saw me of a weekend – those days were sacrosanct. It was our time and, after long Saturdays playing, I would love nothing better than to sit on the couch with the boys in pyjamas, gradually falling asleep on me whilst watching the telly.

I would hate the arrival of Monday, knowing that I would not see them again during the week. I won't be the only father who has sat in his car outside the house where his kids are being put to bed by his ex-wife, not knowing why he is there but knowing he just wants to be close, even if the rules of divorce mean he can't simply knock on the door to kiss them goodnight because it's not his time of the week. Melanie and I were pursuing the divorce through solicitors, and had little reason to see each other. Within a short space of time we had become the 'ex' to each other, even if the legal matters were not finalised.

One Saturday morning Melanie came around to the house to drop off some of the boys' things that I needed. It was a very rare thing for all of us to be in the same room together – the boys were watching Saturday morning TV as I struggled to get them ready to go out.

Our relations had been cordial and, by this stage, we had been living apart for nearly six months, and so in many ways the rawness of the separation had just been replaced by a dull sadness.

'Do you want a cup of tea?' I asked her.

'No, thanks. Are you boys going out?' The boys cheered in the excited way children do when there is no reason in life not to be excited.

'Yes. I know it's a bit wet underfoot, but I thought we would go to the park.'

'Sounds nice.' There was a moment, a pause when she looked at the boys in various stages of readiness, and I could see the regret in her eyes.

'Why don't you come?'

'Yes, Mum, why don't you come to the park?'

'It would be nice . . . for all of us.'

Melanie looked at me, and her eyes had changed. Sometimes, when things hurt too much you have to protect yourself first: if you let your guard down, there is every chance you will get hurt more. We both knew this, and I had let my guard down by inviting her out as if we were still a family. It was clear she was not ready to lower her protection.

'I can't . . . I have stuff to do. You boys have a good time.'

When she left, I tried to carry on with the normal day I had planned with the boys, but suddenly emotion over-whelmed me. It was well and truly over. One day she would meet someone, and I would have to accept another man having a role to play in the boys' lives. That realisation cut me in half. I just slumped on the stairs and couldn't stop the tears from falling as I tried to get Daniel into his wellington boots to go out to the park.

No man wants to cry in front of his sons, but it's even worse when you don't know you're doing it. Daniel was nearly two, so his experience of people crying was vast. He was in nursery full time, where crying was something that all his peers engaged in with varying degrees of frequency during the day, and he had developed a wonderful skill of being able to help. He just put his hands on my wet cheeks and said, 'I'm your friend.'

He must have been surprised to find that what worked in the nursery with two year olds only served to turn his 34-year-old dad into a blubbering, heartbroken wreck. But at least he tried.

•   •   •

Dropping the boys off on Mondays became the hardest thing in the world. At the time, I was the sales manager for Fujisawa, a company specialising in immunosuppression with a product that helped prevent people from rejecting their organs after transplantation.

I had a small sales team and I organised my week so that I would always have a telephone conference on a Monday morning after I dropped the kids off at school and nursery. The teleconference was usually over by 10.30 a.m., which meant I then had the rest of Monday to do what is euphemistically called a 'working from home day', but what should really be called a 'doing very little but being near a phone' day.

It was one of these days that changed my life. Had I gone into the office on Mondays and been surrounded by people, or gone to the gym to let off some steam, I would have perhaps never been in the position to write this book, as I would never have fallen into the depression that led to me sitting at home on a Monday drinking a bottle of wine while watching daytime TV.

If you were depressed, the daytime TV of the late 1990s was not going to help, particularly *Richard and Judy*, who seemed to be a constant reminder of what the world looked like if you were not getting divorced and your life was not in bits. They even read the same books, for God's sake!

The rest of the week I functioned normally, but Mondays were a wipe-out. One week, when I was particularly depressed after dropping the boys off, I opened the first bottle of wine during the telephone conference. It was 10 a.m., and I was already looking forward to the numbness inside that the alcohol would induce as I swallowed it. I was drowning out the pain of the only person I really loved not wanting me any more, and washing away the agony of knowing that my sons would be sleeping in a bed 15 minutes' walk away and I would not be able to see them.

One of the sales team was talking about a clinical study and, as I held the phone to my ear, I looked at the open bottle of wine. The bottle just seemed to stand there, challenging me: 'Take a drink. Go on, if you're man enough, pick me up and take a drink.'

The voices on the other end of the call seemed to fade away. In that moment, the only things that existed in the world were me and that bottle. With startling clarity, I realised I had a choice: to pour a glass of wine, numb the pain and descend on a slippery, downward spiral, or rise to the challenge and try to be a better man.

Whilst the teleconference was still going on, I picked the bottle up, walked to the sink and poured the wine away. I made an arrangement to meet one of the sales team locally, and within 20 minutes I was showered, shaved, in a suit and out of the house.

Little did I know that within 24 hours the way I saw the world would be changed for ever.

CHAPTER 23

FROG AND BUCKET

In pouring the wine down the sink, I'd made a positive step forward and didn't want to lose the momentum by staying in on that Monday night. My usual routine had been to get drunk by the early evening and go to bed early. This Monday was to be a new start.

The problem with making the resolution to go out on a Monday night is that the rest of the world has normally made the decision to stay in. I called various friends, but there were no takers to join me: people were either committed to doing something, were recovering from the weekend or were simply not in the mood. Mel and I had been separated for over six months now, and the novelty of listening to me lament my misfortune over a drink was now well and truly over for most of my mates. Men are not the best at being supportive because we don't really know what to say apart from, 'Hard lines, mate . . . fancy a game of darts?' My mate, John, would ring me on a regular basis with nothing to say, just to see how I was, which I always appreciated, but he lived in London, and on this night I needed to be out of the house. Talking on the phone would not help.

I tried to think of places that I could go on my own and not feel conspicuous. I checked the paper for the local cinema as I am very happy to go to the cinema alone, and still do it today, but there was nothing on I wanted to watch. I couldn't see any concerts advertised. The only thing directed at men alone seemed to be lap-dancing bars, and I didn't think that would help my state of mind. I couldn't imagine sitting there by myself whilst some nubile girl displayed her wares, and all I would have had to offer would have been: 'Nice tits, luv, but I'm only here because I am getting divorced as my wife doesn't love me any more, and I don't want to be sitting at home alone and drunk . . . Nice fanny, too.'

Basically I wasn't great company, and I knew it, so I needed to go somewhere where I could sit and be entertained. I then saw the Frog and Bucket comedy club listed. I had been there once before for a friend's birthday and remembered it was a good night. I had also been to the Comedy Store in London years earlier, and recalled that also as having been a fun night out. That had been my sum total of comedy club experiences: two packed venues, both having excellent line-ups. It made sense to replicate the experience and have someone make me laugh.

I drove to the Frog and Bucket. What unfolded that night I have recounted in my stand-up and interviews since and, although I don't really want to repeat myself here, it was such a momentous night that I feel I must retell it, as it is fair to say no single happening has shaped the person I am today so much.

I hesitated when I reached the door of the place. There was no queue, unlike the only other occasion I had been there, and it looked so quiet I thought it was shut. I stood outside for a while wondering if this was really going to be the laughter-filled night I was hoping for, or if I should go and find that lap-dancer who really wanted to listen.

The bouncer on the door noticed me standing outside. 'If you're coming in, you'd better hurry up. The show's starting soon.'

'I'm just waiting for my mate . . . Tony. He's always late. It was his idea as well, Tony. He loves his comedy.'

'Well, Tony's going to miss the start of the show, and so are you, if you don't come in now.'

'OK, I'll come in. Typical of Tony – what's he like?'

'Right, it's £4 to come in – unless you're having a go.'

'What?'

'Didn't Tony tell you it was open mic night?'

'Who?'

'Your mate, Tony. Didn't he say it was open mic night?'

'What's that?'

'People get up and have a go. If you want to get up, then it's free to get in. If you just want to watch, it's £4.'

In my head I made the quick calculation that the two comedy clubs I had been in had held at least 300 people. If 10 per cent had put their name down, that would be 30 people, and as I was obviously one of the last to arrive it would mean I would be one of the last names on the list. This meant I could get in for free now and, if the show was rubbish, I would have time to leave before my name was called. When you're getting divorced, £4 in your pocket to buy a drink mattered. So I put my name down and walked in.

That spur-of-the-moment decision turned out to be a life-changer.

Once inside, I thought I must have walked through the wrong door. The usual hustle and bustle of the 300-seater venue was, on this occasion, more akin to a doctor's waiting room. Just six people sat on the faded velvet chairs, their voices echoing off the black-painted walls. The tightly packed tables were eerily empty and the stains on the carpet were all too visible without the usual crowds of people to hide them.

Before I had time to consider leaving, a voice announced through the speakers: 'Ladies and gentlemen, please welcome your compère for this evening, Mick Ferry.'

A man walked onto the stage, took the microphone and started talking. I couldn't believe he was actually doing the show without the rest of the audience arriving – surely a coach party was due soon? Mick is now a friend, and a fine comedian: despite everything that suggested the gig should not go ahead, he managed to galvanise us audience of seven into a united body by making us laugh. No mean feat, considering that when I walked in the last thing I thought this collection of people would ever do was laugh.

Mick then announced that five of the audience had agreed to take part in the open mic and would be getting on stage imminently. I couldn't believe that, out of an audience of seven, five people had come to participate. It begged two questions: what were the other two people doing here, and why would five adults present themselves on a Monday night in the hope of making strangers laugh? I had an excuse: I was getting divorced and I was trying to avoid my weekly oblivion drinking. I was just a little lonely and I had nothing better in my life. I concluded the rest of them, unlike me, must have just been sad bastards.

Mick introduced the first act who, instead of getting up to do his set, insisted on going backstage before making his appearance, which forced Mick to introduce him again. He probably shouldn't have made such a meal of his entrance as his act when downhill from there. It was so painful to watch, in fact, that I've tried to block it from my memory, but I remember he kept breaking into chicken impressions. Mick had made it seem so easy to make people laugh that seeing a grown man – who looked at least as old as I was, may also have been in middle management and have had at least one significant failed relationship behind him – resorting to chicken impressions that failed to raise a titter from the audience was excruciating.

The audience by now had begun to resemble a self-help group, as it was becoming clear from the performance of 'Chicken Man' that we were all there because something was wrong in our lives. Some people laughed enthusiastically to encourage him, although this was much more than the performance warranted in my opinion (but then I have never been a great fan of chicken-based humour – not since I was a child, trying to make nurses laugh.) After a finale that involved a simulation of laying an egg whilst driving a van, Chicken Man was supportively applauded off the stage. He seemed quite pleased with himself as he came to sit back amongst the group. Some of the people seemed to know him, and one actually said, 'That was so much better than last week.'

Before I could adjust to the knowledge that Chicken Man had done this before and what I had just witnessed was in fact an improved performance, I heard Mick say, 'John Bishop.'

I hadn't registered what was said before my name was called because I was too busy contemplating how I could leave without causing too much upset to the next act. After all, with only seven of us, it would be difficult to sneak out unnoticed.

After assuming that I would be the last one on the stage, for whatever reason my name was read out second. So, when I heard Mick say, 'Is John Bishop here?' I had a decision to make: either pretend I was not me and allow another name to be called out, or walk on the stage.

I will not lie; before watching Chicken Man's performance I thought it would be great to get up on stage and make people laugh, but it was never something I had considered doing before. My public speaking usually involved a Powerpoint presentation and some sales graphs – I had never been in front of people purely for the reason of making them laugh.

I considered my options. I could go on the stage or I could go home, open a bottle of wine and, the following day, forget it had ever happened. I concluded I had nothing to lose – the empty house waiting for me was a reminder that I was not living the life I wanted, so I literally had nothing to lose. Even if it went badly, only seven people would know, and one of them thought he was a chicken.

'Here, mate,' I said, and Mick invited me on to the stage.

It seemed surreal that my name had been mentioned by a professional comedian, and that I was now about to stand on a stage with the sole purpose of making strangers laugh. I would say I was nervous, but I am not sure that would be correct – I had an excitement inside me I could not recall feeling at any other time in my life. It was the excitement of knowing I was entering a new world and, whatever hap-pened, this first time could never happen again. I could say it was like losing my virginity but in reality it wasn't (when that happened, I knew there was a good chance it would not be the last time), but when I walked on that stage I knew the first time could easily be the last time. I had also not spent every waking minute of the previous two years thinking about it (yes, that does spell 'waking').

When I spoke into the microphone, I said the first words of my comedy career: 'Fuck me, those lights are bright.'

If you have never been on a stage, the lights are the first things that you notice; bright, white lights burning into your face like an oncoming train, letting you know you have crossed the line now – you are on stage and you had better do something.

For the first moment or two, I did nothing; the only thing going around in my head was, 'How the hell did this happen?' I just stood, allowing the luminescence of the lights to settle on the room – and suddenly I realised I had nothing to say. I hadn't planned to be on a stage in front of strangers, but now, with the microphone in front of me, the spotlights on me and an increasingly uncomfortable audience before me, I had to think of something to say.

I often think of that moment when I am touring now because there was a second when my brain said, 'What are you doing, dickhead? You don't belong here – get off, go home and have a drink, and watch *News at Ten*.' Every ounce of my being wanted to run off stage to break the awkward silence, which may have lasted only seconds but to me seemed like hours.

But something stopped me.

Something made me want to stay on there and at the very least say something. 'What's the worst thing that could happen?' I reasoned. Nothing important, I concluded. The consequences of standing on a stage talking to strangers and getting it wrong would not result in much harm. Nobody would get hurt. I wouldn't lose the house, kids and wife I had already lost. All I could lose was my pride, and pride isn't a reason not to try something.

Even now, before walking out in front of thousands during an arena tour, I always think, 'If you mess up, all that will be hurt tonight is your pride.' Obviously, now that things have gone bigger, I could add to that, 'Your reputation, your career and your future happiness,' but I tend not complicate things too much. Now, I am always pretty relaxed before shows because I know I made a choice to be doing this, that night in October 2000 at the Frog and Bucket when the lights were glaring, the audience of seven was staring, the microphone stood to attention awaiting its orders and silence reigned in the room. That was the last time I could have walked away.

'The French, don't they make you laugh?'

I was referring to the French farmers blockading the roads in objection to petrol prices, which meant English lorry drivers were unable to cross the border to return home.

'Wouldn't it have been handy if they had got that angry in 1939 and saved us all a lot of hassle?'

My first joke, which was derived from a conversation I'd had with my mate Jimmy earlier that day, had been born and presented to the world. It was greeted with a laugh, and my life as a 'civilian' was over.

Comedy is the most instant form of communication there is. You say something, and if people think it's funny, they laugh. There is no consideration; there is laughter or silence. I learnt in that moment when you hear laughter, you sense a joy that goes beyond a simple reward – it is an affirmation of your very being. I know that sounds grand, but laughter equals happiness, and giving happiness is surely at the essence of what being a human being is about.

At some point I drifted away from current affairs to talking about my divorce and everyone seemed prepared to listen, provided I dropped the odd joke into what was becoming a therapy session. I became aware of a red light flashing, but thought it must be broken and just carried on, but then, mid-sentence, I heard the Pearl & Dean theme tune sometimes played in cinemas before the adverts are blasted out: 'Ba ba ba baa ba ba baa ba baa baa!'

Mick mounted the stage and my first comedy gig was over. I didn't know that the open spots were supposed to perform for seven minutes; I had done about 25 and was starting to ramble on a bit. The first rule of comedy is that you should know the beginning and end, the middle you can muddle through. I didn't have a beginning when I walked on that stage so I had no end either; I just had a very long middle.

I walked off to some appreciative applause; I think because I spared them any further animal impressions more than the fact that I was any good. But it didn't matter. I was hooked.

It wasn't as if I thought I was ever going to get a job as a comedian; it was just that I now knew that the feeling of standing on a stage and making people laugh, even six people and a chicken impersonator, was better than sitting at home with an empty bottle of wine. It was like realising an ambition I didn't know I had. I did a sky dive once for a television show, having always wanted to do one – it had been at the top of my bucket list for years. I hated it, and would rather do anything else than repeat it. Standing on stage and making people laugh was never on my bucket list, but as soon as I walked off I knew I had to do it again. It wasn't that I was going to add it to my list of things to do before I died: it would be the only thing on the list.

I had no anticipation that being on the stage would feel so natural to me. It was an instant thing, as if it was in my genes, which perhaps it was. Years later, I was to feature in the BBC programme *Who Do You Think You Are?* which retraces parts of your family history. I discovered that my great-great-grandfather, Charles Bishop, had been a performer. He had found his musical talent whilst in the army in the mid-1800s and he changed the whole direction of his life to follow his passion, something I would repeat generations later. He was also the person responsible for bringing the family to Liverpool, where he was engaged to perform in a minstrel troupe. The programme has led to a family reunion and a headstone being placed on his up-to-then unmarked grave. I have also gone back and performed in some of the venues I know he performed in as a kind of homage to him, although I decided that blacking up to do the show may have taken the homage a bit too far.

Mick was great afterwards, giving me lots of words of encouragement. He suggested that I return the week after, but next time I should try to think of something to say for about 10 minutes.

I had found a thing to do which would change my Mondays from lonely days of depression to opportunities to reflect on the week I'd just had in a way that made strangers laugh. But, most crucially, I had found my solace, my life and my future.

CHAPTER 24

SOMETIMES I TRY TO BE FUNNY

From then on, my Mondays were centred around these open spots at the Frog and Bucket. Of course, there was no money in it, but it was a chance to gain experience on the stage and develop more material.

The thing I found immediately striking was that the experienced comedians who would compère these evenings were very supportive if they thought you were good. People like Mick, Tony Burgess, Brendan Riley and Justin Moorhouse would all be happy to pass your name on to promoters of other clubs or advise you who to ring to get more gigs. Comedy is very egalitarian in that way: anyone can have a go at it and, if you are good, the comedy community is ready to recognise that fact.

Within a few weeks, I was asked to do an open spot at the weekend. This meant that the Frog and Bucket would be full, and the line-up would not be made up of other open spots like on the Monday, but of full-time professional comedians.

This was a big step, but I felt ready for it. I had been doing well on Mondays, and I knew if I was to actually get any better I had to be tested on a night where the audience had a higher expectation and were less forgiving.

The compère was Brendan Riley, and the first act that night was Steve Harris, who went on and stormed it. I was due on after the interval, and the audience was in a great mood after Steve's performance, so I knew if I got it wrong I would just make the show go backwards. It's one thing following Chicken Man in front of only a handful of people, but to follow a professional comedian who has just knocked it out of the park in front of a packed audience – that is a different matter.

As I stood ready to go on, Brendan and Steve both gave me words of encouragement, which I really appreciated. There are few industries where people will encourage someone who could potentially take their job to go on and do well. Comedy is a community. If you have the courage to walk on stage, even if I don't think you're funny, you already have my respect, and I think most comedians are the same.

My name was called out and Steve patted me on the back. During the open mic nights, I always approached the stage from the audience as you never knew what order you were going to be called on. So, on this night and on every other night I have done the Frog and Bucket, I approached the stage from the front, which meant I didn't see the audience till I got up on the stage and turned around with the microphone in my hand.

'Hiya, I'm John Bishop. I'm from Liverpool, and I live in Didsbury now.'

'Didsbury's not in Liverpool, you Scouse bastard.'

'It's nice to be in Manchester where even dickheads who shout out are factually correct.'

It was that fast. I spoke, someone heckled, I responded, the crowd cheered, and I was away.

My 10 minutes ended up being 15 and went better than I could have imagined. There was a hen party in from Warrington, and this opened the door to me talking about my marriage and my own new single status.

'I used to be married, but I decided I deserved some happiness in life too, so we're getting divorced. People say money doesn't buy you happiness, but it does buy you a divorce, which is close enough.'

My material seemed a success and, as I walked off to loud applause, I was so relieved. It was my first weekend gig and I had not let anyone down. In fact, I had done well, so well that one of the better-looking girls from the hen party made a beeline for me at the end of the gig. After a brief conversation, I invited her into the small dressing room, which the other comedians duly vacated, and I celebrated my first weekend gig by engaging in some rather satisfying shenanigans backstage.

The old adage of making a girl laugh if you want her to be attracted to you certainly seemed true. I considered myself now well and truly in show business, although Steve did tell me not to expect such fun at every gig.

He was right. It has never happened again, even though I would suggest my act has improved.

CHAPTER 25

WE ALL HAVE TO DIE ON OUR ARSE SOME TIME

Once I started being asked to do weekend spots I faced the problem of managing my time with the boys. The gigs were never anywhere outside the North West; in fact, I was lucky that the comedy scene in Manchester was vibrant enough that the majority of them were within 20 minutes of my house. I didn't change the arrangements and would still collect them on Friday and return them on Monday but, if I had a gig, I had to use a babysitter. However, I was always reluctant to leave before the boys were asleep in bed, which meant I would often rush to the gig, arriving only five minutes before I was due on.

I did my first open spot in October 2000 and was booked for my first headline act in January 2001 by Agraman, a local promoter and compère who was a great supporter of people he thought were good. Indeed, he was later to encourage me to do my first solo theatre show at the 400-seater venue, the Dancehouse, in Manchester in July 2002, 18 months after doing my first open spot. I didn't realise that this was extremely fast progression and that the normal process was to remain an open spot before progressing through the ranks over a period of years. Within the local comedy scene, every-one claims to have assisted those who have done well, but Agraman certainly helped elevate comedy in the North West as he ran the North West Comedy Awards, which had such luminous victors as Peter Kay (Johnny Vegas came second that year), Jason Manford, Alan Carr, Caroline Aherne and a Scouse lad with big teeth.

It gave me a boost to my confidence that someone like Agraman was championing me, although what is unique about comedy is that you know when it's going well, and so does everyone else, because the audience laughs. Even if an individual doesn't like your act, there is no escaping the sound of laughter, which removes the subjectivity of opinion when it comes to promoters booking acts. If they think you will make people laugh, they will book you; if they think you won't, they won't book you – it's that simple.

When I did my first headline slot I thought it was impor-tant to be there for the whole show in order to see what the other acts spoke about. When I did the circuit, I never had a 'set act' as such – I would go on with something in my mind, but allow other things to emerge during the time I was on stage. But since I was headlining this time, I wanted to see what topics had been covered by the other acts, so I could either back-reference them or avoid them altogether.

I had asked my mum to have the boys for the evening, and had been greeted with a knowing look from both her and Dad. At this point I had been single for over a year, and there had been no hint of a girlfriend on the horizon. I still kept the comedy secret, not even telling my mates. I just wanted to have something for me, and I also didn't know when it might end.

I also knew that as soon as I said what I was doing, people would want to come to watch. This would have destroyed me because, although I felt very comfortable on stage, having people I knew within the small audiences I was playing to would certainly have changed things. I would have felt pressure to make them laugh more than anyone else, potentially saying anecdotes that involved them. By keeping the comedy a secret, I was able to be anonymous by being the centre of attention for people who did not know me.

This proved a sensible decision. After my mates found out, some came to watch me during my first run in Edinburgh. I was in a tiny room, and with around 15 people in the audience my five mates made up a high percentage. As the other 10 weren't laughing much and the gig was not going well, my mates decided to heckle me to spice things up. When a third of your audience starts to heckle you about stag dos you have been on with them, you know it was a bad idea to allow them to come.

In not telling people, it never occurred to me that my mum and dad would make their own assumptions about why I would be out that Saturday night. It didn't register what the look meant until I was leaving.

I kissed the boys goodbye and did the same to my mum, after which she followed me out to the gate.

'So, are you off out then?'

'Yes, thanks for having them.'

'So are you going out then?'

'Sort of . . .'

'Or are you staying in . . .?'

I thought it was as good a time as any to break the secret.

'I'm going to a comedy club.'

'Oh, that'll be nice. With your mates . . . or with a girl?'

'On my own.'

'What? Why would you do that?'

'No, I'm not going "going" – I'm going because I'm on. I'm one of the acts.'

'You're what? Oh Jesus, John, don't make a show of yourself.'

'Well, that is the general idea.'

She wished me luck with that worried look that only mothers have, and I knew there and then that I was a comedian. It was the first time I had ever told anyone what I was doing, and now my secret was out. The only other people who were in any way aware of how I spent my free time were the audiences and the people working at the venues. It was a new life, and by letting my mum know where I was going I was merging my two worlds together for the first time.

The gig itself went well. I was on after an excellent Australian comedian called Steve Hughes, who was more experienced than me and better at the job. But if he thought he should have been headlining – as he should have been – he never showed it, and just wished me luck.

Going on stage after great people is always difficult as you have to at least maintain momentum, even though you are not doing the same things. That night, Steve had done such a good job that I managed to just maintain things. I didn't storm it, but I didn't let anyone down and, driving home, I felt satisfied. I knew I had a lot to learn, but I was beginning to allow myself to think I could actually do stand-up and make strangers laugh, rather than just need to do stand-up as a kind of therapy, as it had been up till then. Once you start being booked for paid gigs, the audience has got to enjoy the show. If you enjoy it, it's a bonus, but the audience must come first.

I have been lucky. I can't remember not enjoying stand-up; even on nights when I would rather stay at home or have had a day dealing with the normal stresses of life, once I walk on stage I just feel better. On stage is a great place to be, because you have to focus, and so everything else disappears.

My parents have been to many of my shows since, and there is nothing more strange for a grown man than to have his parents come to a comedy gig where even if things go right they have to listen to you talk about subjects they may not always want to hear, such as your current male grooming techniques.

My mates found out a few weeks later when one of them, Mike, announced the arrival of his second daughter. After a bit of discussion about where to wet the baby's head, the Frog and Bucket was mooted and seemed to gain general agreement.

The only problem was that I was due to do an open spot on the evening in question.

I decided that getting up on stage was the best way to come clean to them all. I knew there was every chance it could go wrong and I might die on my arse, but I reasoned if that happened, then it would still be funny. I felt confident, as I knew the Frog and Bucket, so if my mates were to see me for the first time anywhere, I wanted it to be there.

A table was booked for the dozen or so who were out, and I tagged along. As an open spot, your name is never listed, so as we sat and enjoyed the first act they had no idea of who was coming up next. I slipped away as the compère came back on stage, suggesting I was going the bar. The compère then announced me, to warm and enthusiastic applause from everyone in the packed venue, apart from one table where my mates sat in stunned silence – before in unison exclaiming, 'What the f—!'

Fortunately, the gig went well. I just seemed to settle into being on stage very quickly, which is lucky as, even though my material was not always the strongest, audiences are like a pack of wild dogs: they will sniff out your fear and nerves before you even know you have them. My view is that if you are relaxed, it allows them to think, 'He can't be shit because he isn't worried enough.' This is only a theory, and to be honest I have seen many people die on their arse despite being filled with confidence beforehand.

I was one of them myself.

My worst death came in Newcastle at a club called the Hyena coming up to Christmas in 2001. In the early days I very rarely took gigs away from home because of the boys. But on this particular weekend Melanie was taking them away, which left me with the opportunity to experience my first proper weekend as a circuit comedian, doing a Thursday, Friday and Saturday night in the same club.

I managed my work diary so that I was working up in Newcastle. Thus the hotel was paid for, and I didn't have to take any time from my day job. Back then, the Hyena was a room that contained perhaps 200 people sitting on long benches at tables tightly packed together. There was a local compère, and I was to be the support act for Addy van der Borgh, a very funny, surreal comedian. The compère had previously had some sort of stake in the club and, as he repeatedly told everyone, this was his first gig back since he had stopped being involved in its management.

Comedy is like sky diving: if you get the first few minutes wrong, then it's very hard to recover. I had not done a gig outside the North West, and I was confident and familiar with all the clubs there. But there in Newcastle I began the gig badly and was not experienced enough to turn it around.

I started to lose the audience almost immediately. Though I used what I thought would be clever techniques to win them back, like shouting, 'Go on then, say something, and I'll see if I can make it funny!' the reality is that for a comedian there is no greater indication of a death on stage than an audience having a conversation between themselves. Heckles you can deal with, but indifference from an audience – as in a relationship – is a killer.

I walked off to the hum of people talking, only slightly drowned out by the compère coming back on stage to declare: 'Don't blame me. I don't book the acts any more.'

He continued to win the audience back by reaffirming in their mind how bad I was, whilst I stood in the small dressing room next to the stage with Addy.

There can be nothing more awkward than hearing people laugh at your failure while you're standing in a room the size of a toilet, with someone you have only just met and who has to walk onto the same stage to improve everyone's night out.

The compère announced the interval and then walked into the dressing room. It was the first time, and one of the few times, I encountered the bullying that sometimes goes on in dressing rooms.

It normally takes the form of the established acts all being friendly with each other and saying nothing to the open spot or the new act until they are deemed worthy enough to be spoken to, and every time I've seen it happen I do my best to break the circle. This time, however, there was not even a circle to break. The compère ignored my presence completely, which was difficult considering the dressing room was so small we were all virtually touching, and began to talk to Addy, keeping his back to me.

My disappointment was now replaced by anger at his arrogance. Having laughed with the audience at my failure, I was expecting him to say something along the lines of, 'Sorry, mate, had to do that to win them back. Better luck tomorrow, eh?' Instead, it was clear I was regarded as not being worthy of conversation. So I decided to correct the situation.

'If you ever take the piss out of me again, I'll twat you!'

I may be paraphrasing here, but not much. I don't know what new acts normally do when they have been in a similar situation, but it must be something different, because my comments were greeted with astonishment.

'No need for that, mate! Look, this gig is probably just too big for you, and you shouldn't have been booked. It happens.'

'No, it doesn't. Not to me. If I die on my arse for the next two nights, I will give you my wages. But if you take the piss again, I *will* twat you!' (Or words to that effect.)

I watched Addy's act, and he was brilliant. He reaffirmed to me that my experience had been my fault and that the audience had actually come to enjoy some comedy – I just hadn't provided them with any. I had got it wrong because I had had nothing in my head when I went on stage and had just expected magic to happen. That wasn't all due to laziness or arrogance; it was mainly due to my head being filled with other stuff, so I only thought about comedy when I was actually doing it. A bit like a wife and sex. (Sorry, couldn't resist that one.)

I even went through a period of walking on stage with a stool, sitting on it, and the first thing I would say to the audience was: 'Any questions?' Whatever was shouted out would then form the basis of the act. I enjoyed doing this as it meant literally anything could come up – although this was not always a good thing.

One time doing 'Late 'n' Live', the legendarily hostile Edinburgh Festival show which starts at one in the morning and finishes some time around four, I walked on stage in front of a very lively audience who had already taken heckling to new heights with the previous acts. I proposed to take the hecklers on head-to-head. So I invited the challenge by walking on with the stool and asking an inebriated audience of 200 people at 2.30 in the morning if they had any questions.

'Were you inbred?' shouted a Southern Counties English accent – the kind of accent all students seem to be given when they enrol in drama school.

Having seen a fellow Northern comedian being heckled about his roots, I completely lost my temper. The Edinburgh Festival attracts some people who move around with an air of superiority because they can wear a cravat and not be punched in the nose. It's the place where the bullied can become the bully, whether it's promoters, critics or even comedians who can't get booked on the circuit, but who suddenly get a five-star review from a two-page student mag and take it as an opportunity to look down their noses at the comics who spend every weekend of every year blowing audiences apart in clubs around the country. It's a place I have been to six times, and I have had my fair share of being trampled on. So I was in no mood to allow this to happen again as some tosser tried to suggest that because of my accent I was somehow the result in interbreeding within my family.

I jumped off the stool, looked in the direction of where the comment had come from, and using wit, expletives and the threat of violence, I put him in his place. 'Who the fuck

are you talking to, dickhead? Talk about my family like that
and I will come down there and ram that stupid Southern
head up your arse, although I will have to pull it out of there
first, you prick.'

Not, I accept, the best heckle put-down ever, but it was
par for the course at 'Late 'n' Live'. The baying audience
cheered my rant and savoured the prospect of a comedian
and a drama student having a fight, which probably repre-
sents the least aggressive form of combat there is (two needy
people slapping each other and shouting, 'Not the face, not
the face!').

As the cheer died down, I stood looking challengingly into
the darkness of the audience in the direction of the heckler,
just to assert my authority and let Drama Boy know I was
the victor.

'No, I meant were you in *Bread*, the eighties sitcom.'

The audience once again cheered at the confusion, and my
aggression melted, as I had to accept that as a heckle goes
that was a good one.

So, in Newcastle, on my first proper weekend as a stand-
up, I learnt the importance of at least planning the first 10
minutes – to have something strong to start with to allow the
audience to believe you might be funny. I also learnt the
lesson told to me by Ross Noble, who said that the worst
time to die on stage is the first night of a weekend run. He
said that when you return to the club the following night,
none of the staff want to look you in the eye.

My death had been of a magnitude where this was certainly going to be the case, yet I never thought of not going
back. I had a good job and didn't need to put myself through
the potential humiliation of dying on my arse again, yet it
never entered my head to quit. I could say that that was

because I knew in a comedy career the odd death was inevitable and I wanted to learn from it, but that's not the case. I had no plans for a career; I just wanted to hear people laugh, so, despite the pain suffered the night before, I resolved to return the next night to chase the sound of laughter.

However, before I returned to the Hyena on the Friday, I went out and bought a new pair of shoes. A pair of fake crocodile-skin shoes.

As I approached the entrance that Friday night, Ross's prediction proved to be correct. The bouncers saw it was me and immediately diverted their eyes from my face – to my feet. Once they saw the shoes, they looked back at me with an expression that seemed to say, 'Bloody hell, you've got confidence if you're wearing them.'

At the end of the weekend, I had performed well enough in everyone's eyes to not have to give my wages away, and a truce was called between me and the compère. As for the shoes, I still have them. It's nice to remind yourself never to get too cocky.

CHAPTER 26

LIFE SAVER

Sometimes a heckle is not a heckle, it's a situation. I was talking recently with a fellow comedian, Alistair Barrie, who reminded me of a gig we both did at the Manchester Comedy Store around 2005, which was interrupted in the most unusual way.

Al was compèring, and I was about 15 minutes into my headline act in front of the audience of about 40 people in the small bar there, when a man appeared at the side of the stage. As the stage is less than five foot square, it was impossible for me not to notice him, but it was also impossible for me to see how he had arrived there in the first place.

'Can you help me?' he asked.

I stopped what I was talking about to look at him. The attention of the audience had also shifted to the man, who was now so close that I noticed he was covered in mud up to his thighs.

'I'll do my best, mate, but I'm just at work here.' (I know you can see what I did there – a master at work, oh yes.)

'I just tried to kill myself, but it didn't work.'

If you ever want a comment to stump a comedian, throw something like that in. Some of the audience laughed, assuming he was a plant and part of the act, although a look at the expression on my face would have made it clear he wasn't. Or perhaps they laughed, enjoying the fact that I was completely lost for words. I just thought I would avoid any amusing quips and ask him the obvious question.

'What did you do?'

'I jumped into the canal, but I didn't realise it had been drained, and now I am just covered in mud. Look at me!'

The Comedy Store is situated next to the canal at Deansgate Lock. Once he'd realised he was still alive and had got over that disappointment, he had clearly climbed out of the mud and entered the venue through the side door at canal level.

'So I thought I would come here and get cheered up.'

There are times as a comedian when people make demands of you that can be hard to fulfil, like when you do a corporate gig and they want you to make a joke about the boss, but that is about as demanding as a comedian's life usually gets. 'Can you make me laugh to save my life?' is perhaps the hardest request I have ever had.

As there was only a small audience, we all felt part of the experience. We gave him a seat in the front row next to two ladies who, although sympathetic to the situation, had not come out to sit next to someone drenched in the sediment that only exists at the bottom of canals in Manchester. They moved, so there was a vacant seat between them and the bridge-jumper, and I continued as best as I could with the gig.

Picking up momentum in any gig after you have been interrupted can be difficult, but doing it after a genuine life or death situation is even harder. It was a struggle but, after a few minutes, I was back into my stride and the audience, including the bridge-jumper, began to laugh at the appropriate moments. At the end I took a bow, everyone seemed happy, and I felt that for at least the duration of the gig I had contributed to saving a life.

As I stepped down from the stage, the bridge-jumper stood up and asked if he could give me a hug. We shook hands instead. I don't mind saving lives, but I am not that keen in getting covered in canal mud to do it.

CHAPTER 27

HOW A WARDROBE CAN CHANGE YOUR LIFE

New Year's Eve is one night of the year where you are effectively bullied into having a good time. In other cultures, the passing of one year and the beginning of another is seen as an opportunity to reflect on how your life is progressing and if your dreams and ambitions are closer to being fulfilled. In Britain, it's an opportunity to get pissed and snog someone you don't know.

As I had had the boys with me on New Year's Eve for 2001, it was agreed that Melanie would have them the following year, which meant that I faced the dilemma of what to do with myself. I was single, I had a night off on the one night when you were given a licence to kiss as many strangers as you could, so it was obvious what I should do: I should go to a party.

However, I was still getting used to the idea of being the single man amongst my friends. It felt awkward being invited to events as a single person and sitting amongst couples, so instead of going to a party I went to the Frog and Bucket and did a gig.

Comedy was now becoming my default position, the thing I went to when I didn't know what else to do. It was a separate world to my daytime existence where I was dealing with the machinations of management in the corporate sector, or my time as a single father to my boys.

Everyone knew I did comedy now, though this had led to some situations that I could perhaps have handled better – such as stepping in to deliver a best man's speech when the best man could not make it as his wife had just gone into labour. I was an usher and you would think it made sense that, if the best man cannot make it and one of your ushers is a comedian, then he is the perfect replacement. That is before you realise that to a new comedian even a speech at a wedding is classed as a gig.

I stood up at the top table, families and friends watching, and I held up the best man's speech. 'Paul, the proper best man, has sent me this – his speech all about living with the groom, Mike, and how close they are, particularly after surviving a house fire. It's a good speech, but everyone knows I only do my own material.' I then put the speech down and did a load of gags completely unrelated to the groom, the bride or even the fact that we were at a wedding. I basically did my club set.

It was a wedding, and I was knocking out my Frog and Bucket 'Give me a cheer if you've got kids . . .' kind of stuff, including material about how marriage was basically rubbish. 'I was married till I realised I could be happy without being nagged every day . . .' I gradually lost everyone in the room except 'the lads'. By 'the lads', I mean the large group of mates who were attending. They loved it. Because it was so bad, for them it was even funnier despite their wives and girlfriends sitting as stony-faced as the relatives of the two people whose day it was meant to be. One of Mike's uncles even tried to chip in with a word of encouragement, which I took to be a heckle, so I attacked him with heckle put-downs from the clubs.

'Go on, son, that's funny, that.'

'Funny? I tell you what's funny – wearing that suit and not doing it for a bet. And that wig's not working for you either, unless of course you've just brought your ferret to the wedding.' It was terrible.

As people clapped, as they are obliged to do, Mike leaned towards me and, with the kind of bluntness I would expect from my mates, said in my ear, 'Tit, you just ruined my wedding.'

And I thought I was on for an encore! They got divorced in the end, and part of me still blames myself for it.

In essence, my new world and my old world did not cross paths, apart from the material I used on stage. I was enjoying the gigs, I was being booked frequently across the North West and I had joined Off the Kerb, one of the largest comedy agencies with acts such as Jack Dee, Jo Brand, Jonathan Ross and Lee Evans.

These people seemed in another stratosphere to me. They had been successful for years and, as far as I knew, had been involved in TV and comedy all their working lives. What was certain was that none of them had tried to crack the circuit in their late thirties.

Age and the fact that I had a decent day job made me believe that comedy would only ever be a second income for me. But I could see no reason why I shouldn't try and push that second income as much as I could, because it was like being paid for going out and having a laugh . . . which basically was what it was.

In fact, the extra money from the comedy allowed me to move to a house where the box room actually was a room, and I had a proper master bedroom, although it looked slightly too big when I placed my single wardrobe in it.

•   •   •

At the start of 2002, I was in as good a place as I could wish for. I was managing my job and the comedy, and I was seeing the boys during our precious weekends together. I was also getting on well with Melanie.

She had found out I was doing comedy in a way I would not have wished, but which probably helped soften the blow. I was on stage one night performing some material about splitting up with my wife. This is something many comedians do: they tell an audience that they have just suffered a relationship breakdown, as this is often a gateway to material, and is also a great way to let any interested members of the crowd know that you are single – despite there never being a repeat of the 'hen party from Warrington' incident, I was forever optimistic.

I stood on the stage and went into my routine.

'I've just split up with my wife.'

(*Pause for audience to say 'Aaah.'*)

'No, it's not sad like that. We're not divorced or anything. I've just killed her!'

(*Pause for audience to laugh.*)

'But I knew I would miss her, so I kept her head in the fridge for three months.'

...oe looking cool in a pool, whilst I
...ook freezing.

Luke when he could still fit on my
shoulders.

...aniel trying to show
...e has the Bishop
...eeth.

On holiday in Spain
with the four most
important people
in my life.

Onstage at the Comedy Store, looking more ready to have a scrap than tell a joke.

Outside my first ever one-man theatre show, 18 months after my first open-mic spot.

Dancing with Luke on the Sunshine tour: nice that someone in our family can dance, and it's not me.

My son Joe took this picture backstage when he was on tour with me in Glasgow.

e six Edinburgh shows. Six years of trying to get better.

Fake That: my first exposure to Comic Relief, and in Melanie's eyes the best thing I have done. Ever.

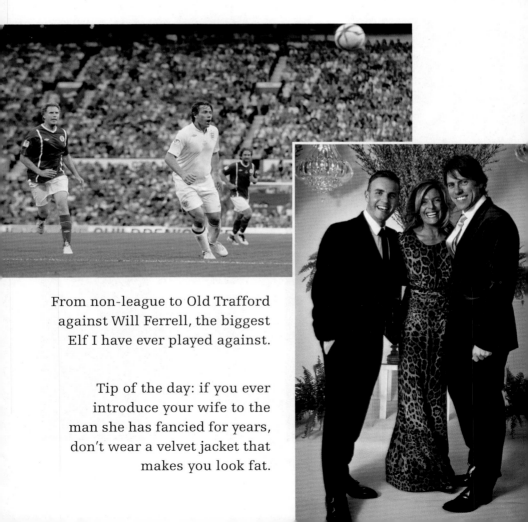

From non-league to Old Trafford against Will Ferrell, the biggest Elf I have ever played against.

Tip of the day: if you ever introduce your wife to the man she has fancied for years, don't wear a velvet jacket that makes you look fat.

The reality of life in Kroo Bay slum: sat with Kadiatu near the open sewer, which runs past her house.

Riding to the coast: ...reg, Gordon and Andy ...n the distance making it look easy.

...hree people who ...aved me when I ...ad nothing left. ...reddie, Davina ...nd Denise will ...lways be my ...eroes.

Freddie decided not to join us in the bad hat contest when we started rowing.

Dot doing something with tape that should be kept behind closed doors.

Eddie, Robbie Savage, Daniel and Luke joining me towards the end of the run just when I needed cheering up.

Chris Moyles – who I love, and who did so much to raise money – surprising me on the run.

The reception on the streets was fantastic and, for me, completely unexpected.

The men who made it all possible: Kevin Cahill, head of Sport Relief; Dr Matt who kept me going; Greg the legend who dragged me through; and Dot who stuck me back together.

s over, and I am with those who matter most.

On holiday in Majorca, August 2013: I am not the best dad or the best husband, but I am the luckiest. They mean the world to me.

The famous sign that hangs in my kitchen and its replacement.

(*Another audience reaction – some laughing, with some 'oooohhs' thrown in.*)

'And it's surprising how handy that becomes after a while.'

(*Another pause and sometimes a cheeky wink to the audience.*)

I would not suggest that is the best piece of material I have ever come up with, but it certainly was effective at that stage in my career. What I had never expected was to say that line and to find the head that was supposed to be in the fridge sitting at a table right in front of the stage (still attached to the rest of the body, I hasten to add).

During my act, I tried not to look in the direction of her table, so at the end I had no idea if she had found anything funny, apart from the fact that no bottles had been thrown.

Melanie had come to the Frog and Bucket with some friends who I didn't know. She had no idea that I was going to be on stage, and I had no idea that she was going to be in the audience. Why would I? We were moving along the lines of divorce, and apart from the occasional childcare situation we had to deal with together, our lives were now firmly moving in opposite directions.

When I came off stage, I couldn't believe that the face I had seen actually belonged to Melanie: as far as I was aware, she had never gone to a comedy club before, certainly not during the 13 years I had known her. I was hoping it was just someone who looked similar, although I knew this was not the case. You do not have three children with someone and not know what they look like, even if the expression I saw from the stage when I first walked on displayed a greater level of shock and discomfort than when her waters broke prior to the birth of one of the boys.

The divorce had been hurtful for all concerned. My way of dealing with the pain was to use it to make people laugh, and I wasn't expecting that to be seen as a positive thing from her point of view. I may not have been pelted on stage, but I was at least expecting a letter from her solicitor the following day demanding a greater settlement due to the humiliation and distress caused by my suggestion of decapitation as a way of resolving our marital disputes.

Instead, when I nervously went out to the bar after the show, I was greeted by a smile – a smile I hardly recognised as it had been so long since I had seen it. Thankfully, Melanie had seen the joke in what I had said. She had been able to laugh with me and the audience about the situation. She had seen the funny side of me cutting her head off and keeping it in the fridge. I would suggest that, within the rawness of a failed marriage, to be able to laugh at the idea of being decapitated by your soon-to-be-ex-husband, you have to have a fair sense of humour.

Melanie had always possessed one, but it had been drowned out by nappies and my indifference, and now it was there again in her eyes. She introduced me to some people at the table who hardly registered in my mind. I couldn't stop looking at her. 'There you are,' I thought. 'I can see you again after all these years. That angry line on your forehead has changed to a dimple in your cheek. There you are, right where I left you before we both became lost in the fog of our marriage.'

There was a brief conversation, and then I said I needed to go. There was a look, a little longer than was necessary, and I knew something had changed in her, too – I just didn't know what. 'Perhaps this is what it is like when you stop hating each other,' I thought. When your life falls apart and you start to hate someone, it doesn't mean automatically you stop loving them. In a marriage, both emotions can coexist with the balance swinging between the two; in a divorce, you never expect the pendulum to swing back from hate.

That night, I realised that sometimes it does. Just before I left Melanie said, 'You were great. You were like how you were when I met you all that time ago. What happened to you?'

'I married you!'

As Melanie now knew about the comedy, she was happy to help if I struggled for a babysitter during a weekend and, in return, I would occasionally babysit for her during the week. It seems a ridiculous thing to write, 'I was *babysitting* my own children,' but the English language has yet to keep up with the ever-changing world we live in and as far as I know it does not yet have a more appropriate word than 'babysitter' to describe a person looking after their own children in the house of their former partner. So the description that best suits a 16-year-old girl will have to do.

Although we were getting on well together, the divorce was still proceeding, and things may not have changed substantially had we not messed up the school holidays when, during the Easter half term of 2002, we both booked the same week off work.

I had already booked to take the boys to a hotel in Portugal, and Melanie was considering either taking them to see her mum in France or going to Abersoch, both destinations that had been our holiday outlets during the years of our marriage.

When the mistake was realised, neither of us was able to alter our dates with work. So it meant the choice between one of us taking the boys on holiday whilst the other one went somewhere alone, or we both took them. We decided that we were getting on well enough to go to Portugal together, but not well enough for me to go to France or Abersoch. To me, revisiting holiday destinations that you went to when married seemed a step too far. Consequently, we spent a week together with the boys in a hotel with other English holidaymakers.

The boys loved it. They were seven, five and three, and while the complications of adult relationships perhaps never registered with them, what did was the fact that they had two parents there for them at once.

When you're a child and one parent is not available to you as they are dealing with a sibling or the million other things that adults do, to be able to turn and find another pair of willing hands to help put your arm bands on, tie your shoes, kick the ball or find your favourite toy all just helps to let you know you are loved.

However, the strange situation in which we found ourselves did not make talking to other parents on the holiday straightforward.

'So, how long have you two been married?'

'We're not married, we're getting divorced and it should all be final in a few months,' tended to curtail conversation.

At the end of the week, it was strange to say goodbye to Melanie and the boys and return to my own home. Although we had gone on the trip purely out of necessity and not because we thought our relationship had reached a new level, it made the home that I had only ever lived in as a single man seem empty when I turned the key and stepped inside.

We never spoke about the effect of having that holiday together, but perhaps it was that week which changed Melanie's attitude. Having been the one who had wanted the divorce, she now began stalling on signing the final documents. We were literally weeks away from the divorce being complete, but my solicitor informed me that the process had halted at her end.

Having resisted the divorce from the beginning, I was now keen to get it done and dusted. Of course, it was preferable to be able to have a relationship where you may be able to go on holiday together, but I had certainly never anticipated anything more than that. Now I just wanted to finalise things.

My solicitor suggested that I talk to Melanie about the delay, as communicating between our solicitors was just racking up bills, which I was not in the best position to pay. After having no joy with Melanie, I decided the best way forward was some form of arbitration. So I arranged for us to go to Relate, and Melanie, much to my surprise – as she can be the most stubborn person in the world – agreed to attend.

Going to Relate is like dogging; there are more couples doing it than would like to admit. I found it a brilliant process because the confusion that often arises when two people live together for years and speak the same language but cannot understand each other's words is changed by the fact that you have to listen. You have to listen because there is a counsellor (or, as I would prefer to call them, a referee) who makes you stop talking.

What may surprise many people who have not been through the process or are not trained counsellors is that when you don't speak you have to listen, and when you listen, what you hear is not always what you might have expected.

Our counsellor was called Susan, and was not the type of person I would expect to be a counsellor, primarily because she didn't have a flowery dress, sandals or a beard. She had auburn hair, a gentle demeanour and a forceful way of saying 'Ssshh!' should you talk when it was not your turn. Slowly, I began to realise my failings in the relationship and to understand some of Melanie's.

Nobody gets married hoping for divorce – they just find themselves on a path that seems impossible to get off. And because you become numb to your partner, everything they say or do simply confirms the need to split up. It's not until you actually hear what is really going through their minds that you realise, 'Bloody hell, some of this is my fault!'

The process was not quick and not always easy, but gradually we began to rediscover the part of our relationship that was not defined by being 'married with kids'. There had been a time when I was a cocky lad in a tracksuit with a twinkle in his eye, and she had been a vibrant young woman who lit up the room with a smile that took my breath away. We had excited each other and had overflowed with potential, which we had then unconsciously set aside for the practicalities of the path we chose to follow into domesticity.

Through a process like Relate, you begin to remember why you loved someone in the first place, even if you can also see why that love had not been enough. I had gone into the process with a view that this was the most expedient way to move the divorce forward, having long accepted that reconciliation was not on the cards. Yet, during the sessions, it became apparent that what we had lost in the relationship was time with each other, and this had led to us drifting apart. This is not a unique situation, and the same thing can be said of a million relationships. But nor had we spent time building a foundation of memories that can sustain a relationship through the tough times: the holiday photographs, party memories or simply a back catalogue of time together which was not in some way tainted by the same pressures, perceived or real, that forced our split.

We decided to spend some time together, but not tell anyone. I certainly wasn't going to tell my mates I was going to counselling. I had the Northern working-class man mindset that telling your friends you were seeing a counsellor would be like telling them you had fallen in love with musical theatre. It's something that some people do, but nobody from my world. My view on this has obviously changed now, and I would encourage anyone who feels that they have problems to talk to someone. The only thing I would say is that it helps if that person is involved in the counselling profession – speaking to people you sit next to on the bus about your feelings generally results in someone feeling slightly uncomfortable.

It is a strange thing to date your own wife. We took it slowly, and a babysitter would be arranged depending on whose turn it was to have the boys. We then would meet and go somewhere we knew we wouldn't bump into people we might know, which made it clandestine and exciting – it was almost like we were having an affair, sneaking around behind the backs of our real lives as separated single parents. We knew it could easily go wrong and didn't want to rush into anything. We both knew the stakes were high: an on-off relationship is OK when there is just you two involved, but it is potentially very destructive when there are children. We were also both protective of our own feelings, and though it was clear we were rekindling lost emotions, neither of us was ready to accept that there could be more to this than two lonely people keeping each other company.

The turning point was when Melanie accompanied me to a gig at Alexander's, a comedy club in Chester. It was a small club with around 80 people in, and I was headlining on the Saturday. I had dropped the decapitation material at this point, which I thought was for the best – I don't know if there is a handbook of advice for people on the path to reconciliation, but I am certain if there is it will say that joking about murdering your partner and then using their body parts for sex will not facilitate a successful reunion.

After the gig, we spent our first night together in years in a hotel in Chester.

For me, that night turned the question from 'If we would get back together . . .' into 'How shall we get back together?' We had two houses, the children were used to this arrangement, and everyone involved in our lives, including friends and family, had moved on and now just saw us as a divorced couple. I also didn't know how to broach the subject with Melanie. What if she felt differently? What if I had read it wrong?

Rather than ask her straight out, I bought a wardrobe. I know that doesn't sound like the most romantic gesture in the world; there are not advertising campaigns suggesting you should 'say it with a wardrobe', or companies claiming that they can deliver a wardrobe to anywhere in the world with a romantic message attached in the same way Interflora do. But I couldn't think of a simpler way to express my intentions.

In my new house, my bedroom dwarfed the single wardrobe I had, so there was plenty of space to put another one beside it. I bought a pine wardrobe, and one afternoon, when I was 'working from home', the boys were in school and Melanie had finished work, I asked her to come around for a coffee.

When she did, I led her upstairs to the bedroom. It was not a place she had not been to before – we were dating at this point, so an afternoon roll around was not entirely a new experience. When she walked into the room, she immediately saw the wardrobe.

'It's about time you bought yourself something better than that tiny thing,' she said.

'It's not for me. It's for you. I want you to put your clothes in it and never take them out again.'

She melted in my arms and with tears in her eyes said she had wanted nothing else more, almost from the moment we split up. By this I mean she had wanted nothing more than to get back together, not just get a new wardrobe. (If it was possible to mend all relationships with the purchase of a wardrobe, Relate would be sponsored by Ikea.)

I felt joy and relief. Relief because I wasn't going to end up with a massive wardrobe I was never going to fill, and joy at the fact the door was now open for both of us to make a go of things. When relationships begin to fall part, arguing is often the only form of communication that exists, and it's often impossible to find a response to each other that doesn't perpetuate the row. Only when the arguing ends is there any chance that you may find something about the other person that does not make you angry. Our shouting had stopped, and now we were standing, embracing, looking at an empty wardrobe and the prospect of being a family again.

The next issue we faced was the boys. We knew that nothing was guaranteed. We could get back together and, after a month of living with each other, all the reasons why we were best apart could re-emerge, so we didn't want to build up their hopes. Melanie was having some work done to her house, and it had already been arranged that the boys would be moving in with me full time for a few weeks. So we used that as the opportunity to have a trial period together.

On the Saturday afternoon after the usual morning of kids' clubs and shopping, I sat the boys on the couch. Melanie had arrived 30 minutes earlier, so I said to the boys we had something to ask them.

At the ages of seven, five and three, you assume children just get on with life without their home environment being anything but wallpaper: they see it, but you imagine they never really consider that it should be anything different. I was to learn that is not the case. They absorb the world around them and know what they would like to make it a better place.

'You know your mum is having some work done to her house, so you boys are coming to stay here full time for a while. I . . . we . . . wanted to know if you boys minded if your mum came too, and we all lived here as a family.'

I don't know what I expected – perhaps a shrug of the shoulders and a request to put the cartoons back on the telly. Instead, Joe threw his seven-year-old body off the couch and flew into my arms, Luke quickly followed, and Daniel, only being three and surely preferring to get the cartoons back on the telly, did what his brothers did (if hugging your dad gets the telly back on, then let's all do it). I was on my knees, with the three most important people in my life in my arms and the most important person to all four of us looking on from the doorway with more tears in her eyes.

In that moment, I knew it was going to be all right.

CHAPTER 28

'MUM, I'M ON TELLY!'

My big TV break came in 2003 on a show called *For One Night Only*, which nobody watched. It was an attempt to bring back variety, and it was shown exclusively in the Granada region in the North West. They made three shows, I think. I say 'I think', because all trace of it seems to have disappeared. Nobody's even bothered to put a clip up on YouTube, and since that is full of videos of people eating yoghurt, it shows you just how poor the show was.

Although I was beginning to develop ambitions that comedy could be more than just doing nightly gigs for £127.50 (which was what I received after my agent's cut), I still never allowed myself to believe I could earn the same as my day job and be able to do stand-up full time. But, as a side line, it had growing potential.

My agent kept trying to bring me to 'television meetings' in London, but I was always too busy working and had very little aspiration to be the token Northerner on things, so I never felt I was missing out. I did get to do some spots as the warm-up for *The Jonathan Ross Show*, which did give me some insight into how good TV worked, but it was to be years before I appreciated the impact television could make on a comedian's career and the rewards that could follow. At this stage, I felt I was winning anyway, as I had a great second income doing something I loved. I was to be further convinced that television was not for me after the disaster of my first appearance.

My agent called me to say that a producer of *For One Night Only* had seen me in Liverpool and thought I would be perfect for the show. At this point, I had been doing comedy for a few years and, as nobody else was interested in me for TV, getting a shot on a programme transmitted at 10.35 on a Friday night in just the Granada region was the best option I had.

The show was filmed in the Batley Carr social club in Batley, Yorkshire, which is a famous social club, having been part of the cabaret scene for decades. I was booked as a new face to offset the better-known acts. These included the host, Stu Francis (not the sharp Canadian one-liner exponent, Stewart Francis, but the Stu Francis of the 'I could crush a grape' catchphrase); pop sensations Smokie and Brotherhood of Man; a very good mainstream comedian called Sean Styles; a magician who looked like a Richard Clayderman tribute act (if you're under 35, Google him); and Bernie Clifton, who is famous for doing his act whilst pretending to ride an ostrich.

I was told to arrive at the club by two in the afternoon. I should have known things were not going to go well when nobody knew who I was when I arrived. The club itself looked like it could generate a good atmosphere: the tables were set out in a semi-circle around the stage and were slightly tiered the further back they went, so they formed a kind of amphitheatre. However, the fact that the backdrop on the stage was the kind of silvery curtain you only ever saw when Jim Bowen revealed the main prize on *Bullseye* meant there was no pretending you were anywhere else but a social club in Yorkshire.

I eventually tracked down David, the producer who had booked me, and though he tried to look pleased to see me I did have the distinct impression he had forgotten I was coming. I was then introduced to the director of the show and asked if I wanted to do a run-through of my act.

The venue was empty apart from a few people setting up cameras, and a lady hoovering. I had been doing well in all the comedy clubs, so I was confident in my ability to perform and I couldn't think of anything worse than standing on a stage in front of an empty room trying to practise being funny. I said I was OK and didn't think I needed a rehearsal. This was greeted with a surprised look from the producer, who was obviously concerned by my lack of professionalism.

'Are you sure?' the director asked. 'Everyone has a run-through.' ·

At that point, a man ran on stage wearing Bernie Clifton's ostrich outfit: the orange legs, the false legs hanging over, the reins on the bird's beak – the lot. He then proceeded to do Bernie Clifton's act, including walking backwards and forwards, arguing with the bird as it turned to look at him and then struggling to control it when it wanted to chase the lady with the hoover and, by way of apology shouting after her, 'Oh, he likes you!'

The director and producer both looked on approvingly whilst all this was going on, occasionally flashing me a look that seemed to say, 'See, now that's a pro.'

'Is that Bernie Clifton?' I asked, thinking he may well just look different in real life than he did on telly. By 'different', I mean a few stone heavier, and at least a foot shorter.

'No, that's his driver. Bernie doesn't do the run-through, he doesn't have to now.'

So I was watching a man pretending to be another man pretending to ride an ostrich. That is the level of professionalism they thought I should aspire to.

Perhaps this was when I should have left, but, as it was to be my first television appearance, I wasn't going to ruin it over a misunderstanding. 'They'll soon see when I get on stage,' I thought.

I shared a dressing room with Sean, who seemed surprised I had no change of clothes. I just had the jeans I was wearing, and a spare shirt. As I still had my day job, a suit meant work, whereas jeans meant comedy or just about anything else that was not work. Funnily enough, when I left the job and could wear jeans all day, I started to wear suits on stage. It just felt right that I should change to go to work, and that is what I have done ever since.

So, on this night, the night of my first TV appearance, I wore faded jeans and a brown shirt. I looked like a dad trying to look like a student. Although when I saw the audience, I could have got away with pretending I was a student.

The moment the audience sat down, I knew I was in for a rough time. I would say the average age was 65. One of the greatest compliments I receive today is when I am told that generations of the same family come to my shows – from grandparents to teenage children – so today I would feel comfortable faced with such a crowd. The problem was that in 2003 I didn't have the same armoury of material that I could shape to fit an audience; I just had some stories that worked for student or circuit gigs in front of people in their twenties. And while 40 years can be a big difference for an audience, that night in Batley it felt like centuries.

I was to go on after Brotherhood of Man and before the magician. I waited in the wings and watched the show. I was more interested than nervous. Stu Francis did a great job as the host as he seemed to be able to get the audience on his side whenever he wanted. If he felt he was losing them, he would simply mention the grape catchphrase and they were back, and I found myself wishing I had a catchphrase or something to fall back on. But before I could think of one, I was introduced.

I walked on to warm applause, but it was at this point I knew I didn't belong. For starters, I was the only person in the building who was wearing jeans. I could actually see some of the audience bristle at my appearance, and I could detect murmurings of 'Who is this scruffy bastard?' in the air, but I decided to crack on with my opening line.

'Hiya, my name's John Bishop. So, who's got kids then, and when I say "kids", I mean little ones, not ones who have driven you here tonight?'

Nothing.

I mean *nothing*. Not a little huff, a grin, half a smile – nothing. It wasn't a great opening line, I admit, but I thought a subtle reference to everyone being pensioners was a good way to defuse the fact that nobody knew who I was. But, as I could tell from the first 30 seconds, nobody cared.

I ploughed on with my material, anyway, which involved a story where I re-enacted the awkwardness that comes when you are a single dad and you have to take young children with you when you need to use a public toilet. The punch-line, which was delivered in a squat position pretending to have a dump – 'I can't leave you out there, kids, there could be nutters out there!' – was greeted with silence.

I can assure you that taking a dump in front of your kids

was not something the audience at the Batley Carr social club thought very funny. There is nothing more humbling as a performer than to be squatting as if to take a dump to try to enhance a story that nobody wants to hear, whilst being filmed for television.

And it was whilst in this position that I heard a response from the audience. It was a whoop. Not the laugh that this killer piece of material deserved, but a whoop. Which was then followed by some talking, more whoops and even a few claps. Before I could begin to think that they were for me, the floor manager walked on and told me to stop.

I had known I was doing badly, but I had thought he would have at least let me finish.

But as I rose from my squat position, I saw the magician dashing on flustered in a sequined shirt, blond hair flowing, chasing a runaway puppy. The audience was now enthralled by what was happening on the stage in a way they had not been moments earlier. After a minute or so, however, the puppy was caught and the audience was left with me alone on the stage again. The boredom returned to their faces when the floor manager said I should carry on.

'Where from?' I asked.

He listened to someone on his headphones. 'Just do that last bit from the start again.'

My heart sank. I had to repeat the same section to the audience, having already endured the fact that they didn't think any of it was funny the first time round.

The only thing worse than being told a joke you don't find funny is being told it twice, and the only thing worse than that is being the person who has to tell the joke. It's at that moment that you really wish the magician was good at his job and could make you disappear. Even I lost enthusiasm, and my squat was barely a bended knee the second time around.

I didn't walk off to the sound of my own feet because Stu got the audience to applaud, they played a sequence of music and the dog barked. The audience must have thought the whole thing was falling apart because the magician came on straight after me, and his whole act built up to a finale where he produced the puppy from a hat. The audience's reaction to this piece of magic was somewhat muted, as they had seen him moments earlier chasing the puppy that he now wanted us to believe he was conjuring out of thin air.

It took Sean Styles to save the show and Smokie to sing about living next door to Alice to prevent a riot.

When the show was edited and transmitted, I watched it through my fingers. If any of my mates watched, they never said.

I knew I had not gone down well when I called in to my mum's the weekend after it was aired.

'We watched you last night,' she said. 'It's a shame they didn't give you very long. I said to your dad, they've cut out all his funny bits.'

That's what's great about my mum. Even though I knew the patched-up remnants of the best bits had been shown on TV, I still left thinking she had a point and perhaps they had just edited it wrongly. The truth is, they had done their best to make me look good, but any editor can only work with what he has and, as a performer, you know that if the most interesting thing on the stage is a lost puppy you haven't gone down very well.

CHAPTER 29

FESTIVAL OF BROKEN DREAMS

With the family unit back together, I could consider going to the Edinburgh Festival for the first time. This was obviously impossible when you share child care, because it requires you giving up the whole of August to do gigs night after night.

Everyone had suggested that I should go up to try it – it was the place where you could be seen by television executives, the kind of people who held the key to you potentially moving on to the next level. The reality for me was I was not sure what that 'next level' was, or even if I wanted it. But my agent advised me it was a good thing to do, and everyone who I had spoken to about the Festival said that no matter what happened, if you did an hour of stand-up every night for a month, you would get better, and that was reason enough for me to go. I loved stand-up, and I wanted to improve.

I first went up in 2003 with a show called 'Freefall'. You have to give a show a title even if it bears little relevance to the content, just so the audience can be assured you have given some thought to the hour that they will invest in watching you.

The truth was that I had never been to an arts festival before I performed there; they had not figured highly during my childhood or my youth, so I turned up expecting to be able to do what I was doing in the clubs – ad-libbing, messing with the audience and saying a few funny things.

I was in a venue called the Cellar, which was what it was: a cellar with about 40 seats. I was on at 9.40 p.m., which was a difficult time because it clashed with some of the bigger acts, however I was pleased because it was a good time, and I was in the courtyard where I had a chance to pick up passing trade.

In the end, though, very few people came, a few shows were cancelled because nobody bought a ticket and what reviews I had made it abundantly clear my show was rubbish.

Being a comedian is like being a stripper: you expose what you have to the world and hope it impresses it. When it doesn't, you can't just put your coat on and leave. You have to cavort around to try and get someone's attention and it can be belittling in a way few other professions are. You alone receive the praise and you alone have to deal with the energy-sapping indifference of a world that doesn't care if you get on stage that night or not. Unless you have lived that life, it's hard to explain, but one of the things that makes you carry on when the world says you shouldn't bother is that we see the moments when it does work; although in the middle of a long, hard Festival, looking for those moments can be like panning for gold.

In order to spend a month in Edinburgh, I had to use two weeks of my annual leave. The other two weeks I worked from the flat I rented, or did field visits with the local sales rep. I would also fly to meetings in the London office on the

6.30 a.m. flight down, and return on the 6 p.m. flight back, before going to do a gig to whatever handful of people turned up to the Cellar. Of all the performers on the Fringe, I have no doubt I was probably only one of a few with a full-time job, and certainly the only one doing the Fringe whilst still engaging in discussions about the next five years' marketing plan with our European head office.

I just felt that I needed to try the Festival, to pit myself against the best around and to learn more about the craft of putting a show together. In order to do this, the support I needed from my company and from Melanie was a lot to ask. And when you consider that, at the end of the month, the only conclusion I could draw was that I wasn't good enough, it was an even bigger commitment.

Melanie and I had just moved into a larger home that was akin to the one we had lived in prior to the split, but this had stretched us financially. To return from the Festival with £8,500 of debt was not what I could dress up in any way as a success, and it was not what I had expected.

Lessons I learnt about Edinburgh for all potential performers:

1) *You will lose money.* This is because you have to pay for everything: venue rental, the venue staff, the flyers, the leaflets they give out, the posters, the PR person who tries to get reviewers to come and see you, your accommodation, your food, your beer (optional, but always more than you think – my advice is avoid where possible), the promoter – some of whom charge a fee rather than take a percentage of sales just in case they don't sell enough. Apparently, you have to take a 150-seater venue and sell it out every night to break even, and I would say 75 per cent of venues are probably smaller than this.

2) *Your heart will be broken.* If you get a bad review, and you will, you will feel as you walk around the streets that everybody in the world has read it. If you get a good review, it will be the day it rained and nobody bought a paper.

3) *Being good in clubs does not guarantee success in Edinburgh.* My first show was not a show; it was me sticking jokes together. You have to do more than that if people are going to watch you in a dungeon.

4) *You will get better and by the end you will be brilliant.* The only problem is, if you were rubbish in the first week, all the reviews and word of mouth will mean that you will be brilliant to an empty room.

5) *You will love it.* Being a comedian is like being a Goth: it's a lifestyle choice not many make, and it can be a very lonely one. Edinburgh allows you to be in the same place as others just like you, and standing in a bar in the wee hours of the morning and looking all around at 'your people' makes it worth being there.

I went home with my tail between my legs, but decided to give it another go the year after with a show called 'Peddling Stories', based on my bicycle ride back from Australia. I just knew that if I wanted to get better as a stand-up comedian I had to keep trying.

By now I had won North West Comedian of the Year, which gave me a boost to my confidence, and also came with a degree of kudos because of previous winners like Peter Kay. It also meant more reviewers came to see the show than the previous year.

They quickly came to the same conclusion as their fellow scribes from 2003: I was rubbish. I wasn't completely rubbish; it was just the show was meant to be about the bike ride from Australia but my ad-libbing style meant that I'd digress from the story and would rarely get past Brisbane, so people felt short-changed.

I was beginning to feel that Edinburgh was not right for me. I gave up a lot to be there and would arrive full of anticipation, but audiences remained low.

Melanie brought the boys up to go to the children's shows and to enjoy the magic of the Festival. On one of these days, I left them in our rented flat to go and do my set, only to be greeted by Helena, the show manager, who told me that I had only five people in the audience.

The venue was a converted shipping container called The Hut. It had a capacity of 50 – which I never managed to achieve during the run. This was the third week, and that is what is so hard about the Edinburgh Festival. You commit to be there for a month, in the same place at the same time every day. However, by the end of the first week it is obvious if it has been worthwhile coming. Audiences and reviewers have already decided if you're any good, and if the answer is 'no', then you still have to keep turning up and trying to impress anyone who bothers to come, who are generally people who can't get into better shows which are on at the same time. But it is these nights that make you a better comedian, as you learn the ability to put on a show in which neither you nor the audience are convinced there is much point.

The thought of doing an hour of comedy to five people who were probably not that interested anyway, whilst the family, whom I hadn't seen for the best part of a month, sat in a flat 15 minutes' bike ride away, seemed pointless to me.

'Can't we give them their money back?' I asked. 'It doesn't seem worth it for five people.'

'No, we can't – only two have paid.'

The logic of not being able to refund people because they had not bought their tickets in the first place brought it all home to me: it wasn't even possible to give my tickets away.

So, I did the gig. Firstly, I dispensed with the microphone, which seemed at best a little unnecessary when you have an audience you can fit in a taxi. I also bought everyone a drink as a thank-you for coming, and we shared a pleasant hour together.

It was not the last time I would buy a drink for everyone in the audience to apologise for the low attendance and to thank them for being there. The last time was at the Leicester Comedy Festival in 2009, when 17 people came to see me, and two weeks before television changed my life for ever.

•   •   •

After the failure of the 2004 show, I decided that I could never go to Edinburgh again until I was free from the constraints of a full-time job. Although the company had been as flexible as they could, I was still running a sales team in a very specialised field, and despite using part of my annual leave to attend, it was not a sustainable situation.

I was also beginning to see people I had been on the circuit with, like the brother and sister team of Alan and Jimmy Carr, move to the next level. I was outgrowing the circuit, but I had nowhere to go.

There comes a point for a circuit comedian where you are being booked to close all the best clubs in the country and, within the dressing rooms, nobody questions that you are at the top of your game. But the reality is that when you reach that point you have to capitalise on it, because sooner or later you will not be regarded as special: someone else

will come along who is just as good and the light will shine
on them.

I had begun to consider leaving the day job but it was such
a big decision. My then agent Danny introduced me to Addison
Cresswell, who owned Off the Kerb and is known within television and comedy circles as having the unique ability to
be a prick and a genius within the same second. Danny had
told Addison that I was unable to commit to the things that
would improve my comedy career prospects because of my
9–5 job. I had even had to give up doing *The Jonathan Ross
Show* warm-ups because it was clashing with sales meetings.

Addison came into the room at such speed that it was clear
this was a busy man who was not going to waste time. In his
Cockney lilt, he declared, 'Danny says you're not sure you
should leave your job. Leave your job. I'll make sure you get
enough work.'

'It's not that simple.'

'Of course it is. What are you on? Twenty-five grand?'

'No, more.'

'Thirty.'

'No.'

'Forty.'

'No.'

'Fifty.'

'No.'

'Keep your fucking job.'

With that, he walked out and hardly spoke to me again
before I left the agency. Yet he was to play a vital role in
changing my life, years later.

I was now facing the option of taking a huge gamble
in leaving my job, or forever being the bloke who head-
lined all the comedy clubs and earned a few quid for the odd

after-dinner speech, but who would progress no further than that. I loved the comedy and was excited about the prospect of making it more than just a hobby but, ultimately, I had a good job and a family to look after. The most sensible thing to do was to stay where I was, and keep doing gigs as a second income to help chip away at our big mortgage.

Then Luis García scored in the semi-final of the Champions League against Chelsea at Anfield, and started a chain of events that resulted in Liverpool winning the Champions League, and in me questioning everything.

CHAPTER 30

WE ARE THE CHAMPIONS!

I can't completely blame Luis García – the rest of the team also played a part, while the capitulation of AC Milan after leading 3–0 at half time, the penalty saves from Jerzy Dudek, the goals from Steven Gerrard, Vladimir Šmicer and Xabi Alonso also contributed. The talismanic performances of Jamie Carragher and Dietmar Hamann also had a role, as did the fact that someone had decided that the American Transplant Congress should be in Seattle on the same date.

It was 2005 and Liverpool had defied the odds by getting through to the Champions League final. I was sitting in the Kop with my mates, Duff, Quinny and Foz, when Luis García poked the ball towards the goal. We all breathed in to try and help it across the line. If it did or didn't make it is now irrelevant because the referee blew, and we exploded in ecstasy.

We had been to all the home games, and the lads had been to many of the away legs, so there was no question we would qualify for tickets and would all be going to Istanbul for the final. Then I saw the date, 25 May: the date of the American Transplant Congress in Seattle. My heart sank.

This was the biggest transplant meeting every year, and it was taken as a matter of course that, as the head of the UK transplant team, I would be attending. After a brief conversation with my boss, it was apparent non-attendance was not an option. They were flexible with me over everything and turned a bit of a blind eye to the comedy, but not attending the biggest meeting of the year to go to a football match would not wash.

I informed my mates, who all suggested I tell them to stick the job up their arse. But ultimately they knew that wasn't going to happen. We were all entering our late thirties and all to a greater or lesser extent were learning to toe the line. That is what happens in life when you reach an age of responsibility.

My ticket went to one of the other lads, Sam, and I instead went to the congress. Only to find that some of the meetings which would have kept me there on the 25th had been brought forward, so that I was now able to leave on 24 May.

Had the congress been anywhere else in America, there was a chance that I could have made it to Istanbul. But the travel agent looked at all the options, including flying the opposite way around the world, and the best he could do was to get me home for the kick-off, although even that would involve 19 hours of travelling and a tight connection in London. I took the flight, thinking it would be better to be at home to watch the match rather than in some Irish pub in Seattle at four in the morning.

I made the connection and walked into my house to find it full of children: Quinny had gone to Istanbul, so had sent his wife and kids to my house. The game kicked off with me perched on the edge of the couch whilst our wives chatted and little girls did cartwheels in front of the telly. My only other option was to watch it alone in the pub, but since I was still living in Manchester I didn't really think that was a good idea.

By half time, the depression was only made worse by the fact that Liverpool was losing 3–0. You'd think this would've softened the blow of me not being able to watch the game in Istanbul, but instead it made me more depressed, because I had killed myself to get home and watch it on TV, and Liverpool was getting battered. Had I made the effort and been at the ground, I could have shared my disappointment with my mates, I could have joined in the chorus of 'You'll Never Walk Alone', I could have been part of it. Instead, I was sharing plates of sandwiches and cakes with the kids.

The second half I hardly watched as each goal Liverpool clawed back made me walk into the garden to keep my head. After the extra time and the penalty win, I was both ecstatic and deflated. The best game of football ever and Liverpool had won; the best game of football ever and I had not gone because I had toed the line.

That night, I walked the streets till 4 a.m as the jet-lag kicked in, and I spent the time speaking to my mates on their mobiles as they waited at the airport in Istanbul.

I am, however, now glad I didn't attend what was arguably the greatest football match ever because, had I done so, I may not have ever reached the conclusion that I did.

In that moment, I knew that I had to leave the day job to try comedy full time. I couldn't conform any more, and I couldn't keep blaming my situation on circumstance. Yes, I was married with a mortgage; yes, I had a responsibility to the boys and Melanie; yes, I had a good job. But I knew if I didn't try it, then in years to come I would be in my fifties and bitter because the boys would have left and I would be thinking I could have had a shot at show business but didn't try because of them.

There is no greater coward than one who hides behind his own children. I concluded it was better they see me try to make a go of it but fail, than have me place responsibility on their shoulders in later life. I also knew I had to give it a go for me. As my dad had said when I wanted to do the A-levels all those years ago: 'You have to try it. If you don't, you will spend the rest of your life wondering what would have happened.'

I did try it, and a lot happened.

CHAPTER 31

ON TOUR

Melanie knew how much it meant to me to give the comedy a go, and she never once suggested I shouldn't do it. Prior to our marriage split, the option would never have been considered; we were both too conservative for that. Now we knew that for the benefit of the relationship we had to try new things, although, to be fair, leaving a well-paid job to be a comedian is a bit more than trying 'a new thing'. It is a leap of faith, and we jumped at it together.

When I left the office for the final time, I was doing so with the support of everyone I left behind. Nobody said, 'Are you mental?' which you would have perhaps expected; instead, people patted me on the back and wished me luck as if they would have liked to do it themselves. Having said that, people do the same to boxers on the way to the ring, but that doesn't mean you are ready to get punched in the face.

The truth was, I was leaving a salary of nearly £70,000 a year to go and do gigs, which paid £200 a slot. If I got it wrong, being punched in the face would be the least of my problems.

The first thing I had to work out was how much money I needed to earn to try and reduce the impact on our family. I figured that if I had one sportsman's dinner a month, for which I charged around £750, and I worked every weekend with a couple of mid-week gigs, we could cover our bills. That was my target – to meet the existing bills. Anything above that would be a bonus, but anything below it would be a problem.

It was September 2006, two months before my fortieth birthday, and I was now solely dependent on my ability to make people laugh to earn a living.

There is nothing more likely to sharpen the senses than to realise this, and so I sat down with Danny to draw up a plan. I suggested that since I was not getting any TV work, perhaps I should do a small tour, possibly of arts centres around the North West, where I had a small following.

This was greeted with less than lukewarm enthusiasm. As my agent quite rightly pointed out, there was no reason for anyone to buy a ticket to see me, so I would probably lose money. Not a situation I could afford to be in. Instead, he suggested I should just carry on working on the circuit till something came up.

I realised then that the agency no longer saw me as a person of potential. They had signed Alan Carr and Michael McIntyre, both of whom had more exciting prospects than me. The message was loud and clear, and so with no hard feelings I decided I should leave and try things on my own.

So, within a short space of time, I had left my job and my agent. Most mid-life crises result in people getting a sports car, a tattoo or a new young girlfriend; mine resulted in me leaving my job and leaving the only person who had got me any work in my new profession. I was well and truly in with both feet now, and I had to make it work.

I put a little tour together called the 'Going to Work' tour. It began on 4 March 2007 at the Brindley Arts Centre in

Runcorn and was due to finish on 26 April at the famous Leeds City Varieties. I managed to get 15 venues to agree to take me, which was encouraging, as they would only do so if they thought people might come to watch. In the end, I only did 13 dates as two, one in Bradford and one in Rochdale, cancelled as nobody had bought a ticket.

Overall, the tour did well because of reasonably sized audiences in Liverpool and Manchester. The biggest crowd was at the Royal Court in Liverpool, where 745 people came along – not bad for someone nobody had heard of. It was nights like those that made me feel I might have had an audience out there somewhere. Yet five of the 13 venues sold less than 100 tickets. It was hard to justify the effort.

The final date was to be a celebration. Leeds City Varieties has a great reputation as a venue to perform in. Virtually every comedian of note from as far back as Charlie Chaplin has played there, and I really wanted to finish my first ever tour with a bang.

The problem was, it's very hard to generate 'a bang' when you have only sold 15 per cent of the tickets.

Faced with doing a gig for 55 people in a 563-seater venue, my heart sank. The box office assured me there would be some walk-ins, but unless something dramatic happened – like every television in Leeds breaking, thereby forcing people to go out to be entertained – there was never going to be enough spontaneous custom to fill the place.

I sat in the kitchen totally dejected. The tour was supposed to have been the launch pad that was going to generate interest in me beyond being a good club comedian; it was supposed to have got industry people excited and add fuel to my career, endorsing my decision to leave the day job.

The reality was that it was not going to be the tour that changed things for me. And it also had to pay, as I had to at least make the same as I would performing in the clubs. My commitment to Melanie had been that I would manage to cover the bills; now I had to end the tour in a venue where the majority of the seats would be empty. There is no greater indication of failure in show business than empty seats, and my triumphant finale to the tour was to be played out in front of a sea of them.

Melanie came in and saw me sitting, deflated, drinking a cup of tea that I had been staring at so long it had gone cold. That only served to enhance the misery of the situation. Tea is what we give people in England to make things better or to make them feel welcome. Cold tea is what you drink when life feels so shit you can't even be bothered to put the kettle on.

'What's wrong with you?' she asked.

'Nothing.'

'You're drinking cold tea – you're depressed or mad, so what's wrong?'

'Hardly anyone is coming tonight.'

'How many?'

'Hardly any.'

'How many?'

'Fifty-five now, maybe a few extra.'

'Well, that's good, isn't it?'

'It would be if there weren't four hundred and fifty more empty seats looking back at me. Over eighty-five per cent of the seats will be empty.'

'Well, don't tell the empty seats any jokes. You chose this job, so you have to make sure you're good at it. Go and make the people who have come laugh, and they will tell people they know to come next time. Walk on there with a face like the one you've got on at the moment, and nobody will come back. Hurry up, you're going to be late.'

That was it. A straightforward, Northern wife's view of the situation. There was no pandering to creative sensitivities; this was my job and, just like a plumber who didn't want to unblock a drain, my feelings were secondary. It was my job and I had to get on with it.

I got in my car and drove to Leeds.

CHAPTER 32

IT'S ALWAYS BETTER WHEN IT'S FULL

I would love to say that the gig was fantastic and that I was carried out of the venue shoulder high, but that would be a lie. It did go well, apart from a heckler who kept interrupting. When you are performing in an empty venue, it is hard enough to generate an atmosphere, but when someone keeps butting into the show it makes it even harder.

I tried every normal heckle put-down, but he still kept getting involved, to the extent that it began to affect the rest of the audience, so I just let him have it with both barrels. All my angst and frustration were let loose on him, and I embarked on a character assassination of his hair, his clothes, his teeth, his face, his job, his accent, his very being – at the end of which, he stood up and said:

'There was no need for all that. I'm leaving.'

The small audience cheered, and the man turned to leave, at which point I heard myself say:

'Don't go. I think you're a complete tosser, but you do make up a significant percentage of the audience, and I can't afford to lose anyone!'

He left, and the gig genuinely did go well afterwards.

The tour was over, and though I had proved to myself I could do it, I also proved that I could not do it very well on my own. It was time to find a new agent.

I spoke to three people. One said to me she could not see anything to work with and didn't think I had much to offer. One said if I was ready to come to London he could try to get things moving, but he had a big client who had just got a part in a movie and so was expecting to be in LA a lot over the coming months. Only one made the effort to come and see me on tour. And she was also the only one who said, 'I will take you as you are.'

Lisa Thomas was Jason Manford's agent, and Jason was then, and still is, one of the people I met on the circuit whom I consider a friend. It was through him that we met; he had told me about her and her about me, and had suggested that we would work well together.

First off, I went to Lisa's office for a meeting with one of her juniors, who didn't impress me at all because she spent the whole time asking me if I was as funny as Michael McIntyre. Then Lisa called me to apologise for not being at the office that day, and asked if she could come to one of my gigs in Manchester.

She came and saw me do two hours to 500 people, and met me in the bar afterwards, along with Melanie and my sister, Carol.

'What do you do?' Carol asked Lisa.

'I'm an agent,' she replied.

'So you've come to try and rob our John of all his money,' Carol said, before I could stop her.

'No. I hope to make him a lot more,' Lisa batted back.

There was someone I needed to say hello to so I left them talking. Some 10 minutes later they were all laughing and, if nothing else, I was impressed that Lisa had made the effort to come up from London, had managed to overcome my sister and wife, and was clear about what she wanted to do: she wanted to move me up. I agreed to join her and, within a very short space of time, I knew it was one of the best decisions I had ever made.

For her part, Lisa has since told me that she could not understand how I could attract a fair-sized audience for a one-man show, while nobody outside the North West had ever heard of me. She knew there was something to work with; she just wasn't sure what, as everyone she spoke to within television had written me off.

Being on television was still not a priority for me, but it has become obvious that TV exposure brings more people to see you live. The catch-22 was that the more people who came to see you live, the more likely you were to be asked to be on television.

Lisa had spoken to the handful of people who booked most of the TV shows in the country, and the overwhelming feed-back was that I had three main problems:

1) My accent. Some of the bookers saw this as a real barrier, but there was nothing I could do about that unless I tried to be something I wasn't.
2) I was too old to be new. Television, particularly television comedy, is always looking for the next new thing. It's very rare that the next new thing will be a married man in his forties with small children. That is not the next new thing, that's the bloke who lives next door and washes his car on a Saturday.

3) I don't tell jokes. Instead, I tell stories – anecdotes which are not punchy and quick like jokes, but which require an investment of time. This style of comedy was never going to work for a panel show, which by now was the universal access point to television exposure for most comedians.

So, unless I wrote a sitcom about a bloke from Liverpool who was married with kids and enjoyed telling his mates stories, there was little chance I would break through on to the small screen.

A couple of TV executives also apparently said I didn't look funny enough, whatever that meant. It was what I immediately liked about Lisa: the honesty. She had decided to become my agent, but had been told there was no place for me on the only medium that could actually raise your profile quickly, so she felt it was only right she should tell me.

Nothing was going to happen fast. I listened to each of the points and decided that I couldn't change points 1 and 2, and even though I could change number 3 I didn't want to. If I changed to suit the tastes of others, I would forever be changing, so I decided it was best to continue just being me and try to make my stand-up as good as it could be. I reasoned that if you are funny, people will come eventually.

I made the decision that year to return to the Edinburgh Festival. I had no job, so I could really give it a push. Lisa introduced me to Ed Smith, who was going to promote the show and try to get me a decent time slot. He came back with 11pm, a bad time slot. My last two attempts at Edinburgh had resulted in poor audience numbers, so they basically gave me what they had left.

I was to do a month in a venue called the Beside, which held 80 seats when it was full. I decided to do a show explaining how I ended up in this position: being 40 years of age and performing my third show at the Edinburgh Festival in another disused shipping container. The show was called 'Stick Your Job Up Your Arse'.

This time I prepared properly for the run. Those critics who had already decided they didn't like me came back again simply to reaffirm their dislike, but others suggested the show had promise and the audience numbers were up, also. The story touched a few people, who wrote to me afterwards to say they had used the tale to re-evaluate their lives and a few of them subsequently left steady jobs to fulfil their dreams. If any of those people are reading this, I hope everything worked out as you would have wished. If it didn't, then it was not my fault and refunds are not provided.

Having decided that there was no point in waiting for my big TV break, and buoyed up by the fact that Edinburgh was not a complete disaster, I took the show on tour. Five of the venues sold less than a quarter of the tickets. At Leeds City Varieties, I scraped by with less than 50 per cent of the venue being full, but the Memorial Hall in Sheffield sold just over 50 seats at a venue holding 500. No matter who you are and how much the audience is enthusiastic, when 90 per cent of the seats in the venue are empty it is hard to feel that your career is moving forward.

A few years later I received a letter from Leeds City Varieties asking people who had performed there if they wanted to contribute to their planned refurbishment, perhaps by sponsoring a chair. For £350, I sponsored chair G10 in the stalls, on the back of which is a plaque saying, 'It's always better when it's full. John Bishop.' I hope that chair will be there long after I can get booked there, just as a reminder.

After the tour, I began to prepare for my return to Edinburgh the following year with a show called 'Cultural Ambassador', a reference to Liverpool's status as the European Capital of Culture in 2008.

It was my fourth solo run in Edinburgh, and it marked a real turning point for me. For once, people bought tickets prior to any reviews, and even when some bad reviews were written, it still did not stop people coming. I was finding an audience or, more to the point, they were finding me, despite me being a story-telling, middle-aged man with a Scouse accent.

CHAPTER 33

OPPORTUNITY KNOCKS

The year 2009 was when doors began to open and opportunities I never thought I would have fell into my lap, all through a combination of luck, being in the right place at the right time, taking a chance and Jonathan Ross.

By the end of the year, I had been in a successful play, acted in a film made by one of the world's most famous directors, acted in one of the UK's most popular television programmes, been nominated for the most prestigious award at the Edinburgh Festival, started a sell-out tour, been on two of the best-loved stand-up shows on TV and received a commission to make my own stand-up show for the BBC.

So much happened that to make sense of it I think it would be best to break it all down as follows:

1. ACTING

I have never trained as an actor and I'm really grateful that I have had the opportunity to do it at all. In interviews I have always played it down, suggesting that I could only ever see myself acting if the character happened to look and sound a lot like I do, and, to an extent, it's true. While I'm no Johnny Depp, I would love the opportunity to do more of it, because I enjoy being able to take myself out of the equation. As a comedian, you are always the source of everything, whereas acting allows you to place a character before the reality. I will stop going on now, as I am beginning to sound like a luvvie.

In July 2009, I appeared in *One Night in Istanbul*, a play based on the story of some Liverpool FC supporters going to the Champions League Final in Istanbul, the irony being that my character never makes it to the game despite having a ticket. The play was well-received during its run at the Liverpool Empire and, at times, the audience looked more like they were going to a match than to a play as they would come in wearing replica shirts, scarves and carrying banners, which they draped around the theatre.

My only previous experience of acting had been two appearances in pantomime. The first one was at the Royal Court in Liverpool for the Christmas of 2005, where I played Herman the Henchman in *Snow White and the Seven Dwarves*. The producer decided we couldn't afford real dwarves and instead employed children with false heads on. This was OK until one matinée, when I was chasing the 'dwarves', and Sleepy tripped over and his head fell off into the front row, causing multiple children to scream and be sick with fear.

The second occasion was the following Christmas at the Lowry Theatre in Manchester, where I was Captain Cutlass in *Dick Whittington*. Chesney Hawkes played Dick, Darren Day played King Rat and Frazer Hines in his 25th consecutive panto played Alderman Fitzwarren. That occasion was to be the inspiration for the 90-minute comedy drama that I wrote and which appeared on ITV1 years later.

I was under no illusion that I was being asked to play these parts because of my acting ability. I was at the time on Radio City in Liverpool, hosting a weekend show imaginatively called 'Bishop's Sunday Service'. It was basically a shambolic show where I messed around with the producer, Kelvin, and tried to have as much freedom as you can on a commercial radio station. I ended each show with the Jim Reeves song, 'Bimbo' – something that had never featured, nor would ever feature, on the station's play list again. Being on the radio meant that I could give the panto free publicity, which is why virtually every panto in the country has someone from the local station in it.

Being in *One Night in Istanbul* meant that I was in Liverpool when Ken Loach started auditions for his new film, *Route Irish*. When my agent got me an audition, I was full of excitement. I have always been a Ken Loach fan, ever since I first saw *Kes*, while in my student days I would always seek out his films at the art house cinema because whatever the subject matter he made you part of the world. I have never watched one of his films and not been moved in some way, so I reasoned that even if I didn't get the part – which I very much doubted – at least I was going to meet the great man himself.

I was told that the film was about three main characters: two men, Fergus and Frankie, who were boyhood friends from Liverpool and who, after careers in the army, became private security officers in Iraq; and the girlfriend of one of the men, Rachel. It was that vague. Ken is famous for keeping his actors in the dark and nobody gets to see the full script till the end of the film, to ensure the reactions are all genuine.

I was overjoyed the day my agent called to say that I had got the part of Frankie. Mark Womack was to be my best friend, Fergus, and Andrea Lowe was to be my girlfriend, Rachel. I had no idea how I managed to secure the part, and never asked about the fee – I would have paid to be in a Ken Loach film, so that was of little concern.

I then received a voicemail from Ken Loach himself, explaining that he wanted to tell me something about my character that I could not tell the rest of the cast.

I called him back and, after thanking him and letting him know how excited and privileged I felt, I waited for the information about my character that I could not reveal to anyone. 'This is the famous Ken Loach directing technique,' I thought, 'allowing actors to be more naturalistic as they will hold character secrets that nobody else will know.'

'You're dead.'

'What?'

'You're dead, and the film is about how your best friend Fergus finds out who killed you.'

So that was it. My big film break was playing a dead man.

We flew out to Jordan, where we filmed the Iraq scenes. Watching Ken work was a master class in directing and energy. The man is in his seventies and would do 16-hour days in the heat without flagging for a second. I had mixed emotions about being out there, however, as I knew that when we flew back, that was my part in the film finished.

As the filming in Jordan drew to a close, everybody said they were looking forward to continuing the filming in Liverpool. I had become close to Mark, so it seemed odd to tell him I would see him on the set on Monday, knowing full well I wouldn't be there.

Mark said later that he turned up to film for what he thought was going to be a family reunion scene with the actors who were playing my family members, when Ken walked in and told them that Frankie was dead. They would not see me again and they were to get ready to go to my funeral. My on-screen mum apparently cried at the news, delivered so bluntly.

Straight after filming *Route Irish*, I went on to do *Skins*, where I played a frustrated father of teenage kids with a wife who was not sure she liked him any more. (I know, type-casting.) It was a great laugh and was possibly the first opportunity to try and be a bit cool in front of my own teen-agers, although the fact that I was playing a bit of an idiot didn't really help me in that regard.

My character was called Rob Fitch, who was a fitness instructor. This was ironic as at this time I was doing less exercise than ever and was starting to get a little paunch, which Melanie thought was amusing as it meant I was offi-cially middle-aged. I am not built to be slim and, like my dad, I am naturally stocky, but I have never been overweight.

However, as a man, when you pass 40 you wake up fatter than when you went to bed. Something just happens, and before you know it you're a bloke who looks like he has a ball up his shirt as you catch sight of yourself in the mirror and see a little pot belly looking back. Melanie is always trying to correct my posture and telling me to straighten my back, presumably working on the theory that if I was taller I would be thinner, which sounds daft but actually works.

Anyway, *Skins* came along just as my little pot belly was expanding. I had to wear tight T-shirts with the words, 'Don't Get Fit, Get Fitch' on them, which might have been OK had they not been a size too small so that, on occasion, if they were not tucked in tight enough, my belly would pop out of the bottom, somewhat shattering the illusion I was any sort of fitness instructor.

I also had my first screen kiss in *Skins*. It was with Ronni Ancona, who was playing my wife and is a very attractive woman. It came after a scene where we agreed to get back together after splitting up – again, art mirroring life, as they say. It was an emotional moment and took place in the family kitchen. All the film crew were crammed in there as well, which was quite off-putting, and this was just a snog! How anyone does a sex scene without laughing their heads off is beyond me.

I kept asking the cameraman and the director where they wanted me; I asked Ronni which way she wanted to tilt her head; and I asked the make-up woman if I was going to smudge anything. I was basically like a teenage kid at a party who knows he is going to snog the girl he fancies and spends ages building up to it before going for it.

And go for it I did. I just thought, 'I am getting paid to kiss an attractive woman.' I used to be a sales rep, I have to make the most of these opportunities. Also the story mirrored my own so much it was relatively easy to connect with what the character would be feeling. I walked into the kitchen, grabbed Ronni in my arms and snogged her face off.

After a long lingering kiss and passionate embrace, the director shouted, 'Cut.' We disentangled our bodies and I stepped back, hands on my hips, somewhat proud of myself. Nobody could say I didn't give it all when it came to snogging.

The problem was that, as a fitness instructor, I was wearing tracksuit bottoms. And the 'wardrobe problem' that had occurred in the university library years before was now apparent for all to see, the difference being that in the library there was not a full film crew looking at me.

There is nothing more embarrassing than being the last person in the room to know that you have an erection.

As I blushed red, Ronni laughed it off and just said, 'I'll take it as a compliment!'

2. JONATHAN ROSS

Having allowed me to be his warm-up man, Jonathan was about to inadvertently change my career completely. When he and Russell Brand became embroiled in 'Sachsgate', the BBC decided to suspend Jonathan for a period of time, which left a gap in their scheduling. This gap was filled by Jonathan's agent, my old agent Addison Cresswell, who offered the BBC the opportunity to work with one of his other acts, Michael McIntyre.

Live at the Apollo was by far the biggest stand-up show on TV at the time. Addison's company made the show, and the BBC was keen to try something new. It was decided that Michael would travel to theatres around the country and introduce acts, most of whom were unlikely to get on to *Live at the Apollo*. It was a simple sell: the channel wanted to work with Michael, as he was very hot; they needed to fill the slot left by Jonathan; and it would be made by the company who already produced the most successful stand-up show on TV.

The deal was done, and I was booked to appear on the Manchester show of *Michael McIntyre's Comedy Roadshow*. It was being recorded in May and would go out in June. As I was going to the Edinburgh Festival in August, and then starting a tour of small venues in October, which would run for the rest of 2009, it was potentially a great platform for me to generate some ticket sales.

Television is so fickle that I knew, if I messed up, the likelihood of being able to get on TV again would be massively diminished. I was still deemed unsuitable for telly by some

TV execs, and the reality was that had the show not required at least four comedians for each episode I would not have got on. Nobody knew if the show was going to be popular, but it had a primetime slot, so if you did well, millions of people would see it. If you did badly . . . even with clever editing, a death on stage is a death on stage.

It was filmed at the Manchester Apollo, a great venue for comedy. After a sound check, I was standing outside at the catering truck having a cup of tea with Anthony, the show's producer, when Addison came out.

'Bish, my son. I told you I would get you on the telly.'

For a moment, I didn't know if he had remembered that I had left his agency two years earlier, but I decided to make the most of his apparent good mood.

'This is nearly telly. You don't know if people will watch this, so if you want to put me on telly, put me on *Live at the Apollo*.'

There was a slight moment of silence as Anthony looked into his teacup. He also produced *Live at the Apollo*, and had suggested my name on a few occasions, only for it be rejected by the BBC or, perhaps, by Addison.

After a moment's thought, Addison broke. 'OK, you wanker. If you do well tonight, we'll have a think about it.'

He turned around and walked back into the theatre, and I just assumed I had been given another one of those, 'Don't call us, we'll call you' brush-offs, which I had heard for years.

That night I went on stage and decided that, regardless of the potential consequences, I should just treat it as a normal gig. Anything else would mean I was trying to be something that I wasn't.

Sometimes in life things are all as they should be, and so it was on that night. Jason Manford was the headline act and

Michael the host. Those two names ensured that the venue was full with an enthusiastic audience. The line-up was very strong, and I went on after Sarah Millican and Mick Ferry who had compèred my first ever gig and now we were sharing our first prime-time TV slot together. The headliner was Jason Manford. It meant that the show was already going well, and everyone was enjoying it.

The Apollo is a brilliant place for comedy so, as I walked on, I knew that the only thing that could go wrong would be me. My only other television appearance as a stand-up had been interrupted by the magician's puppy getting out of his bag, so I felt on this occasion I had more of a fighting chance.

My mum and dad came to watch with Eddie, Kathy and Carol, and Melanie was also there with a few friends, so I knew I had support in the audience. But I also knew there was near enough 3,000 people who may never have heard of me, and a potential audience of millions of people watching at home.

If it was going to be a bad gig, it was going to be a *really* bad gig.

Michael introduced me and I walked on to warm applause. I paused to take a moment and began to feel my mouth go slightly dry, the first sign of nerves. To calm myself, I put one hand in my pocket, tried to be casual and said, 'Hello, good evening. How are you?'

There was a small reaction from the audience.

'Good, good, good. Don't worry, I've never heard of me, either.'

This got a decent laugh.

'Got to be honest with you, ladies and gentlemen, it's lovely to be here, and for those who haven't yet worked it out, I'm from Liverpool.'

This was greeted with some cheers and boos in equal measure.

'It just shows the BBC's commitment to ethnic diversity.'

There was a decent laugh at that.

'They could have put me on anywhere but they thought, "No, let's put him on in Manchester and see what happens."'

A huge laugh that moved to applause. My dry mouth was gone and I felt at home. I was doing a gig, something I had done perhaps thousands of times before. But no matter what the stakes are, all you can do is make the people in the room laugh, and I seemed to be doing that.

The gig went much better than I had allowed myself to hope for. Lisa had come to watch, but apologised afterwards, telling me she hadn't been able to see all of my set: halfway through her phone had rung; it was Addison, calling to say he wanted to book me for the next series of *Live at the Apollo*.

Had Jonathan and Russell not engaged in their misjudged banter on Russell's radio show, then *Michael McIntyre's Comedy Roadshow* would never have been commissioned and, without it, I would not have been booked for *Live at the Apollo*. And if it weren't for *Live at the Apollo*, I wouldn't have been invited to be a guest on Jonathan Ross's show when he returned to the air the following February.

It was an exciting time for all of the family. We sat and watched *Michael McIntyre's Comedy Roadshow* together – Melanie, the three boys and I. Melanie had been to the recording so she knew what to expect, but the boys – then aged 14, 13 and 11 – hadn't and I wanted to be there when they saw the show.

My part came on and they did laugh in the right places – although I don't know if Melanie was kicking them under the table, as sometimes their response was half a second after she laughed.

The show ended and, together, the three of them got up to leave. I couldn't believe it! They were just going to go and do whatever kids do these days, and I couldn't help myself.

ME:

'Well, what did you think?'

THEM THREE:

'What?'

ME:

'What did you think about the show?'

JOE:

'Michael McIntyre's really funny.'

LUKE:

'And the man with the long hair.'

ME:

'Mick.'

LUKE:

'Yes, and the Sarah woman. She's funny.'

DANIEL:

'I like Jason Manford.'

JOE/LUKE:

'I liked him, too.'

I just looked at Melanie. My own kids were now my biggest critics. Then Joe laughed.

JOE:

'You were great, Dad.'

LUKE:

'Yes, you were really funny.'

DANIEL:

'Yes, Dad, you were dead good.'

MELANIE:

'But you weren't on long.'

So I was nearly as funny as everyone else, but hadn't been on very long.

I was on tour by the time *The Jonathan Ross Show* was aired in February 2010, so I never got to watch it as it was transmitted. By this point, I would not say that the family had become used to me being on TV; I am not sure that ever becomes normal. But the text I received from Melanie when I got off stage perhaps reflected how life was becoming for us:

'Saw you on Jonathan Ross. It was very good :-) I think the dog has worms :-(x'

3) ELVIS

At the start of 2009, I was 42 years old which, I discovered, was the age that Elvis died. This gave me pause for thought. It made me reflect on my own life: what I was doing, where I was going and what I hoped for in the future. These thoughts were to develop into the show I took to Edinburgh that year, 'Elvis Has Left the Building'.

This time I had arguably the best venue at the Festival, the Cabaret Bar, which all comedians love because it feels like a comedy club. The stage is small, the audience is close and, with standing room, you can get in about 175 people. That means that if you sell out there is a chance that not only will you not lose money, you may even make a profit for the month. I also had a great time slot of 9.30 p.m. so, once again, everything was as good as it could be. The only thing that could go wrong would be me.

The show marked the first time I received more positive than negative reviews. Every night sold out, and I was nominated for the main comedy award at the Festival. It was great to feel that I was making strides. It wasn't so much recognition as validation: audiences were enjoying it, as were critics, and the judges of what is arguably the biggest award for comedians thought I was amongst the best there that year. It felt like all the hard work from the previous years was now worth it. The award used to be called the Perrier and, when it was that, people knew what was meant by it. Unfortunately, the year I was nominated there was no sponsor, so it was just called the 'Main Award' which, to be honest, sounds a bit like Employee of the Month.

All these things were positive, but for me the best thing about the Edinburgh Festival that year was that it was the first time the boys came to see me perform. In previous years they had been too young and the time slots too late for them to attend. Also, nobody would like their children to see them perform in venues where they would represent a sizeable proportion of the audience: it is hard enough to impress your children; imagine what it would be like if they came to see you in a converted shipping container as you struggled to try and make half a dozen people laugh. But, that year, with the shows selling out, it felt like the best possible opportunity I was going to have.

Melanie brought them along and they sat at the back whilst I turned our domestic life into material to make strangers laugh. I could see them laughing and occasionally nudging each other when I referred to something that had happened in our home. For any father, 'performing' in front of your kids is an odd thing to do. You are taking your standing as the head of the household and giving it up as you publicly seek the approval of others. There is a vulnerability in performing that really does break down the mystique of superiority that most parenting is built upon, but for me that gig was one of the most important ones I have ever done. Having my family sitting watching me in a room full of people was the point of no return. It was me saying to my sons, 'This is what I do,' and once you do that there is no changing your mind.

Their dad was now a comedian.

CHAPTER 34

2010 . . . NO GOING BACK

The momentum of 2009 carried on into 2010 and I brought out my first DVD, called *Elvis Has Left the Building*, filmed at the Liverpool Empire Theatre. It sold well, so well that it recouped the entire advance I had been given to make it.

Having a DVD in the shops suddenly took me out of the relatively niche comedy environment to the high street, and it was strange that Christmas when I did my annual last-minute dash one evening around HMV to get stocking-fillers for the boys and Melanie to see my face on the front of my own DVD.

It was bloody cold, so I was wearing a woollen beanie hat with a scarf around my chin. As I went to the DVD chart to pick something for the boys, I was stunned to see that I was Number 1 in the overall DVD chart. Without thinking, I reached up and took my DVD off the shelf.

I was looking at the back, remembering the night of the recording in the Liverpool Empire, when a man aged about 20, with a crew-cut hairstyle, wearing a black hoodie, washed-out grey tracksuit bottoms with black training shoes

– a combination which, as far as I can see, is the most public way of telling the world you don't care what they think of you – leaned into me and said:

'I wouldn't buy that. He's shite.'

I laughed it off, assuming he knew who I was, until an old lady at the till made a similar assertion. It made me realise no matter how successful you may become, someone, somewhere still thinks you're rubbish.

Not only did the success of the first DVD bring home to me that things had changed, but it did for all the family, too. You cannot walk into HMV and see your dad on posters on the walls without it entering your head that some people think he is worth spending money on, even if you don't. It never occurred to us how deep these changes were likely to be and that we would have to get used to the things you normally associate with other famous people, like being stopped for autographs. I am proud about the way Melanie and the boys have adjusted. I think we are as down-to-earth now as we would have been had none of the impending fame happened. I've never stopped thinking that this could all end at any moment and, though we should enjoy it for what it is, we should also recognise that it could disappear tomorrow.

One aspect of the DVD's success was that I could pay off our mortgage, and move my mum and dad out of the council house they had lived in for the last 30 years. These two things had been my biggest material ambitions and, once achieved, I didn't need to do any more.

I am not a very materialistic person. There is not a single thing that I own that I would not give up tomorrow. Of course, I like pleasant things, but I am not driven by them. When I realised I was in a position to buy my mum and dad a nice house, I asked to meet with Eddie, Kathy and Carol to ask them what they thought: the last thing I wanted to do was to act without their support. Helping my mum and dad would have been something any of us would have done; it just so happened I was able to do it first, but this had to be a joint thing.

We met at Eddie's house and, as we sat around the table, I suddenly realised that the last time I had done anything like this was to let them know Melanie and I had split up, so I wanted to clear that up:

'Melanie and I are not splitting up.'

They all just looked at each other. Why would anyone get their siblings together just to say, 'Everything's OK'?

Before anyone could ask what I was going on about, I said: 'I have some money, and I was thinking of buying Mum and Dad a house, unless you object.'

Again they just looked at each other.

'Why would we object?' Eddie said.

'I don't know, in case you thought I was being flash and you thought I was a dick.'

'Driving a flash sports car and leaving Mum and Dad in a council house – that would be being a dick.'

Kathy and Carol agreed. I was not a dick, and we went out for a walk looking at homes together that evening. It was the first time the four of us had walked anywhere alone since childhood, and we were looking to see if we could find a nice place for our parents to live. It felt good. Like the most natural thing in the world, as if we had all been waiting to do it one day.

Mum and Dad took the offer in the way I expected. The estate was very good, but the option to have a detached home had always been a dream. If any of the children helped to make that happen, then in many ways we had all achieved something as a family. There are not many things I allow myself to be proud of, but the day they moved I have to admit to pulling over in the car when they called to tell me they had the keys. I got out and leaned on the bonnet and, after speaking to them both, took a deep breath. I breathed in the moment. I had done all I had ever wanted, and as I breathed out, trying to suppress the rising lump in my throat, I remembered the doors of Preston Prison being shut behind us, and the look of the guards as they checked who we were visiting. Nobody would look at any of us again that way.

•   •   •

Within two years of becoming my agent, Lisa had changed my life. She had put me in a position that I could never have imagined possible when I left my job to try and earn enough money to cover the bills by making people laugh. The Elvis tour ran until June 2010, and then I immediately started work on 'Sunshine', the next show that I was taking to Edinburgh that summer.

A comedian like me tends to use his own life for the comedy – if something happens to me, then I talk about it. The previous 12 months had been a whirlwind, so to try to put it in perspective I talked about it on stage, being very careful not to fall into the trap of appearing to be bragging, or boring people with tales of the famous folk I now knew.

At that year's Festival I was to be in a new venue, the McEwan Hall, which had a staggering 1,100 seats – a massive leap from the Cabaret Bar, the 175-seater venue I had been in the year before. Once again, it emphasised how far I'd come in such a short space of time.

Although I was concerned beforehand about filling the McEwan Hall throughout the month, in the event I had no reason to be worried. 'Sunshine' had virtually sold out before I arrived, and I ended up doing extra shows. This was helped by the fact I was by now a familiar face from television, as the first series of my own show on BBC1, *John Bishop's Britain*, had aired earlier in the year. It was a programme I was proud of, particularly the second series the following year, where I was able to apply some of the lessons I had learnt from the first – such as don't wear shiny suits.

By the end of that summer in Edinburgh, I was told that 'Sunshine' had sold the most tickets ever for a single run at the Festival. I am not sure if this is actually true, but it felt nice to hear it when I could still recall so vividly the empty seats that had looked back at me just a few years before.

'Sunshine' graduated from theatres into arenas and catapulted me to a higher level in terms of ticket sales. Being in an arena I think gives you a responsibility to try to do something you cannot do in a theatre, and in this show that involved a dance routine at the end – a dance routine that involved my son Luke, who was allowed to take time off school to do it as part of his work experience. There are surely not many work experience placements that involve you taking a bow in front of thousands of people with your dad dressed as John Travolta.

Lisa bought me a watch to commemorate the success of the show, and every time I look at it I think of performing in The Hut to five people. It seems a lifetime ago, and like it was yesterday, all at the same time.

CHAPTER 35

SPORT RELIEF

When James Corden rang me one morning in July 2011 and suggested we do a sporting challenge together, I have to admit it was not a phone call I ever expected.

During 2010 I had appeared on a sports-based panel show called *A League of Their Own* on Sky. It had very little to do with sport and often ended up with me sitting in an ice bath, but I loved it. I was on every show with Freddie Flintoff, Jamie Redknapp and Georgie Thompson, with James as the host.

The show was a massive success, although regrettably I am no longer a part of it. Though I don't miss days in the studio making the show, I do miss being with the lads, as I regard them all as friends: James I see as often as I can; Freddie is part of my five-a-side crowd; and I even go on holiday with Jamie, which is not something I would recommend as it normally involves me breathing in for two weeks.

Part of the reason I left the show was because of that phone call I received from James, because what was to follow became a commitment whereby I could not guarantee to being around for filming the next series, so I said I would leave. As it happened I managed to do half of that series, but for the subsequent series the producers had moved on and regardless of my availability, I was not asked to be a full-time team member again. That's television, I guess.

'You and I should do something for Sport Relief,' he said.

'What like?'

'I don't know. I'll call them, and we can go and have a chat.'

James then called them and we arranged to meet Kevin Cahill, who is the chief executive of Comic Relief, and can be best described as looking like a cross between Harry Potter's granddad and someone who plays a ukulele in an Irish folk band. He has Santa Claus white hair, little round glasses and a look in his eye that suggests he has just had a Guinness, although I have hardly ever seen him drink.

I had met Kevin the year before when I had been asked to participate in a Take That video for Comic Relief called *Fake That* where, along with James, Catherine Tate, Alan Carr and David Walliams, we pretended to be members of Take That. Whatever happens in my career, Melanie was never happier than seeing me in a Take That video as she is a massive fan, and at a variety of times in our marriage I have had to pretend I was various members of the band, anyway!

At the time, James was in rehearsals for a new play called *One Man, Two Guvnors*, so we met Kevin in central London and suggested we would be up for doing something for the charity.

Kevin then called Professor Greg Whyte, who was the sports scientist who'd supported all the great challenges that Sport Relief had done in the past, from Eddie Izzard's marathons to David Walliams's epic swim. We sat around the table whilst Kevin put his phone on loudspeaker and Greg explained that he thought we could do an adaptation of an existing challenge called 'the Arch to Arc'. This is a race starting at Marble Arch and ending at the Arc de Triomphe in Paris, and involves a combination of running, swimming and cycling. It was obviously difficult, because Greg said only seven people had completed it.

As Greg spoke, James and I both looked at each other with expressions that said, 'You must be bloody kidding!'

During the conversation it was agreed that, whatever form the challenge would take, we must end in London: there could be no greater anti-climax than to round off the hardest physical challenge of your life surrounded by apathetic French people. The meeting ended with the conclusion that Greg was going to look at the challenge and how it could be adapted, and James and I were going to look at our diaries to see when we would both be free.

This was done and, following a quick fitness test with Greg, we agreed to do the challenge the following February 2012. That gave us five months to train, which everyone thought would be enough.

I had never sought celebrity, but now I had it I could use it to make a difference. I know that sounds naff, but it's true. There are not many opportunities in life where someone says, 'Can we borrow what you represent for a while, and if it works, a lot of people you have never met will have a better life?' How could you say no to that? From what I can see, it is the best possible use of this thing called fame.

Celebrity is an odd thing to experience. There came a point, and I don't know when it happened, where I stopped noticing people noticing me when I walked in somewhere. The first time fame hits you is when you see people acting differently because you are there. Not the obvious things of asking for a photograph or an autograph, but nudging each other, watching what you do, the phones coming out as they text friends your whereabouts and, perhaps the most invasive thing of all, taking a photo surreptitiously.

Then, after a while, that becomes normal and you stop noticing. You learn to walk without catching people's eye, you learn to move quickly through public places like airports and, if you are stopped, your family learn to walk on. It just becomes part of your life, and you know it will change one day. One day the nudges and the looks will be accompanied by the question, 'Didn't that used to be . . .?' There will be a point where your star has waned and people will have no interest in you. What would once have been the hassle of being unable to go anywhere without someone wanting a photo will become a privilege. You will go home to your wife and say someone recognised you today in the supermarket from a television show you did decades ago that is now being repeated on an obscure satellite channel, and for a fleeting moment you will think the good days are coming back and the phone will ring again. Until the silence reminds you that your time is over, you are a has-been and the obituary is getting shorter with every passing year.

Celebrity is the candyfloss of life: sweet, but in and of itself worthless. I am a comedian, and it was through being a comedian that I was put on television. It was through being on television that I became a celebrity. It was through being a celebrity that I fitted the profile required by Sport Relief. 'A famous celebrity does something' is a better headline than, 'Someone you probably have never heard of does something.' That is why Kevin was interested in the first place, because if both James and I were involved it was like doubling your money. 'Two celebrities – one very famous and his mate – doing something' is a great headline.

A lot can happen in a short space of time in show business. After a while, I realised I could not stay off the stage for the time I had originally planned. I had been touring constantly for four years and to suddenly stop doing gigs just made me irritable at home. It was Melanie who made the decision that I should consider another tour, although I think the way she put it could have been more subtle than, 'God, you're a miserable bastard. Why don't you get out of the house and go to work?'

I spoke to Lisa and my promoter Ed and decided to go on tour again later in 2011. The Sport Relief challenge was already booked in for February and the tour was scheduled for September through to November.

I wanted news of the tour publicised and the tickets on sale ahead of any Sport Relief announcement, to avoid any cynics suggesting that I was in any way trying to capitalise on the charity. I became almost paranoid about ensuring there was a clear demarcation between the two things. I never allowed mention of my tour in any interviews to do with the challenge, and we delayed the actual launch of the tour marketing to avoid it being out at the same time as Sport Relief activities. All of which was probably rather unnecessary; after all, watching a man in agony doing a physical challenge probably doesn't make you think, 'I bet he's funny. Rather than donate to charity, let's go and see him on tour.'

The tour needed a name to put on the posters, so over dinner one night I asked Melanie and the boys for suggestions.

'What's it going to be about?' one of them asked.

'I don't know, just the ups and downs of the last year or so. But I want a punchy name, ideally one word, like "Sunshine".'

'And not a poster where you look like a dick.'

'That's right, son, a poster where I don't look like a dick.'

The poster for the 'Sunshine' tour was of me holding a microphone. The single worst, most cheesy thing any comedian can do is to stand holding a microphone grinning at the camera. It screams, 'Look at me! I speak into a microphone, like I am doing now, and people laugh!' It also screams, 'I have no imagination, and I think you are so thick I have to hold this magic stick so that you can understand why people can hear me when they are so far away.' My particular picture seemed to scream, 'Hi, I'm John, Sagittarius, and I am available for walks in the park and dinner dates in between my stints as a bingo caller.' I hate that picture, and now it will be on DVD boxes in bargain bins looking back at me for years to come.

It was Daniel who proposed calling the new tour 'Rollercoaster'. It was to be the biggest tour I had ever done and was to be the most fun. We had a crew of 13 travelling with us all the time, so we formed a five-a-side team and challenged each of the venues to a game. This was a great bonding thing for all of us, and though some of the lads had not played football since school, and from the way they played some had not even played football in school, it was great fun, and by the end of the tour we had even started to win games.

But all of that was to come. What had to happen first was the completion of the challenge.

It was the middle of September 2011, five months before the challenge was due to begin, and James phoned me up to say he might not be able to commit to it, after all. Things had gone ballistic with the play, he'd received rave reviews, and there was talk of him taking it to Broadway. If he did this, then his insurance would not allow him to take on such an event.

This changed the complexion of everything: I was now committed to something that I had only thought of doing because James was participating. Now, if there was a chance that he would not do it, I wasn't sure that I wanted to; in fact, I didn't think anyone else would be that bothered if I did it either. James was the big star who would attract the media attention so, without him, I had doubts that it was actually going to be worth doing at all.

I spoke to Kevin and he suggested a few alternative names, all of whom I refused. Not because they weren't great people, but because I didn't know them. The challenge was going to be a thing between mates, and suddenly replacing that mate with a celeb face would have been like finding your friend had cancelled his stag do but sent you to Amsterdam anyway, with people you had never met before: the end result may be the same, but the process is certainly not as much fun. I said that if the challenge was to happen I would want to do it alone, although I'd need Greg to give the go-ahead that I could manage this, rather than in the tandem way we had planned.

In October, James confirmed that he was going to Broadway and was out of the equation. He was both gutted and excited at the same time. He was very committed to the challenge and had a long relationship with Comic Relief and Sport Relief, but the chance to go to Broadway does not come along often in anyone's career. He went and, as expected, was a blistering success, so it was without any doubt whatsoever the right decision for him.

Kevin, Greg and I had our own decision to make: should we go ahead with it or not? After a lot of intense discussions, we all agreed we should. Greg drew up a 12-week training plan for me, and Kevin got the wheels in motion for the documentary to be made for the BBC, of me visiting some of the projects in Africa.

It is only when you get involved with Sport Relief that you become exposed to the machinery that is behind it. My day-to-day contact was Bex. I could call her any time for anything and, provided it was aimed at making the challenge successful, she would get it. Kevin is an incredible wheeler-dealer, and from the moment he was recruited by Richard Curtis to head up Comic Relief he has been driven to make the charity as effective as he possibly can. Without doubt, the greatest way of doing this is knowing how to manage people in the best possible way to ensure you gain their commitment.

It was January 2012 when we went to Sierra Leone. I was six weeks away from the challenge and, after a Christmas of self-denial where I had even trained on Christmas Day – sitting on a rowing machine in my freezing cold garage for 90 minutes – I have to admit to feeling slightly disillusioned. Training alone twice a day in the dead of winter was no fun at all.

Greg came up for the occasional session to check on my progress, and I had been able to join my friend, Martin, and his mates for bike rides. They were a great set of lads who made the effort to come out with me and fit into my training schedule during one of the coldest winters on record. They called themselves The Big Dogs and had had cycling kit made with their club name emblazoned across the front and back: whenever they walked into a café or pub during a ride they looked like a Hell's Angels gang in Lycra. They all fitted the description of middle-aged blokes on bikes, a new social phenomenon that has replaced the darts or dominos teams as a form of social interaction for men; I cannot have imagined my dad going out in tights to spend time with his mates. I am not even sure what my kids thought of me doing the same, but I got an inkling when they laughed at me. But, I enjoyed it and still do it now.

Whether Kevin had purposely planned the Sierra Leone trip to coincide with my potentially losing faith in the challenge or not I couldn't really say, but it wouldn't surprise me. We arrived with the documentary team at our hotel late on the first night, so we just had time to check in and sleep before – the following morning – being taken to the country's only children's hospital.

Those who have seen the documentary will know some of the stories that emerged during my time in Sierra Leone, so I will not go over them again here. Suffice to say, I left with renewed commitment to drag myself through the challenge, no matter how reluctant I was.

We have all watched scenes from the appeal films that Comic Relief and Sport Relief make, but it's difficult when you are sitting in the comfort of your own home to take in the complete picture. Even when they are well done, there will always be things that you cannot capture without being there. In the hospital, I saw deceased children swaddled in sheets and left in a cot in a corridor that formed a makeshift morgue, as the hospital did not have the staff available to take the bodies down to the basement. So parents were tending to their own child within feet of one that had lost its fight for life, generally from a disease caused by poverty – death caused by the absence of £5 to pay for vaccinations or a mosquito net. I paid £5 for a coffee recently in London, and though I nearly choked at the cheek of the price, I never died because I didn't have the money.

Some things in the film we couldn't show. Some things television cannot show, such as the smell from the slum in Kroo Bay where I sat with 11-year-old Kadiatu, whilst raw sewage stagnated in an open sewer next to her home.

Other things were simply too difficult to capture and

bordered on voyeurism because they would not help people watching at home to understand the situation more – they just moved things on to another level of pain. I was standing in the hospital ward talking to the camera and explaining what was around me when I heard a sound that cut to my core. A mother had just seen her child breathe its last breath. She had spent days travelling to the hospital by any means she could, only to find it was too late. The malaria was too advanced.

There is something about being a parent that is impossible to explain. It is an overwhelming feeling that makes you wake up in the middle of the night to check your child is still sleeping in their cot. It is smelling their clothes before you put them in the washing machine so you can have the last vestiges of their scent because, as a single dad, you will not see them again for a week. It is standing in the freezing cold beside a football pitch holding their hand and waiting for them to be brought on as a sub. It is the apologies you give to schools for behaviour you can't understand. It is the hollow self-hatred if you overreact to their provocation. It is the pride when you see them walk in and light up a room. It is that small crack in your heart when you realise they like you, not just need you. It is the joy of dancing with them. It is the hospital visits where you wish you could make it all better. It is the frustration of mobile phones not answered and the reassurance of the key in the door as you lie awake trying not to wait up. It is listening to dreams and ambitions and hoping they realise them all.

It is the sound that leaves your body as the final breath leaves theirs. A sound that cannot be shared via a television screen because it is too visceral; you don't hear it, you feel it in your gut. You want to help and you want to run away and hold your own children, all at the same time. It is a sound I shall never forget.

CHAPTER 36

A FAMILY DAY AT WEMBLEY

The week of the Sport Relief challenge came around very quickly, but it coincided with Liverpool playing Cardiff in the Carling Cup Final at Wembley. Although the Carling Cup is not one of the major cups, it is still a cup. I have referred to it as a drunken girl in a nightclub at ten to two in the morning; she may not be your first choice, but in the absence of anything else you can't help but be grateful to be in the game. As Liverpool supporters, we used to expect to be in a final every year. That isn't the case any more, so you enjoy the opportunities when they come. I was not about to break the promise I made to myself after missing the final in Istanbul just because I had a busy week coming up.

I wanted to go to the match before travelling to Paris on the Eurostar to start the challenge, so Bex made all the arrangements necessary in terms of getting me and my mate Duff, who was coming to the start line with me, from the ground and onto the train by motorbike taxi. The plan was to film some footage by the side of the pitch, which could then be used in the documentary to illustrate what a busy life

I had: 'Here's John, who goes to football matches, too' – that kind of thing.

The game ebbed and flowed, and at the final whistle it was a 1–1 draw, which meant there would be extra time played. Beth, one of the directors working on the documentary, came up into the stand to our seats to say we really had to get near an exit to catch the motorbikes or we would miss the train, which would have been a disaster.

As we were led by staff through the bowels of Wembley, we had no sense of where we were until we reached a pitch-side entrance leading to one of the corner flags. As the doors opened and our little group stepped back into the daylight and walked towards the corner flag, the ball fell to the Liverpool striker, Dirk Kuyt, who promptly fired the ball into the Cardiff net.

Elated, we all jumped to celebrate: Daniel and my nephew Lee running around the corner, Eddie, Duff and me hugging as we leapt. And then, at that moment, we turned to see a mass of blue and white behind us.

We were right in front of the Cardiff supporters, whose disappointment at conceding a goal was compounded by Liverpool supporters dancing in front of them.

Before we could even adjust our response to the situation we had found ourselves in and walk away quietly, the abuse began. The usual finger-pointing, vein-bulging-in-the-neck rants that you see football supporters do when they are angry. The stewards quickly appeared, as did the two police officers who provided our escort through the ground, and tried to get us back through the exit.

I don't blame the Cardiff fans for their initial response, but when I saw someone throw a plastic bottle that just missed Daniel I lost it. I could see the culprit, who looked like he was in his thirties, with close-cropped hair and glasses, and a face so red and strained it looked as if he was trying to lift a car, anger and frustration etched across it. The bit I couldn't understand was the glasses. Whilst he was voicing threats of violence against me when I came to Cardiff on tour, I kept thinking, 'You can't be that mad, you've remembered to put your glasses on.'

Everyone else had been led away so I was the last one left, looking at the mass of angry blue, but all I could see was the bottle thrower. Just before the police officer came to get me, I managed to shout, 'Fuck off, four eyes!'

There is nothing more satisfying than seeing a grown man lose total self-control after being called a playground name. His head looked like it was going to explode, and even the people around him started to step away as he raged even more.

When I went to Cardiff later that year on tour, I had nothing but the brilliant time I always have had there. Mr Angry had actually been in correspondence with my nephew, and once it was explained that where we were at the time of Dirk Kuyt's goal was not something of our making, and we had reacted without knowing our location, it all cooled down and apologies were exchanged. He even said that he was coming to see me on tour, although I would not have recognised him unless he painted his face red. He probably went back to his life as an accountant, where nobody has ever seen him about to burst a blood vessel in frustration. I mean, football is not so important that it should influence your life that much, everybody knows that.

We boarded the motorbike taxis, said goodbye to Eddie, Daniel and Lee and raced through the streets of London to Paddington. When we arrived, Bex was waiting for me with a worried look on her face.

'What happened?' she asked.

'It went to extra time, but I just had a text to say we won on penalties.'

'Not the result. Lisa has just rung to say call her straight away as Radio 5 Live have phoned to say you were arrested for crowd trouble at the game!'

Can you imagine worse publicity for a charity event? That, the night before, the main protagonist is 'banged up for kicking off' at a football game?

I called Lisa and the misunderstanding was cleared up and, along with Beth and Duff, I boarded the train to Paris, a football game behind us, and a week of hell ahead.

CHAPTER 37

WEEK OF HELL

In a period of five days, I did what I consider to be probably the most significant thing of my life. Significant not because it was challenging or physically difficult; not significant in any particular way that was unique to me being there, but significant because of the efforts of others. Literally millions of people donated money to Sport Relief as a direct result of those five days, and it was they who made something that could have just been a celebrity challenge into an event that raised enough money to ensure that some people are alive today as a direct result of it.

The challenge had been adapted to start in Paris and end in London. This meant that the first day was a 185-mile bike ride. I had not slept well in anticipation, but now I was to be seen off by Lisa and a small band of friends, as well as a contingent from BT, who were the sponsors, and Sport Relief.

I was wearing all the appropriate Lycra Sport Relief-branded clothing to let the world know I meant business. I was to have a phone call with Chris Moyles on Radio 1's breakfast show, whose support proved integral to the success of the event. He was to sound the klaxon that signalled the start of the challenge. As my feet were clipped into the pedals of my bike, in order to talk to Chris on the phone and leave promptly when he sounded the klaxon, I had to continually ride around in circles. This meant the obligatory photographs and video links would not work, so I ended up being propped up by Sport Relief staff. I looked like I was being taught how to ride without stabilisers, rather than being prepared to face the biggest sporting challenge of my life.

I rode the first few miles with Olympic Gold medallist Chris Boardman, before setting off towards the coast. It was so well organised, we had motorbike outriders holding back traffic where we needed to. Behind them rode two bicycle outriders, Andy and Gordon, who, along with Greg, acted almost as targets for me to try and reach, although they were usually more than a kilometre ahead of me; I was not allowed to ride too close to anyone in case I was seen to gain an advantage from a drag in their slipstream. If I was going to do this, nobody wanted to be accused of making it easy.

After 90 miles I was joined by mates Martin, Bomber, Chris and Andy from The Big Dogs cycling club. It only seemed right that they should take part in the ride since they had helped prepare me for it, and it was a great lift to see them at the point where I was really starting to tire.

The ride was taking longer than anticipated due to factors that were out of our control, such as the need to pause and do radio interviews and press – all things that help raise money but which interrupted the progress. The distance of 185 miles is also a very long way, so if you are behind on time at the 90-mile mark it's very difficult to pick it up; you can only go as fast as you can.

What made it worse was that in rural France there are no street lights, not even cats' eyes in the road, so as night fell we were riding into complete darkness. You had no idea you were going uphill until you started to slow down; then you only knew you had passed the apex when you found yourself suddenly going faster.

Like everybody else, I had assumed the road to the coast would be flat, and it probably is if you're sitting in a car. But if you are getting there by peddling it may as well be the Alps after the first hundred miles. We eventually rode into Calais at 4 a.m., at least four hours late and with a wake-up call at six, which didn't leave much time for rest and recovery. On the one hand, I was pleased one leg was over, but I knew it represented only a fifth of what I had set out to do, so there was no time for slaps on the back.

I went to the hotel room and started what was to be my nightly routine: I had an ice bath for 10–15 minutes, before putting on compression tights to stop my legs swelling. This part was never captured by the documentary crew; a man in his forties wearing compression tights is not a sight that would encourage people to donate to Sport Relief; instead, they would be more likely to want to help the poor fellow with rickets and squashed genitals. Then I had a massage from the physio, Dot.

When I say 'a massage from the physio, Dot', I mean a proper massage. Dot is not, as his name may suggest, a dainty lady, but a six-foot-three ex-serviceman who is built like a barn door. If ever you need someone to straighten your body out, he is the man, whether your body wants it or not.

The second day, I was woken after an hour's sleep. I was tired but excited: I was going to row the English Channel, which was never something I could have even conceived of doing when I was at school. I was going to do this once-in-a-lifetime experience with four great people: Freddie Flintoff, Davina McCall, Denise Lewis and Mike, an experienced cox who had done the Channel crossing a few times. We'd trained for half a day with Mike near Portsmouth so had some grasp of what we were doing, but we four rowers were in a boat that normally needed six oarsmen.

The recommended way to cross the Channel is with a team of 12 people, six rowing, and rotating with the other six every 2–4 hours. It made an afternoon on the water seem not very much preparation at all, but it was all we'd had time for, so there was no turning back.

What we didn't know was that the Channel crossing had been a problem right up until the night before the start of the challenge. What I didn't realise is that you are not allowed to cross the Channel from France to England in anything less than a suitable ferry or boat. If you want to swim it, row it, water-ski it or cross it in whatever fashion is deemed unusual, you have to start in England – the French simply don't permit it.

Perhaps the fact that the destination is England rather than France means that nobody has been incentivised enough to challenge this law. At least if you go the other way, there will be a chance of a topless woman on the beach or decent wine and cheese at the end. Climbing out of the water in Dover to a bag of chips and a nursing-home day-trip is hardly the same.

Kevin had reassured me that this would all be sorted before we started the challenge but, as I was learning, Kevin had a habit of being reassuring about things that were not yet in place; after all, if he didn't take those chances, a lot of things would simply not happen. However, if we could not row across the Channel, we would have a real problem.

Kevin had asked Gordon Brown – with whom he had a good relationship since he had taken part in a Smithy sketch for Comic Relief a few years earlier – to help, by calling the

French president, Nicolas Sarkozy. This was done and, unbeknown to me, it was only the night before I left for the challenge that Kevin had received a message that the Admiral of Calais (a title which sounds like a name you give a pub) had given approval for us to row on Tuesday morning.

It is a great illustration of the respect that the organisation commands that Kevin was able to ask a former prime minister of the UK to help, and that he was then prepared to pull his weight with his counterpart in France. I am not so sure this would have happened had Nicolas Sarkozy been aware that my first ever joke as a comedian was about the French not stopping the Germans in 1939. Still, let's not mention the war.

We boarded our boat and started rowing at around eight in the morning. It was to be some 13 hours before we would climb out of the boat again. Thirteen hours is a long time doing anything; 13 hours rowing seems even longer, like dog years. The reason is that rowing a boat in the sea quickly becomes boring. Mike was counting our strokes, which after an hour also starts to get dull, but he was using this technique to keep our pace up. The problem with the Channel is that as soon as you reduce your pace you start to drift off course and then have to work hard just to get back to where you were in the first place. After the first hour, during which we were happy to joke and laugh, we settled down to the slog of the row. Freddie summed the tedium up perfectly: 'Rowing is shit. No wonder they give people knighthoods for doing it.'

A few hours in, and fatigue was beginning to take its toll. As I was rowing, I was falling out of pace with the other three and even Mike shouting to keep me focused didn't seem to help. I kept shaking my head and trying to concentrate on the rowing action, but when I looked into the water at my oar I was beginning to see double.

The problem with seeing two oars is that you don't know which one to put in the water. If you get it wrong, as I did, it has the same effect as a boxer throwing a punch that does not connect – you just carry on going. I fell back and was helped back into my seat by Freddie, who was very nice about it: if only four of you are rowing and one keeps falling out of his seat, it must take a lot not to want to throw him overboard. But all three of them just kept encouraging me on.

After four hours I had to take a call with Greg James for Radio 1. The phone was handed over from the support boat and I recall hearing Greg's voice, but I have no idea what I said – the tiredness was such that I could hardly speak. Davina quickly intervened, took the phone from me and did the interview on my behalf. My accent is not great on radio at the best of times, but, four hours into rowing the English Channel after an hour's sleep, I sounded like I was walking out of the dentist with that silly pink water still dribbling down my chin.

There is a moment when exhaustion and drunkenness have the same effect. You start slurring your words, you start rolling your head, your blinks become 20-second naps and you are useless in a boat. The support boat was summoned and, after a quick look and a discussion between Greg and the doctor, Matt, a bunch of tablets were put in my hand.

To this day, I don't know what they were, and perhaps the discussion between the two was to see if we had reached international waters, so that everyone knew what laws were being broken when I took them. I ate an energy bar, drank some fluid and let the pills kick in, and we started rowing again, us band of four with our cox, Mike.

The reality was that I could not have given up; I knew I would have let so many people down. I am sure the charity would have managed to salvage something from the situation, but these things are not set up to fail. Who wants to donate to someone who nearly did something? Knowing the benefits the money could bring spurred me on; not wanting to let my kids or Melanie down by failing spurred me on; not wanting to face the world as someone who couldn't complete something spurred me on; but, most of all, the four people in the boat spurred me on. Mike did his job admirably as a cox, but the bond between the rowers was something that moved me. In that boat and on the day, I could not have wanted to be with better people.

At my lowest point, Freddie leaned forward and patted me on my back: 'Don't worry, mate, we'll get you home.' Had it been Denise or Davina who had said that, I would have kissed them, such was my gratitude that I had these special people with me. But as it was Freddie, I just said, 'Thanks, mate,' and attempted to carry on rowing.

The sun was setting as Dover came into sight. Being in a rowing boat and seeing your eventual destination is almost worse than not seeing it, because for ages you feel that you aren't getting any closer.

We had been rotating around the boat every hour to balance out who took the front position and set the pace, but for the final three hours we just sat and rowed as Davina set the pace, showing all those fitness DVDs are the real deal, and we kept up as much momentum as we could.

Freddie and Denise have been world-class athletes because they have that thing inside that makes them winners. They would never have stopped until we reached England, no matter how long it took. Davina is one of the most determined people I have ever met, and led us into the port under Mike's direction. Meanwhile, I was doing all I could to not let them down.

As we neared the dock, we saw a small crowd had gathered. Then, as we approached, we realised it was not such a small crowd at all, but a sizeable contingent to welcome us home. This was a surprise, as I had told my friends and family that I would see them at the end of the challenge – if I made it – and not before. However, when I saw the other members of the boat greet their friends and family, I wished I had asked them to be there. But then I realised I was not even halfway and, for me, the time to celebrate had not yet arrived.

We rowed up to the berth where we docked the boat but, before we climbed out, we shared a moment. A cricketer, an athlete, a television presenter and a comedian had just rowed the Channel. None of us had ever thought we would do something like that, and we all knew we were likely never to do it again. I also knew that in the middle of the Channel, when I had had nothing left, they had carried me through. To the press, this may have been four celebrities in a boat; but to us, it was four friends, and I will always owe a debt of gratitude to them all. I kissed Davina and Denise goodbye, then I turned to Freddie, looked in his eyes and shook his hand.

He may have saved me in the middle of the Channel, but there was still no way I was going to kiss him.

After an ice bath and a heavy night's sleep, I was woken up by Dot bringing his treatment table into my hotel room. I had a massage, got dressed, ate breakfast and prepared for three days of running. This was a daunting task, as I had never run more than a half-marathon prior to training, but I felt confident that I had a chance to do this. Running is putting one foot in front of the other. I had been doing it for most of my life, so I convinced myself that this was all I had to do.

It was not to be too long before I realised it would not be that easy. As a surprise, Comedy Dave from Chris Moyles's show turned up to run the first five miles with me. A small crowd had gathered to send us on our way, and we started the journey towards London.

Within the first few hundred metres I noticed vehicles on the road were beeping their horns at us: cars, school buses, lorries, motorbikes – it seemed like everyone was beeping at us. At first, I just thought that this was what people in Dover did: a kind of early warning to signal to anyone who had just driven off the ferry to let them know what side of the road they were on. It was Dave who told me that the beeps were for me.

Having spent the last two days out of the country, I was unaware of how many people knew what I was doing. Of course I had done interviews, and Radio 1 was playing a massive role in supporting the challenge, but you don't think that will automatically result in people being bothered. Everyone has a busy life, so you could easily miss a radio interview. I wouldn't have blamed anyone for wondering why two blokes were being filmed whilst they ran, particularly as the pace they were running at hardly meant that they were training for the Olympics. It was a great lift to have people beeping their horns as I passed, and it continued right till the end, although at times I was almost too tired to acknowledge it.

After Dave left, I continued to the halfway point, where I was to meet Dermot O'Leary. Dave I knew from going on Chris's show; Dermot I had only met once before, but he is one of those people it is virtually impossible to dislike. We ran together for 10 miles.

I realised that the advice of running with someone made sense. Gordon was still ahead on his bicycle checking the route was OK, and Greg, for his sins, was also running virtually the full distance – just for fun, and to be there in case I needed a pep talk, a quick reaction to an injury or simply company.

However, there is a point, I find, when you are running long distance, that it is best to be alone. I never trained with headphones, so even when I had nobody with me I never played any music. I just wanted to concentrate on putting one foot in front of the other. As I had done all those years earlier on the bike ride home from Australia, I wanted to get to the state of mind where I moved without thinking about it.

Around lunchtime, we made a quick pit stop in a village to get some food and for Dot to have a look at some niggles I was feeling in my Achilles' tendons. Lisa had visited for the day and Melanie was due to come and join me in the hotel that night, so I asked if Lisa had heard from her. Just as I opened my mouth, her phone bleeped on the table in front of me. It was a text from Melanie. We both laughed at the timing, and Lisa said I may as well read it.

The text began with the words, 'Whatever you do, don't tell John . . .' Clearly, a sentence like that is never going to be good news but I had to read on. It transpired that Joe had been involved in an accident in which he had crashed head-on into a bus whilst riding his bicycle in Cape Town, where he was at college.

The previous few years had not been easy for Joe. He had been diagnosed with a rare auto-immune condition that affected his hearing: some days he would wake up deaf, and this could last for hours or days. The fluctuations meant that hearing aids could not easily be set and the constant tinnitus kept him awake some nights, so that it was difficult to know how much sleep he had had.

Joe was 15, and would raise his voice when he was talking to me, which drove me mad as I just assumed he was being a disrespectful pain-in-the-arse teenager. 'Who do you think you're shouting at?' would be replied to with, 'I'm not shouting at anybody,' and then him walking away. Not coming back when I told him to would send me into a further rage. But, of course, he didn't know he was shouting because he didn't know he was losing his hearing. You know that you can't see, but you don't know that you can't hear, so what I took to be defiance was just a symptom of his deteriorating hearing. He simply couldn't hear me when he walked away.

Whilst I had been touring and making television programmes, smiling for promotional posters, signing new DVDs and receiving applause, Melanie had been sitting in hospital waiting-rooms hoping to find someone who could help give our son his hearing back. She had been holding the family together and battling to keep our priorities right. Nobody receives applause for being a mum. Some people have said that being alone on a stage as a comedian is a lonely place – sometimes being at home is a lot lonelier.

Attempting to remain calm, I tried to call Melanie, but her phone went straight to voicemail. I phoned Joe's phone but it, too, just rang until the voicemail kicked in. Then I realised I had no other numbers with me to call, and my heart sank. In a world with a myriad of communication methods I didn't know anyone who I could contact.

I didn't want to make a scene or create a drama because it had become apparent to me that this challenge was bigger than me, but nothing is more important than your own children. We had to start running again to keep up with the schedule, which couldn't afford any delays – to delay would alert the world to the fact that something was wrong. I had no choice: I had to start running without knowing what had happened to my son.

I asked Lisa to keep calling them and to see if she could discover what hospital Joe had been taken to. Then I went outside, smiled for a few photographers, waved to the crowd and started running. I just didn't know what else to do.

By the time I reached Faversham, the place where I was going to end the day, two hours later, Lisa had spoken to Melanie. Somehow Joe had managed to smash the windscreen of the bus, but, apart from being shaken, he was fine. After an examination for any serious problems, he had been released from hospital and would make it over for the end of the challenge on Friday, but would not be able to run with me as the other two planned to do.

I ran into the centre of Faversham tired, but feeling so much lighter than the previous 15 miles. The knowledge had lifted a weight of my shoulders, and as I began to allow myself the belief that I could complete this challenge I started to notice the crowds lining the streets, cheering as I went past. And, when we turned the corner, it was clear we had literally stopped the traffic. The town was full of people cheering. I was greeted by the mayor, someone tried to give me a beer and others tried to push cash into my hand. Any doubt that the beeping was for me was now well and truly gone. This was already bigger than I thought it would ever be.

Any charity event is measured by the money it raises and you can only know what this is at the end, but by the time I reached Faversham it was clear that we were capturing people's attention, and this could only mean that donations would come in. Beyond thinking I could do it physically, I began to believe the support we were being given would result in a decent amount of money being raised. Basically, I began to think it would all be worth it.

That night, when Melanie arrived, it felt as if I hadn't seen her for weeks, so much had happened. I was stiff and was walking with a slight limp as we approached each other in the corridor outside my room.

She held on to me tighter than I can recall her ever doing. 'He's OK. I've spoken to him and he's OK,' she said.

'I know,' I replied.

'You look shit,' she said, as she wiped a tear away from her eyes. I am not sure it was there to indicate her relief about Joe or because I looked so 'shit', but we both laughed.

After the ice bath and massage, I put on my compression tights which, I have to say, did nothing to inject spice into a 19-year marriage. I was like an exhausted Max Wall (again, if you're too young, Google him), and would have slept heavily had my stomach not decided to reject everything that I had eaten for dinner that night.

At breakfast the next day, when I told Greg and Dr Matt about throwing up, Greg simply said, 'We thought that might happen.' Apparently, when your body is exhausted, the blood in the stomach exits to feed the overworked muscles, leaving a higher concentration of acid, too high to digest food.

With that knowledge on board, but nothing else, I started my run from Faversham to Gravesend, a distance of around 28 miles. Melanie joined me for the first half of it, which was good, but without any food inside me I was running out of energy and was also becoming increasingly affected by the pain coming from my Achilles' tendons. They were both incredibly tight, and each kerb-stone I had to step over sent a stabbing sensation up the back of my legs. What was worse was that the treatment Dot favoured involved the use of blue tape and, when I say blue, I mean Smurf blue. I had the tape all the way up the rear of my legs as I ran. They looked like the oddest varicose veins known to man.

That day I was helped along by Frank Skinner, whom I had never met before but really liked, and Chris Moyles, who surprised me by turning up. He had done so much for the appeal, it was great that he was there whilst I did it.

I was tired when we reached Gravesend, but was also on a high. I knew I only had one day left, and then it was all over. The following morning I started from the town centre in Gravesend where I had finished the previous evening and, as a small crowd waved me off, I began running. Within a few hundred yards there was sharp pain in my right shin – an excruciating stab that felt like a burning knife, but I knew I couldn't stop: I was still in sight of everyone who had just waved me off. You could call it pride, you could call it ego or you could call a desire not to let anyone down, but I didn't want to stop after they had all made the effort to come and cheer.

I carried on, then hobbled around a car and, when I was sure nobody could see, I stopped. Greg, Matt and Dot came to look and decided that it was probably shin splints – anything worse and I would need to stop. There was no way I was going to stop, so we decided I should run to the scheduled pit stop nine miles away and see how I was when I got there.

Before I got there, I was joined by Greg James, the Radio 1 DJ who had interviewed me on the boat, when I could hardly speak. He had come to run a few miles, but I think also to see if I was as close to death as I had sounded.

I also had another surprise. As I was running, someone came to run alongside me. This had happened a few times and I had engaged in pleasantries, although this time I was in too much pain. So I just said, 'All right, mate,' and glanced over – to see my own face staring back at me. The person running alongside was wearing a mask of my face. Before I could decide if this was funny or not, he lifted the mask and I saw that it was my brother Eddie, who ran the next nine miles with me and gave me a great lift.

I reached the pit stop and received what treatment they could offer. The shin was causing some concern, the type of concern where people say it's not causing them any concern but then whisper to each other. I heard 'hairline fracture' being mentioned and decided to let everyone know that, no matter what it was, there was no way that with 15 miles to go before the end I was going to quit.

Dot did what he could, and I was back on the road and heading to the big city. Robbie Savage joined us for a section, which at first I hadn't been keen on. Everyone else who had run with me I either knew or I liked, and he didn't fall into either of those two categories. For some reason, as a footballer he always wound me up, and as a person I always envisaged he would be annoying. However, he is another person to be added to the list of those I got wrong before I met them. He was funny, and had played football against many of the people Eddie had when he was a professional, so I was able to direct my concentration away from my legs to listen to their anecdotes.

The problem with London is that it is simply too big for anyone to give much of a toss about anything that anyone else is doing. After two days where whole towns had seemed to come and greet me, I was now entering London where, apart from the odd shout from a builder on scaffolding – and, to be fair, that could have been directed more at Robbie than me – there was no reaction. We could have been a very slow jogging club who happened to be getting followed by a camera crew for all the people of South London cared.

As we entered Greenwich, my sister Carol met us to hand over Luke and Daniel, who ran with us for a few miles. It was great to see them, as I'd been so preoccupied with maintaining the challenge and what had happened to Joe that I had hardly spoken to them. But although I wanted to catch up with them properly, I knew I just had to carry on going. I was in agony, but didn't want anyone to know, and I was aware that if I stopped there was every chance I would struggle to make the final pit stop.

However, your kids know you better than you imagine.

'You OK, Dad?' asked Daniel, when I grimaced going down some steps.

'He's in agony, stupid.'

'Don't call me stupid, idiot.'

'Who are you calling an idiot?'

It's amazing how quickly domestic life can walk back into your head, even as you come to the end of the hardest week of your life.

At the final pit stop, Joe was there, slightly bruised but mainly unscathed. I had seen a photograph of the damaged bus; he was lucky to be there, and we both knew it. There was a quick hug, I called him a dickhead, and we moved on.

The shin was now extremely painful to touch, but Dot administered whatever treatment he could, and I got up to run the last seven miles into London. Before starting, I thanked as many people as I could who had been with us during the week, and then I set off with just Greg for the final leg.

I would have been happy to have run the whole way and crossed the finishing line with Greg, but the director of the documentary, Matt, kept asking Greg to move aside so he could have a solo shot of me. The third time he did this I told him where to shove his camera, and after he realised I wanted to run with Greg we were left to run side by side until we reached the Embankment.

I knew we were finishing in Trafalgar Square and that all we had to do was turn right. However, Greg said we had to split up at this point as I had to go the long way round to enter it down The Mall, but he would see me at the end.

I had been moving virtually every waking hour for the last five days and now someone had decided to add on another mile to my run so I could run down The Mall. I was fuming, thinking that if this was something Matt had set up because I had told him where to shove his camera, then I would duly complete the task when I had finished.

I had turned the corner in front of Buckingham Palace and started to run down The Mall when I noticed there were no cars on it. I looked behind me, and noticed two police cars holding up the traffic as I progressed up one of the most famous roads in the world – a road that had been closed for me. Normally when I find a road has been closed, I feel like screaming. This time, I felt like crying.

I turned into Trafalgar Square to the sound of 'You'll Never Walk Alone' and people cheering. I wanted to shake people's hands and thank them for their support but I still hadn't finished. Even though it was few hundred yards, I would not allow myself to stop till I crossed the finishing

line, which I could see at the top of some steps. In my knackered state, I remember thinking I couldn't believe after the
week I had just endured, somebody had thought, 'Let's just
make him climb some steps at the end.'

A yard from the finishing line, I finally stopped running.
I took a step and walked over it. It was done. As I raised my
hands in the air, Melanie and the boys joined me and we
hugged for a moment on our own before turning to face the
press and the crowds. It was our moment: for better or for
worse, my 'Week of Hell' was over.

All of my friends and family were there, and my mum's was
amongst many of the most important faces in my life glisten-
ing with tears as I looked at the people gathered there. Jason
Manford led me to the podium and revealed that the challenge had raised £1.6 million. By the time I hosted a section
of Sport Relief with James Corden, the documentary had been
shown and the total had reached £3.4 million, and by the time
Sport Relief closed the account the challenge had raised
£4.2 million. That is nearly a million children immunised.

A few weeks later, I turned up at the Comic Relief night at
the BBC and everybody kept asking me how my leg was and
how I was recovering. Then I saw David Walliams who, up to
that point, I had only met a few times before. 'How's your
head?' he asked. He was the only person to ask that, because
he was perhaps the only person who would know what it's
like when you take on such a huge public challenge. You take
your body and you train it, prepare it to do a job, to perform
a function, and it does it. What nobody sees is the weight of
responsibility you try to sleep with for months before; how
your whole focus is to do something which is not actually
what you do and is actually something you're not even sure
you can do; and yet everybody you know and millions you

don't are going to know if you succeed or not. Then it's over, and you get back that head-space you had devoted to completing the task. You can now think of something else; the problem is, you don't know what.

I will always feel proud of my participation in the 'Week of Hell' because, while I learnt a lot about myself, I learnt more about people. Nobody had to make a single donation to Comic Relief for what I did. There are many more people who have done much harder physical challenges without the recognition, and I personally don't think the physical side was that important. My leg wasn't fractured, and after a few weeks with a plastic cast the swelling went down. A few months later I was jogging again, so there was no significant damage done. What will always stay with me, however, was that people chose to be involved, to phone, to make a donation to help someone they would most likely never meet to have a better life. For one week, people took a second to think of someone else, and I was part of that process; something for which I will always feel humble and proud.

POSTSCRIPT

We arrive at Dublin airport straight from the O2 Arena. We have just finished the 'Rollercoaster' tour in Dublin, where the audience's reaction has made me feel as close to a rock star as any comedian should be allowed to feel. The standing ovation is still ringing in my ears as we pass through the small checkpoint and then board the minibus that will take us to the plane. Handing over what luggage we have, we board: David, my cousin and now my tour manager; Dean, who has been part of the tour and is now going to be part of the filming to take place in Lancaster the following day; Lisa, my agent and now business partner in the production company we'd formed.

Our first project, a collaboration between us and the esteemed production company, Baby Cow, is due to start filming the following day. We will be starting the filming of *Panto!*, a 90-minute special for ITV1 that I have co-written with screen writer Jonathan Harvey, which is based on my experiences doing pantomime in Manchester in 2006. While performing in the panto, I had developed the idea of a comedy-drama based around the efficiency of what goes on behind the scenes contrasted with the chaotic fun of the panto for the audience.

I had written the first draft six years ago and nobody had wanted it, so it had been a long journey of knocking on doors and being turned down. Now it was being made. Like everything else in my career, had I listened to what I was told it would never have come off the shelf.

Chesney Hawkes is even in it, as is my youngest son, Daniel. My character has a son, but we couldn't find anyone who fitted the bill. The producer, Lindsey, suggested that the director, Chris, should meet Daniel, and he was cast. Strange to think that when I started performing, my sons thought I was a 'knob'. But Luke has performed on stage with me, Daniel has acted on screen with me and this book contains an excellent picture Joe took of me on stage during one of my tours, so they seem to be more interested in what the 'knob' does than perhaps they are prepared to let on.

As the plane holding us four takes to the sky, I look away from the fading streetlights of Dublin below and look across at Lisa, remembering what it felt like when nobody wanted to represent me. I remember the tours where I performed to rooms filled with empty seats; I remember when everything about me was wrong for TV: my accent, my age, my face. I remember sitting with Melanie and calculating if we could afford for me to leave my job. I remember the times I have not been the perfect father or husband. I remember the sessions in Relate trying to stitch a family back together. I remember what it used to feel like going home to an empty house when I didn't have the kids. I remember riding the bike home from Australia and long summers spent in America coaching football. I remember travelling in my dad's yellow van to Newcastle, the first time I left home and the subsequent decision to go to Manchester where I made friends for life. I remember the conversation trying to convince my mum and dad that leaving a job to do A-levels was a gamble worth taking. I remember getting up at six to be a mail lad in ICI.

I remember my mum holding my hand as I lay in a hospital bed, not understanding the concern in her eyes, but knowing she made things better by being there. I remember having to wait for someone to unlock a door so I could hug my dad. I remember being a kid on a council estate wanting to be like my older brother and having no idea where girls went when they weren't skipping or in the kitchen. I remember being scared that whatever it was that compelled me to do things that were different to the rest of the people around me may lead to a dead end. I remember so many things that remind me not every day has been like this one. I sit back and look at the dark shape of Ireland fading behind me and think, 'How did all this happen?'